JOHN
FREDERIC
OBERLIN

Ah friend, what is our life, if it is to be used only for our pleasure and prestige! . . . I do not wish to live one moment more than I can be useful. . . . So long as I can learn, . . . capture, devise, apprehend, copy or acquire from others, anything by which the needs, the sorrows, and the miseries of so many oppressed people can be alleviated, I will let no ingratitude, no opposition, . . . no expense . . . restrain me. . . . Thus my life, in spite of countless adversities, . . . is a constant joy, and my death will be but a transition to continuing happy activity in the afterlife.

John Frederic Oberlin

Dessiné d'après Nature et gravé par Ch. L. Schuler en 1803.

JEAN FRÉDÉRIC OBERLIN

*Ministre à Waldbach au ban de
la Roche âgé de 62 Ans.*

JOHN FREDERIC OBERLIN

by John W. Kurtz

WESTVIEW PRESS
Boulder, Colorado

Copyright © 1976 by Oberlin College.

Published 1976 in the United States of America by

Westview Press, Inc.
1898 Flatiron Court
Boulder, Colorado 80301
Frederick A. Praeger, Publisher and Editorial Director

Library of Congress Cataloging in Publication Data

Kurtz, John W.
  John Frederic Oberlin

  Bibliography: p. 321
  Includes index.
  1. Oberlin, Johann Friedrich, 1740-1826.
BX4827.03K87   284'.1'0924 [B]   76-25211
ISBN 0-89158-118-9

Printed in the United States of America.

To the memory of
William Henry Kurtz, country pastor,
and
Minnie Louise Kurtz, née Grosshans, daughter of Alsace

Contents

Preface

The first book written about Oberlin was an English biography entitled *Memoirs of John Frederic Oberlin*. It was published anonymously in London in 1829, three years after Oberlin's death. Since then 101 books and more than 300 essays, articles, and tracts about Oberlin have been published in thirteen languages. In the face of such redundance, how can the publication now of yet another Oberlin book be justified?

To that question there are several answers. (1) Each of the existing biographies in English is little more than a rehash of that first publication of 1829, even to the extent that the historical errors made by its author are in all innocence repeated over and over again. (2) Of the two basic works in French, Ehrenfried Stoeber's of 1831 and Camille Leenhardt's of 1911, the first is now almost totally inaccessible, and the second is only slightly less hard to come by. (3) All the books since Leenhardt's seem to me to have failed to exploit adequately not only those documents now lost that were still available in 1911, but also other archival materials that are still to be found in Strasbourg and Waldersbach. (4) None of the previous biographers has adequately detailed the relationships between Oberlin's life and work and the social and intellectual currents of his time. (5) Practically all of Oberlin's biographers have emulated not only Stoeber's hortatory, propagandistic purpose, but also his rhapsodic, inspirational style, so that the traditional image of Oberlin created by them is that of a sculptured saint rather than of a living man of flesh and blood. After reading through the mass of adulatory prose, one feels impelled to try one's hand at rescuing Oberlin from his idolators. (6) There are aspects of Oberlin's life that have seemed unorthodox, and therefore an embarrassment, to both socially and religiously oriented commentators. In recent years one of these anomalies, namely, the seven-year period of his dalliance with spiritism, has recently become a cause of contention within the small coterie of Oberlin scholars. In chapter nine, "Of Mysteries and Dark Enchantments," I have tried to contribute elements of impartiality and rational perspective to the argument.

I gratefully acknowledge my indebtedness for help and support to the following: to Oberlin College for two leaves of absence, for a research grant, and for permission to quote the passage from Robert S. Fletcher's *A History of Oberlin College* on page 281; to Mme Anne-Margrit Meyer for much help and countless favors; to Mme Claire Richardot, of the Waldersbach museum, to M. Georges Klein of the Museum of Alsace, and M. Josef Fuchs of the Municipal Library of Strasbourg for aid in research; to Professors Frederick B. Artz and Robert J. Soucy for reading the manuscript and for valuable criticisms and suggestions; to the John Frederic Oberlin Society for its support of this publication.

Picture Credits

Introduction

The century of European history from 1750 to 1850 was a charismatic era. In philosophy it was the age of Hume and Voltaire and Diderot, of Kant and Fichte and Hegel, of Schelling and Schopenhauer. In politics and statecraft it was the era of Franklin and Washington, of Jefferson and Adams, of Frederick the Great and Catherine the Great, of Maria Theresa and Joseph II, of Napoleon and Alexander I. In science and technology it was the age of Watt and the Industrial Revolution, of Linnaeus and Malthus. In exploration it was the time of Humboldt and Cook and the Montgolfiers. In music it was the era of Haydn and Mozart, of Beethoven and Schubert. In education it was the age of Rousseau, of Campe and Basedow, of Pestalozzi and Froebel. In literature it was the time of Blake and Burns, of Wordsworth and Coleridge and Byron, of Lessing and Schiller; it was the age of Johnson and the age of Goethe. In religion it was the time of Wesley and Methodism, of the Moravian Brethren and the German Pietists, and of Jonathan Edwards and the Great Awakening. It was, withal, an age of transition: from rationalism and enlightenment to sentimentalism and romanticism. It was the age of revolution.

John Frederic Oberlin, whose life from his adolescence to his death covered three-quarters of that "century of the uncommon man," was not one of those who, in that optimistic age, designed the philosophical systems or promulgated the social concepts and principles that charted the course of

1

Western civilization from the time of the aerostatic balloon to the age of interplanetary exploration. But as a well-educated burgher of his time, he read the treatises of the masters of science and philosophy and social theory; and in his everyday life as a country pastor and a social and educational reformer he found ways to convert the precepts of the thinkers into practical measures for the improvement of the life of a deprived people in the Ban de la Roche, the remote and backward community in and for which he lived and labored during the entire threescore years of his ministry. He made of his backwoods parish a living, working exemplar of the ideal **community that has been envisioned in many a utopian novel** and tract. The story of his remote little community lies before us as a kind of laboratory demonstration of what social improvements could be accomplished by the imaginative utilization of the best wisdom of his time.

Oberlin's life was fundamentally guided not by any systematic philosophical ratiocination, but by his deeply religious nature. His religion was more Christocentric than, say, the deism of Rousseau's Savoyard Priest. It was more akin to the "religion of the heart" proclaimed by the German Pietists; to the discipline of the Moravian Brethren with their emphasis on a life of prayer, of devotion to Christ and to the responsibility of the individual. But, all organized systems and confessions aside, Oberlin turned, first, last, and always, to the Scriptures as his guide to the temporal salvation of his parish and the eternal salvation of its members. Even among his Bible-oriented fellow clergymen, who based their preaching mostly on the New Testament gospel, he was unique in his devotion to the Mosaic law as a model for social organization in his own time.

It is an interesting coincidence that Oberlin's tiny community was developing at approximately the time when a new nation was being formed out of the thirteen British colonies in North America. This coincidence may allow one to presume for Americans of the twentieth century a degree of empathy with the backwoods reformer in the Vosgesian wilderness. Most of us will find it easy to understand and to accept Oberlin whenever his talk is in accord with that of the models and heroes whom we fondly call the founding fathers and whenever his actions demonstrate the practicability of those egalitarian ideals that we ourselves have inherited from his contemporaries. But many of us, in this less religiously oriented age, will see his fervid religiosity as a barrier between him and us. We will find it hard to understand him when, as often happens, his talk is in the emotional idiom of Puritanism, of Pietism, and of revivalism. And there are many, no doubt, who will feel not only indifferent or perplexed, but actually alienated as they read in the course of this narrative about a phase of his life when he was captivated by some of the more esoteric, more recondite doctrinaires of his time: the clairvoyants, the spiritists, and the whole tribe of eschatologists and millenarians and other speculators on the postmortem state of man. But this, too, is an important phase of Oberlin's multifaceted character and life and should neither be suppressed (as it has been by some writers) nor passed over lightly by anyone who wishes to see this man both plain and whole.

The reader who wishes to understand the private feelings and musings and fantasies of Oberlin will have to make a sustained effort to put himself in Oberlin's position. He will have to remember Oberlin's loneliness, his sensitivity to various hostilities and criticisms. He will have to keep in mind that one trait of Oberlin's extraordinarily complex personality was a preoccupation with thoughts of death and a constant desire for a higher existence. And finally, the reader will have to resist the natural, common tendency to measure and evaluate historical personalities by the modes of thought, the fashions, and the prejudices of one's own time. With a reasonably open-minded attitude, the modern reader will be able to comprehend John Frederic Oberlin as a unique figure in whom the wisdom of the Enlightenment, the enthusiasms and excitements of religious fanatics, and the inspiration of the prophets and saints of the Old and the New Testament came together in the shaping of that community which so uniquely bears the stamp of Oberlin that it may be said to be a projection and extension of his personality.

Part 1

From Strasbourg to Waldersbach: 1740–1767

1

Heritage and Childhood

The first known appearance of the family name Oberlin in any public record in Alsace is in the registry of the church in Sundhofen, a town near Colmar, which belonged at that time to the Württembergian earldom of Hoburg. The entry in the registry states that one Jacob Oberlin (also known as Oberle and Offerlin), an emigrant miller and baker from Messkirch in Württemberg proper, then resident in Colmar, had presented his son Johannes to be baptized on June 7, 1574.[1] It seems likely that Jacob Oberlin, who was a Protestant, had gone out to the little town of Sundhofen for the christening because the Lutheran faith had not yet been introduced in Colmar. Thus the Oberlin family tradition of Lutheranism goes back beyond the time when that faith was firmly established in the city of their residence; and Jacob Oberlin and his descendants persisted in it even during the Thirty Years' War, when Colmar, in the changing fortunes of battle, was swayed back and forth between Protestantism and Catholicism.

In 1632, the second Johannes Oberlin, a son of that Johannes who had been baptized at Sundhofen in 1574, transferred the family seat to Strasbourg because Protestantism was more securely established there and he and his progeny could worship God according to their conscience and practice the family trade in peace.[2] Through two more generations the Oberlins were bakers, until, early in the eighteenth century, perhaps in a maneuver toward upward social mobility, one Johann Georg Oberlin broke with the family tradition, studied at the university, and eventually became preceptor of the sixth form at the renowned Protestant *Gymnasium* in Strasbourg. He married Marie-Madeleine Feltz and became the father of two daughters and seven sons, two of whom made names for themselves in the history of Alsace. The eldest of these was Jérémie-Jacques. He became a colleague of his father at the *Gymnasium* and later a professor at the University of Strasbourg and a distinguished historian and philologist; he counted among his friends and students at the university Johann Wolfgang Goethe, who accords him high praise in his autobiography, *Dichtung und Wahrheit*.[3] The second son was John Frederic, the subject of this biography, born on August 31, 1740.

The family traits that seem to have been dominant in determining John Frederic's peculiar talents and professional interests came mostly from his mother's side.[4] The ancestry of Marie-Madeleine Oberlin, née Feltz, has been traced beyond the beginning of the fourteenth century. The most interesting among all the known Oberlin forebears is one Marx Heyland. He was born in Vaihingen-on-Enz in Württemberg about 1500 and died in Basel in 1550. He first practiced the trade of tailor and then became, like Martin Luther, an Augustinian monk. Heyland, however, perhaps emulating his illustrious *frater,* soon repudiated Rome and the celibacy of his monastic order, and married in 1525. His wife was Mergeli Iselin, daughter of a wealthy Jewish family of Basel. After leaving the monastery Heyland became a printer; when the Augsburg Confession had been established in Basel, he became a Lutheran minister. Thus the family tradition of the Lutheran ministry was not only initially but also durably established; in the nine generations from Marx Heyland to John Frederic Oberlin there were seven Lutheran ministers, and six of them took ministers' daughters to wife.[5] Among the later maternal ancestors, the first one who did not become a clergyman was Oberlin's grandfather, Johann Heinrich Feltz, a jurist and professor.

Oberlin's father was a man of imposing appearance, well educated, enlightened, vivacious, conscientious, and possessed of a strong and firm character.[6] One of his favorite diversions was to take his large family on weekends to the country estate and chateau named Haegeli, at Schiltigheim near Strasbourg, that belonged to grandfather Feltz. He spent hours there instructing his children in the practical aspects of botany and agronomy and leading them in instructive games and amusements of various kinds. The favorite among these, with both the father and young Fritz, as John Frederic was invariably called by parents and siblings, was playing soldier. Father Oberlin would line up his seven sons according to their height and would march and countermarch them across the farmyard, alternately beating out normal marching cadence and double time on a battered old drum. This military sport aroused in Fritz a lasting interest in and admiration for the soldier's life, while the agricultural lore that he acquired during those weekends became the basis for later intensive study and experimentation in the Ban de la Roche.

In the childhood home of Oberlin's mother, literature and the arts had been cultivated. One of her sisters, Mme Link, whom Oberlin's brother Jeremie-Jacques once referred to in an academic disputation as "femina scientiis et morum elegantia conspicua," distinguished herself as a translator of French literary works into German. Mme Ernest Roerich, a great-granddaughter of Oberlin, wrote in 1910 that Oberlin's mother had received "a good education *à la française,* that is to say, the best that a young girl could receive at that time."[7] She had been sent to a private boarding school in Nancy, where she had become an intimate friend of Marie Lescynska, daughter of the unfortunate Stanislaus I, the exiled king of Poland. The two friends exchanged intimate letters for many years, even after the princess had become the wife of Louis XV and queen of France.

Oberlin's mother kept up her cultural interests despite the heavy demands of housekeeping for her large family. She avidly read the best French authors and, like her sister, translated some of their works into German. She was an excellent housewife and mother, a woman of great vivacity, imagination, and warmhearted piety. It was her daily practice to gather her children around the family table in the evening, not only for prayers and pious devotions, but also for conversation and to read to them from contemporary German authors, among whom her favorites were Klopstock and Gellert.

Concerning Oberlin's childhood there is little documentary evidence except that he was born on August 31 at Strasbourg, was baptized at St. Thomas Church on September 1, and was given the name Johann Friedrich. The only authentic information that we have beyond that is a small collection of anecdotes told to Oberlin's first French biographer, Ehrenfried Stoeber, by Oberlin's daughter, Mme Louise Witz, who must have heard them as reminiscences of her father and other relatives. After Stoeber they have been repeated by virtually every biographer, often with such dramatic embellishments as "reconstructed" dialogue.[8] Around them there has grown a hagiology about Oberlin. Their trite patness, however, seems so obtrusive that taken together they yield only a stereotype of a piously exemplary boy rather than an authentic picture of a particular youthful personality. They tell, for instance, how little Fritz saved his meager weekly allowance in order to use it for many acts of charity: returning it to his generous father to help him meet a financial emergency; pouring his whole treasury into the lap of a peasant woman whose basket of eggs had been upset on the market square by his naughty playmates; making a contribution of two sous to a poor woman who seemed inconsolable because she lacked just that amount for the purchase of a coveted petticoat. They also tell of deeds of heroism: how, for example, he once won the applause of bystanders by shielding a hapless beggar from the blows of a wrathful police officer. And they tell finally of Spartan habits of austerity: handicapped even as a schoolboy by the weakness of memory of which he complained all his life, and observing that he could memorize his lessons most easily early in the morning, he would put sharp-edged pieces of firewood in his feather mattress so that the comfort of a soft bed would not beguile him into oversleeping but cause him to rise up at dawn, with the motto "Aurora musis amica" on his lips.

The military garrison, which has always been a conspicuous presence in the frontier city of Strasbourg, afforded many a martial spectacle during Oberlin's adolescence and increased the interest in soldiering that had begun with his father's marching games. He was often seen at the barracks gate and is said to have been a favorite among the officers passing in and out there. But his father had chosen an academic career for himself, though his own admiration of the military had been great, and Fritz felt constrained to do likewise. Yet the military discipline which he admired so much he adopted as his own way of life. The designation "soldier of Christ," which he sometimes applied to himself, was more than a mere metaphorical cliché.

2

Preparation

Oberlin attended the Protestant *Gymnasium*. He finished the course at the age of fifteen (with an only moderately good record) and went from there to the university. His intention was ultimately to study theology, but in the early semesters he ranged over a broad field of general studies. The best information we have about his studies is from a letter written in 1820 in response to an inquiry from an admirer, a beginning theological student at Nancy, about his studies in preparation for the ministry. Oberlin, while asking his correspondent to "make allowances for the weakness of my octogenarian memory," gave, under the heading "general studies," the following list: Latin, Greek, Hebrew; logic, rhetoric, metaphysics; arithmetic, geometry, trigonometry, astronomy; ancient and modern geography, physics, natural history; history of philosophy; natural law; Egyptian, Greek, Roman, and Hebraic antiquities.[9] The omission of medical studies from the list of scientific subjects must have been inadvertent, for it is known that he attended lectures on medicine and also had some experience in the dissecting room.

Among the professors under whom he studied were Jean Daniel Schoepflin, historian and "Strasbourg's greatest eighteenth century scholar"; J. M. Lorenz, historian; Brackenhoffer, mathematician; Spielmann, professor of medicine and anatomy; Silberrad, professor of law.[10] Furthermore, Oberlin often visited lectures on medicine by Professors Laut, Pfeffinger, and Daniel. Though each professor is here

11

identified with a particular subject, none should be thought of as an authority in only one field. It was not an age of specialization in scholarship. For instance, the renowned expositor of Enlightenment, Christian Wolff, lectured at Halle not only on logic, metaphysics, and ethics, but also on cosmology, physics, mathematics, politics, natural law, and philosophy of religion. The universality of his competence may not have been matched by any of the Strasbourg dons, but it was probably approached by many of them. The academic fashion of the time both for students and for professors was general studies, and Oberlin's diaries and letters amply show that he kept up a lively interest throughout his fourscore and six years in just about all of the diverse subjects to which he devoted his first three years at the university. Both from his verbal testimony and from his lifelong avocations we know that his favorite studies were technology and the natural sciences.[11]

The importance of school and university studies in the forming of Oberlin's character and attitudes is matched, if not outweighed, by that of the religious influences that dominated his childhood and youth. His parents were attracted to the movement within the Lutheran church known as Pietism, which emphasized a religion of the heart as opposed to mere acceptance of the dogma of a more intellectual religion. This strain of Lutheranism, which was vigorously opposed by the established church authorities in Alsace as elsewhere, had nevertheless a considerable group of followers consisting of church members who, in addition to their attendance at regular church services, held small group meetings each week for Bible study and devotions. One of these fellowships was wont to base its meditations on the writings of Count Zinzendorf. These Friends of the Congregation of the Brethren, as they called themselves, were led by two young theologians. One of them was Magister Franz Christian Lembke, evening preacher at Old St. Peter's and a colleague of Oberlin's father. It was through this connection that Lembke had been one of Oberlin's sponsors at his baptism.[12]

Another admirer of Zinzendorf's teaching was Johann Sigismund Lorenz, preacher first at St. Nicolaus, then at Young St. Peter's. It is worthwhile to describe this man in some detail, for he, among all of Oberlin's teachers, influenced him most in his theological thinking and his preaching style. In his youth Lorenz had been stirred by Friedrich Eberhard Rambach's *Meditations on the Passion* and had "decided to consecrate myself with all my heart to my Savior."[13] As a young curate he was obliged to be content for years in modest posts, for the churchwardens were wont to hold at arm's length all candidates for livings who were suspected of Pietistic leanings. After several years as preceptor in the house of the Prince of Nassau-Saarbrücken, he became a professor at the Protestant *Gymnasium* and evening preacher at St. Nicolaus. The emotionalism of this young preacher, his constant appeal for true "conversion" in the Pietistic sense, his insistence that Christians must be doers of the Word and not hearers only, and especially his preaching against ostentation in dress and against attendance at theater and balls, aroused the opposition of the leaders of Strasbourg society. On Oberlin, however, he made a deep and enduring impression. In 1768 Lorenz became a member of the university's theological faculty, though he was watched closely by his orthodox colleagues; in 1769 he became director of the theological school of St. Guillaume and evening preacher at the Temple-Neuf; and finally, in 1771, minister of Young St. Peter's. In his academic teaching Lorenz opposed particularly two "intellectualistic" conceptions of religion: a lifeless, traditional "ecclesiastical respectability" based upon the profession of "one correct and true doctrine"; and the moralistic rationalism which was spreading from England to France and Germany among the educated class. He sought to instill in his students, as future ministers, a religion of the heart, a personal and fervent attachment to Christ and a total consecration to His service.

The idea of personal dedication also pervaded his preaching, which became ever more effective, especially among middle-class citizens and artisans, who honored him with the sobriquet "Jesus Prediger." But the more influential elite, captivated by the rationalism and humanism of the Enlightenment, remained hostile to his demonstrative conception of Christianity. He was eloquent in his advocacy of the pragmatic and individualistic religion expressed in a personal dedication to God and in a Christianity of deeds, of good works, of sacrificial devotion to one's fellow men through the faithful fulfillment of one's vocation. An unusual feature of his sermons was that the practical application of the biblical text, which in the standard Lutheran sermon was generally limited to a brief paragraph, constituted virtually the whole discourse. His sermons were often specifically addressed to particular vocations. Thus a sermon on Jesus in the temple was addressed to school children; one on the centurion at Capernaum to soldiers and the constabulary; and one on St. Paul to artisans and tradesmen. It was a preaching technique that Oberlin would often emulate in his own ministry.

By these qualities, beliefs, and talents Lorenz aroused the respect and affection of young Oberlin, inspired him to enter the ministry, and continued always to exercise a strong influence on his theological attitudes and his preaching style. Eventually, however, the friendship between master and disciple came to grief because of Lorenz's insistent belief that everlasting hellfire awaited all those who did not submit before death to a revivalistic conversion. The break came in 1770 when Oberlin's father died. "The death of your beloved father, my dear Oberlin," Lorenz wrote on that occasion, "must surely cause you great sorrow; and all the more, indeed, because, though he was a perfectly good and righteous man, the gates of heaven will not be opened to him because he is not counted among the host of those who have been reborn." Thus confronted with an image of divine cruelties to a person he loved, the ardor of Oberlin's devotion to his master suddenly cooled. We shall have occasion to recall his revulsion against that restrictive conception of the limits of divine redemption when, some years later, in a particularly eloquent sermon, he himself will seem on the point of embracing that doctrine, but will be brought up short by the reaction to it of one of the least of his parishioners.

Having completed the traditional *triennium academicum,* Oberlin received the baccalaureate degree on April 6, 1758. Thereafter, having chosen the ministry as his profession, he continued his studies in the theological faculty. In the previously quoted letter of 1820 to the young theological student, Oberlin listed his specifically theological studies as dogmatics, exegesis, church history ("in conjunction with the relevant geography"), history of dogmas ("the teachings of various churches or communions in conjunction with the teachings of Holy Scripture"), pastoral theology, and "daily study of the Bible from beginning to end." His professors of theology were Lorenz, Beyckert, Reuchlin, and Elie Stoeber.[14]

On the first day of the year 1760, at the beginning of a new decade of the century and shortly before the beginning of the third decade of his life, Oberlin wrote down a "Solemn Act of Dedication to God." The inspiration for this action probably had come, either directly or through Lorenz, from the English dissenter Philip Doddridge, who, in his *Rise and Progress of Religion in the Soul* (1744), which had appeared in a French translation by Rambach in 1751, recommended that every earnest believer strengthen his resolve to serve the Lord by making a written declaration of his intent to do so.[15] Such declarations, to be written by all true believers and periodically reviewed and renewed throughout their lives, were also recommended by the Moravian Brethren. Oberlin's declaration runs to a thousand words and is replete with utterances of religious fervor such as pervade the writings of the Pietists:

> Eternal, infinitely holy God! I desire fervently, with feelings of deepest humility and with a contrite heart to come into Thy presence . . . to make a covenant with Thee. . . . I pledge myself most solemnly to Thee. . . . I declare that I am Thy child. . . . I renounce all other lords who have hitherto held dominion over me, the joys of the world . . . the lusts of the flesh. . . . I dedicate to Thee all that I am and all that I have: the faculties of my mind, the members of my body, my portion, my time. . . . Grant that in the moment of my departing . . . I shall remember this covenant and shall employ my last breath in Thy service. . . . Let the name of the Lord be my eternal witness that I have signed this covenant with the steadfast and earnest will to keep it.

Some biographers have interpreted this document as evidence of a conversion, a sudden spiritual awakening such as the Pietists demanded as being prerequisite to a godly life. Though Oberlin was reared and educated in the Lutheran doctrine, he did not interpret it, as many Pietist theologians did, to include belief in the utter depravity of man through Adam's sin. Though he found much to admire and emulate in the theories and practices of the Pietists, he did not share their belief that before the education of a child could begin, the evil that has been innate since Adam's fall in every human child must be eradicated and destroyed root and branch. He rather leaned toward the vast optimism that characterized enlightened men in that charismatic century who, under the influence of Locke and Kant, proclaimed the fundamental goodness of man. He probably accepted Leibniz's proposition that this is the best of all possible worlds; but yet his optimism, like that of Leibniz himself, was not absolute, for he knew that evil must be an inevitable ingredient even in the best of all possible worlds. Oberlin therefore saw the necessity of constant vigilance against such temptations to evil as "the joys of the world," "the lusts of the flesh," slothfulness of body and of mind, selfishness and greed; and in his struggle against these and similar all-too-human weaknesses, he recognized the strategic value of keeping before him a positive goal toward which he could strive with his whole being. He found such a goal in the moral perfection exemplified by the Mosaic law and in subservience to the will of God.

Within this context, Oberlin's declaration is more than a monument merely to a sudden conversion; it is a sober, sincere statement of attitudes and resolutions that began to be formed in his childhood and were explicitly articulated in his "Act of Dedication" as he entered manhood. It remained the guiding rule of his conduct until his death. At the age of thirty, ten years after he had first inscribed it, he endorsed it by subscribing the words: "Renewed in Waldersbach in 1770"; and fifty years after that, at eighty, he read it through again and wrote in the margin: "God have mercy upon me! Waldersbach 1820." It was an act of dedication gravely conceived, soberly planned, periodically renewed, and methodically and conscientiously executed.

This explicit dedication of his life to God was reinforced by rules of conduct that he imposed upon himself, as indicated in various entries in his journal from 1760 to about 1765. In one of them he pledges to exert himself always to do the opposite of what his sensual inclinations may desire; to eat and drink but little and never more than is necessary to maintain good health, and to eat less of those foods that he particularly likes than of others; to seek to control the impetuosity which often takes possession of him; to abjure all invective; to perform his duties as a student with the utmost exactness and the greatest punctuality; to keep sacred all hours left free for study; to be content with a minimum of clothing and furnishings in order that he will not find it necessary to give many lessons and will thus be able to give better lessons to those pupils whom he has, while his studies will be less interrupted.

These resolutions are supplemented by the following rules: "Always save a part of your income for the poor. . . . Be as frugal as possible. Pay those who serve you in such a way that they will be content, but at the same time seek to avoid unnecessary expenditures. Do things for yourself. See to it that your clothing and your furnishings are simple but clean."[16]

There is testimony that Oberlin actually lived by these austere rules: he ate but two meals each day, a full meal—but mostly without meat and wine—at noon, and only bread with water in the evening; he allowed himself but a few hours of sleep. Throughout his life he repelled the "temptations of the flesh" with puritanical rigor. That he learned early to withstand pain is indicated by an incident in December 1766. There developed an abscess on his leg which grew alarmingly and caused him great pain; but he had promised to preach at the early morning service in one of the churches of Strasbourg. So, despite the bitter cold of that morning and the pain, he walked to the church and preached at seven o'clock. Thereafter he went back to his room, lanced the abscess, and then sat down to continue his studying where he had left off the night before.

In 1763, having completed all the requirements, he received, on July 21, the degree of doctor of philosophy.[17] He never made use of the doctoral title, and all but his most recent biographers have been unaware that he possessed it. Perhaps he was motivated by his natural humility and his desire to minimize any intellectual or social superiority that might separate him from the simple folk of his parish; the only titles that he ever employed were *Pfarrer, pasteur,* and *ministre.* Having reached this milestone, Oberlin abandoned his studies for a time in order to take a position that would give him practical experience.

It was common practice in the eighteenth century for noblemen and other highly placed personages to entrust the education of their children, especially their sons, to private teachers, usually called *Hofmeister* in German and *précepteur* in French, rather than to have them mingle with the mass of children of common citizens and peasants in the schools. Students of theology were most in demand as preceptors because of the high respectability of their calling; and probably many a calculating candidate sought such employment hoping that he might be placed in a household whose head had influence in his community as a patron of the church and who could therefore help him to a good and satisfying benefice. Such ulterior motives should not be ascribed to all preceptors, however. Among those who temporarily practiced the vocation of *Hofmeister* were some of the very great among Oberlin's contemporaries, including Klopstock, Hamann, and Wieland. No doubt there were also many among the students of such tutors who, like Wilhelm and Alexander von Humboldt, spoke of their teachers with affection and appreciation. Still, the stereotype of a preceptor as it is reflected in literature—for example in J. M. R. Lenz's drama *Der Hofmeister*— is the forlorn, lonely, and sometimes angry man exposed to the contumely of his employer and the humiliation of being treated by children and parents as a servant on the same social level as the valet or even the stable boy, while he, for his part, complains bitterly of the obstreperousness and the stupidity of his charges.[18]

Oberlin had the good fortune to be employed as *Hofmeister* by an intelligent, generous, and kind man who in no way resembled the caricature of the contumelious employer. Daniel Gottlieb Ziegenhagen, the son of a Lutheran pastor of Brandenburg, had emigrated to Strasbourg as a student of medicine. After completing his studies he remained there as a medical practitioner. By 1762 he was generally considered the foremost physician and surgeon of the city. When seeking a preceptor for four of his eleven children, he thought of Oberlin, whom he knew through his connection with St. Nicolaus Church.

The connection between Oberlin and the Ziegenhagen family proved profitable for both parties, though it had in the beginning seemed destined not to come about at all because of the maladroitness of a friend whom Ziegenhagen had commissioned to recruit the young candidate in his behalf. Certain specifications laid down by the intermediary are recorded by Stoeber. Some of them are of interest because of Oberlin's responses.

Condition: The children must always be washed and dressed in clean clothing.

Response: I shall urge cleanliness upon my charges . . .
but I shall not assume the duties of a domestic, which
would only rob me of time for my teaching, as well as
for my studies.

C.: The *Hofmeister* will go for a walk with the children
three times each week.

R.: This will be done more or less often as time and
occasion offer.

C.: During the walks the *Hofmeister* will converse with
the children upon useful subjects.

R.: This is my usual custom, whenever the circumstances
are favorable.

C.: The *Hofmeister* will carve the meat at table.

R.: This I will not do!

Thus Oberlin made his first assertion of that sense of the
dignity of teaching that he was to proclaim many times and in
many ways throughout his life. It must be put down to Dr.
Ziegenhagen's credit that he did not construe the unabashed
responses as portents of insubordination in a prospective
household servant; on the contrary, they seem to have pleased
him, for he employed Oberlin forthwith. During the three
years of his residence in the Ziegenhagen household, Oberlin
enjoyed the respect and affection of the learned doctor, who
remained his good friend and generous supporter until his
death in 1771. Oberlin's position gave him not only the
possibility to gain valuable pedagogical experience while still
having time for study, but also an opportunity to acquire other
knowledge and skills that proved of value to him in his life's
work in the Ban de la Roche. His generous master initiated him
into the mysteries of *materia medica* and trained him in the
rudimentary skills of surgery, particularly the then indispensable art of bloodletting. Stoeber tells of his first surgical
operation. One day, after a conversation about medical theory
and practice, Dr. Ziegenhagen suddenly removed his jacket,
turned back his sleeve and said with a smile, "I feel that I need
to be bled and I want you to do it for me. So, prepare yourself
for your first surgical exploit." Oberlin hesitated, fearing that
he might injure his beloved master, but Ziegenhagen insisted,
and the novice completed his initiation with faultless success.

Oberlin's chief duty in this household was, of course, the
teaching of the children, and to it he devoted himself with the

But, in keeping with his austere way of life, he was determined to renounce any prospect of a comfortable living in the easy circumstances of a well-established parish and to seek instead a post where there would be trials and troubles to cope with, hardships and privations to endure, oppositions and enmities to overcome; in short, a place where he could show the profundity of his devotion to God and of his love for God's children in a life of toil, humility, and sacrifice. An assignment that had seemed to promise possibilities for the attainment of some of those purposes had been offered to him when, after he had completed the *triennium academicum,* he had been invited to apply for a post as a military field chaplain; but after long consideration he had turned it down "with an unquiet heart." Why had he done that? Hadn't he always felt a predilection for the military life? Some eight years later he wrote in a retrospective letter to his mother that the prospect had filled his heart with terror, but without identifying the specific causes of his fears. One can only surmise that at the time he had not yet felt adequately prepared to cope with the crass materialism and atheistic braggadocio of the "enlightened" officers' corps, attitudes that were so alien to his posture of pietistic humility. He knew that the officers made it their sport to ridicule their chaplains and to thwart and frustrate their purposes, and he may have felt himself to be not yet mature enough to match his wits with theirs. Furthermore, his self-confessed weaknesses of "vivacity, impatience, and importunity" may have raised doubts in his mind about his amenability to military discipline. Perhaps also the desire to complete at last his theological studies had made acceptance of the opportunity seem premature. Whatever the impediments may havé been at that time, they either did not recur or did not seem insurmountable now, in 1767, when the prospect of a chaplaincy presented itself again. He prayed for the gift of complete submission to God's will and then filed his application. Thereupon he procured books by the *philosophes,* whose names he had often heard spoken by his acquaintances in the garrison of Strasbourg. He immersed himself in the writings of Voltaire and Rousseau, of Diderot, Holbach, and La Mettrie.

His judgment about these savants of his time was always ambivalent. He found many admirable and useful insights in their writings, applauded the humanitarianism of much of their social theory, and appropriated much of their pedagogical wisdom for his own use as an educator; but he abominated their religious skepticism, their deistic anti-Christianity, their materialistic atheism. Having observed the enthusiastic interest of the young officers in the writings of these men and their ready acceptance of the rationalistic world views expressed in them, Oberlin, in his fanatic youthful religiosity, saw the "godless *philosophes*" as the Antichrist whose sway over the minds of the soldiery it would now be his duty to exterminate. He wanted to know the enemy in order to smite him more effectively.

The expected commission was inexplicably delayed for weeks. Were the higher military authorities perhaps uncertain about the wisdom of confronting the officers' corps with this zealously pietistical soldier of Christ? Or was the delay a signal from God that this was not the work that He had in mind for him? Then, one wintry day early in 1767, there was a knock at Oberlin's door. Upon opening it with a friendly "*Entrez!*", he found himself facing a short, frail, yet dignified and somehow distinguished-looking man who introduced himself as *Pasteur* Stuber of Waldersbach.[21] As he came in, Stuber noticed a couch behind partially opened paper curtains. It looked dishevelled; Oberlin had been resting on it, nursing a toothache. "*Voilà,* just like a room in the Ban de la Roche," Stuber said to himself. As Oberlin bustled about making his guest as comfortable as possible and putting the couch in order, Stuber joked with him in a friendly way about his newspaper curtains. "And what," he said, "is that iron pan hanging over your writing table?" "That is my kitchen," Oberlin answered. "At noon I dine with my parents; they allow me to take a piece of bread away with me. At eight o'clock in the evening I put the bread in the pan, pour some water over it, salt it, put my lamp under it, and continue my studies until about ten or eleven, when my hunger reminds me that it is time for supper. Then I eat my homemade soup; and it tastes better to me than the finest delicacy." "Ah," thought Stuber, "this is my man!"

Oberlin had never visited the Ban de la Roche, nor had he met Pastor Stuber; yet he was not totally unfamiliar with either the place or the man. His maternal grandfather, Johann Heinrich Feltz, representing St. Thomas Church, had attended the installation of his brother-in-law, Johannes Rapp, as minister at Waldersbach in 1728 and thereafter had returned often as a visitor. Furthermore, Dr. Ziegenhagen had become acquainted with the parish when his stepson had been minister there from 1747 to 1750 and had kept up an active interest in the progress of the parish. So, from his grandfather Oberlin had heard much about the Ban de la Roche, and from Ziegenhagen he had learned also about Stuber and his work, and was therefore pleased at the opportunity to make the acquaintance of the man and to hear more about the parish. Good rapport having been thus established, the two men talked long and earnestly together about the Ban de la Roche.

JEAN-GEORGES OBERLIN
père de Jean-Frédéric

3   Jean-Georges Oberlin

2   Marie-Madeleine Oberlin née Feltz

5   Jérémie-Jacques Oberlin

4   Jean-Georges Stuber

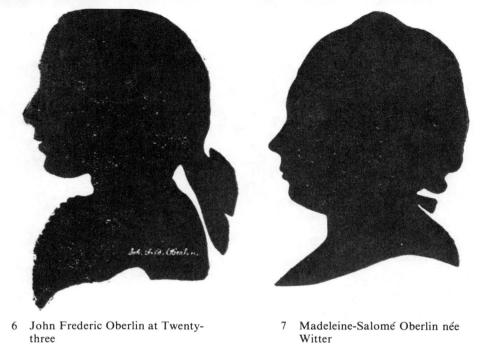

6 John Frederic Oberlin at Twenty-three

7 Madeleine-Salomé Oberlin née Witter

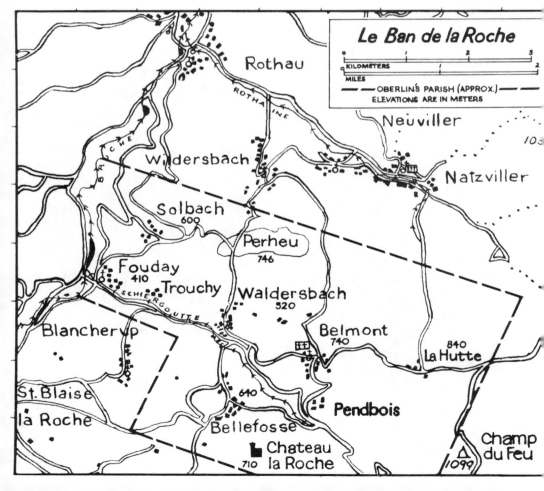

Le Ban de la Roche

KILOMETERS

MILES

OBERLIN'S PARISH (APPROX.)
ELEVATIONS ARE IN METERS

Rothau

ROTHAINE

BRUCHE

Neuviller

Widersbach

Natzviller

Solbach
600

Perheu
746

Fouday
410

Trouchy

SCHIERGOUTTE

Waldersbach
520

Blancherup

Belmont
740

La Hutte
840

St. Blaise
la Roche

640

Pendbois

Bellefosse

Chateau
la Roche
710

Champ
du Feu

1099

3

The Ban de la Roche

The Ban de la Roche lies within the old province of Alsace near its border with Lorraine and in the present *département* Bas-Rhin of the Republic of France. It is a small valley situated between the easterly and westerly ridges of the Vosges Mountains. It is bounded on its north and south sides by two small streams flowing to the river Bruche, on the west side by the river itself, and on the east by a high mountain called, in French, sometimes *Haut Champ* and sometimes *Champ du Feu,* and in German *Hochfeld.*[22] Within these borders are contained eight villages divided between two parishes, each of which is designated by the place of residence of its ministers: Rothau with Wildersbach and Neuviller; Waldersbach with Bellefosse, Belmont, Fouday, and Solbach. In Oberlin's time Waldersbach also had the two still existing hamlets, Trouchy and la Hutte, plus a third, called Pendbois or Hangholz. Scattered between the villages and hamlets and nestled in the folds of the higher hillsides there were, and still are today, many isolated farmsteads, some of them inaccessible to vehicles at any time and sometimes in winter even to pedestrians because of the heavy snowfalls. Both the French name *Ban de la Roche* and the German, *das Steintal,* are derived from the name of the medieval fortified castle, *Château de la Roche, das Schloss zum Stein,* whose ruins look down from a lofty crag above Bellefosse on all the villages save Solbach, which is hidden behind a high plateau above Waldersbach called Perheu.[23] The differences in elevation above sea level in the Waldersbach parish are great. In descending order they are, in meters: Champ du Feu, 1,100; Château de la Roche, 955; La Hutte, 840; Perheu, 746; Belmont, 740; Bellefosse, 640; Solbach, 600; Waldersbach, 520; and Fouday, 410. The straight-line distances between Waldersbach and other villages are, in approximate miles: Belmont and Solbach, 2; Fouday, 1.8; and Bellefosse, .75.

In the Ban de la Roche of today one is never far from the sound of running water. The predominately westerly or southwesterly winds grow cold in their rising course over the westerly range of the Vosges, thus causing heavier precipitation over the valley than is experienced in other regions of Alsace. Agriculture in the area benefits from the abundance of moisture. The Chirgoutte, which arises in the forests of the Champ du Feu, takes up along its course the waters of many brooks and rills and rivulets. These flow through and irrigate fields and meadows, keep the water-troughs along the village streets in front of the peasants' houses brimming with fresh water, sustain a plentiful stock of trout, and drain the superfluous waters from areas that in Oberlin's day were marshes or bottomless quagmires. In the winter the heavy precipitation caused grave problems in communication. Oberlin's journals describe a winter when the snow was "three shoes higher than the beginning of the roofs of some houses in Bellefosse and twenty-five shoes deep on the ground in Belmont."[24] Furthermore, the weeks of isolation caused by such deep snow covers are prolonged because the orientation of the valleys and gullies leading down to the Chirgoutte allows little direct exposure to the sun during the winter months.

In the Middle Ages the Château de la Roche was occupied by a succession of robber-knights. A local legend tells of three noble ladies who came for a time into possession of the château and led their men out to ravage the region more cruelly than any of their predecessors had done, until their robber's den was overpowered and the three robber-baronesses were captured one foggy night in 1099 by their neighbors, the masters of Schirmeck, Salm, and Colroy-la-Roche. The event was believed to be commemorated in a scarcely traceable frescoe that Oberlin described in 1808 as having been visible on a wall in the old chapel at Fouday until it was painted over in 1776 or 1777. But this romantic legend probably has no basis in historical fact, for neither Schirmeck nor Salm existed in 1099, and the Château de la Roche was probably built in the twelfth century on the foundations of a Roman fortress.[25] The earliest documentary evidence of its existence dates from the middle of the fourteenth century, when the knights of Ratsamhausen occupied it as feudal lords of the Ban. Following the medieval tradition, they terrorized the region as robber-knights and highwaymen until the citizens of Strasbourg raised an expedition against them. In this action the château was reduced to ruin, but the Ratsamhausens were allowed to continue to rule over the Ban. A hundred years later they sold the fief to the Counts Palatine of Veldenz-Lützelstein. Upon the demise of that house, the fief reverted to the French crown. In 1720 it was granted to the king's military commissar for Alsace and later minister of war, d'Angervilliers. In 1723 d'Angervilliers transferred it to his daughter, Marie-Jeanne-Louise, who later married the Marquis de Ruffec. In 1758 the Marquise de Ruffec passed it on to her son-in-law, Count Antoine-René de Voyer d'Argenson, Marquis de Paulmy, minister of war to Louis XV. Soon thereafter the king honored d'Argenson by elevating the Ban to the status of an earldom. In 1770, the third year of Oberlin's ministry, d'Argenson sold the fief for 330,000 francs to another favorite of the king, a sturdy, highly honored patrician of Strasbourg, Baron Jean de Dietrich, who proved to be an enlightened, gracious, and generous ruler of the previously tyrannized region.

After the Revolution had wiped out all patents and privileges, the entire Ban de la Roche was incorporated in the *département* Bas-Rhin; later it was divided and part of it was assigned to the *département* Vosges. After the war of 1870, when Alsace, together with Lorraine, was incorporated in the German Reich, the Steintal, as it was then officially called, became a part of the administrative district of Molsheim. Since 1919, when Alsace again reverted to France, the entire Ban de la Roche, reassuming its old name, has been a part of the *département* Bas-Rhin. Thus, like the whole province of Alsace since the days of the Roman Empire, the Ban de la Roche has been successively German, then French, then German again, and since 1919 French once more.

Remote and isolated though it is in its geographical location, the Ban de la Roche has had to suffer more than its share of military destruction and pillage. More often than other regions of Alsace, the Bruche Valley has been the scene of bloody feuds and military actions. Especially the Thirty Years' War and its aftermath laid waste the land and nearly exterminated its inhabitants. Their situation was particularly bad during the Swedish occupation. Even after the Peace of Westphalia, tranquility was not restored; the people were heavily taxed for war tributes *"pour satisfaction suédoise"* as stipulated in the treaty. Two years after the treaty, Weimarian troops passed through, and thereafter the populace again was forced to pay tribute "for the subsidy of the Empire and the maintenance of the soldiers." The population of the entire Bruche Valley, including the Ban de la Roche, was nearly extinguished by the depredations of the soldiery, the death of multitudes from plague and famine, and the execution of presumed witches who were tortured to death or beheaded on the plateau above Waldersbach called Perheu in such great numbers that the ruling prince expressed surprise that the small area could have harbored so many.[26] Church records show that there were only six marriages in the five villages of the Walderbach parish in all the eighteen years from 1640 to 1658. The lowest point of population seems to have been reached in 1650, when the entire parish had been reduced to about fifty inhabitants and the population of Fouday consisted of only two persons, a widow and her seven-year-old child. The woman's name was Milan and she is said to have come there at some earlier time from Italy. By 1655, returning exiles had increased the number of households in the entire parish to thirty-eight, but in the next five years only five more were added.[27] This slowness of growth is not surprising; the everlasting scourge of poverty caused by the infertility of the soil and frequent crop failures in that harsh climate was exacerbated by almost continuous military depredations and compounded by the impositions of tribute and villainage by rapacious feudal lords, which continued in the Ban de la Roche long after feudalism had been eradicated in the rest of Alsace and in nearly all of France. The last feudal lord of the Ban was dispossessed by the Revolution of 1789. A second cause was the isolation of the area, imposed by its geographic situation and intensified by peculiarities of language and religion.

French or German? In the history of many an Alsatian community this question presents itself. The upper reaches of the Bruche and all its tributary valleys with the exception of the Ban de la Roche were settled by Alemanni. Thus the language of all areas contiguous to the Ban de la Roche became German, but that of the Ban itself has always been French.[28] For want of communication with the world beyond its narrow confines, the vernacular deteriorated to a peculiar patois. Its vocabulary was a compound of standard French infused with archaisms, of German infiltrating from the surrounding areas, and of Italian borrowed from workers imported by the overlord from Italy and Switzerland. Its sound had the gutteral undertones of the Alemannic Swiss dialects. Here is a letter written by a young man reporting his safe arrival in Strasbourg after a hard trip, together with a translation in standard French:

> Biyet. Mis dchers pére et mére! Dje sò errivé è Chtrose-bourgue è bouonne santé, si nò que dj'ons brâmon èvu lè piooue et que dj'ons ètu bin hôdés. Dj'ons errivé è chéz-houres do sà.

> Lettre. Mes chers père et mère. Nous sommes arrivés à Strasbourg en bonne santé, si non que nous avons eu beaucoup de pluie et que nous avons été bien fatigués. Nous sommes arrivés à six heures du soir.[29]

Oberlin's brother, Professor Jérémie-Jacques, after a summer vacation in the parsonage at Waldersbach, during which he collected material, published a book on the patois of the Ban de la Roche which many later French linguistic scholars acknowledge as a pioneer work in dialect studies. On the subject of the patois there was disagreement between the brothers: John Frederic wanted to stamp it out as a hindrance to communication between his people and the outside world; Jérémie-Jacques, as a scholar in linguistics and a folklorist, wished to see it preserved and nurtured.

Some writers have tended to exaggerate the backwardness, the decadence, and indeed the "savagery" of the residents of the Ban de la Roche before Oberlin's time.[30] In their defense it may be said that if they spoke a patois that was incomprehensible to outsiders, it was because isolation and changes in the ethnic composition of the population had wrought changes in their mode of utterance; but it made their speech no more subhuman than that of many other regions that one could name in France, Germany, and elsewhere, whose dialects even today seem barbarous to unaccustomed ears. If their literacy rate was

lower than that of the rest of Alsace, it was because the daily
struggle for continuance of life occupied their energies to the
exclusion of such intellectual pursuits as reading and writing,
not because they were of a lower order of intelligence. If there
were times when they subsisted on grasses and herbs, they did
so because of famine in the land, not because they had reverted
to the feeding habits of beasts; and if some writers have claimed
that they lived like savages in caves, they are simply wrong, for
there are no natural caves in the area and the nature of the soil
is such that they could not be created without great labor,
engineering skill, and expense. And, finally, if the roads were in
bad condition, they were no worse than the streets and
highways in other regions of Europe; for do not many
travelogues and diaries contain records of broken wheels and
axles and whippletrees because of the wretchedly kept, deeply
rutted roads? Are there not many literary works of that time in
all the European languages in which situations of tragedy or
comedy are the result of such accidents? And as for other more
primitive areas, consider the following from the *American
Annual Register* of 1797: "The roads from Philadelphia to
Baltimore exhibit, for the greater part of the way, an aspect of
savage desolation. Chasms to the depth of six, eight, or ten feet
occur at numerous intervals. A stage-coach which left
Philadelphia on the 5th of February, 1796 took five days to go
to Baltimore."[31]

Another cause of isolation was the fact that the Ban was a
Protestant island in a Catholic sea. There is no documentary
evidence available concerning the coming of the Reformation
to the Ban de la Roche, but it is generally agreed that it was
definitely established, under the principle of "cuius regio, eius
religio," when the house of Veldenz assumed tenure in 1570.[32]
The change of faith created no great disturbances. The parish
priest at that time was a man named Papellier. He is said to
have been a gregarious and merry man who at weddings
danced with the peasant maids of his parish "as passionately as
any other bachelor," often removing his clerical coat and
camisole if the evening was hot. When he heard the news of the
new disposition he accommodated himself to it without com-
punction, put on the new costume, and conducted the services
according to good Lutheran doctrine "to the extent that he
understood it."[33]

During the Thirty Years' War, one Nicolas Marmet was the

sole clergyman of the entire Ban de la Roche, which at that time had not yet been divided into two parishes. He had come there in 1625, lived most of the time in Wildersbach, where he owned a small property, and died in Rothau in 1675. Marmet seems to have been a kind of precursor of the Enlightenment; he sought to eradicate superstition and idolatry from his parish, once almost losing his life in the effort. Stoeber tells the story as follows: Although Protestantism forbids iconolatry, the church at Fouday nevertheless displayed a wooden effigy of the head of John the Baptist. According to an immemorial custom, upon entering the sanctuary the women either kissed this image or at least threw it a kiss with their hands. Marmet, disturbed by such acts of idolatry, removed the image. Thereupon the women, motivated by feelings of outrage and revenge, stormed the parsonage, captured the parson, and were about to fling him into the Bruche when fortunately some men came along who rescued him from the furies. But the head did not appear again. Thus have the good Ban de la Rochois ever been inclined to deal with enlightened outsiders intent on reforming them; even Oberlin was to have a similar experience in his time.

Two important steps toward cultural recovery from two-score years of depradation were taken fifteen and seventeen years, respectively, after the war's end; beginning in 1663 there were schoolmasters in the Ban de la Roche again; and in 1665 Pastor Marmet received the help of a vicar who resided in Waldersbach.[34] From then on the Ban was divided into two parishes, Rothau and Waldersbach. The church at Waldersbach was elevated to a "mother church," and the names of the ministers of both parishes are known to this day in unbroken succession. In 1700 one Pierre Christophe Morel became minister in Waldersbach. He called himself *Ministre du Ban de la Roche du côté de Waldersbach* and was the first to reside in a regular parsonage, a structure little better than a hut, which had formerly belonged to a huntsman. This remained the Waldersbach parsonage until a new one was built long after Oberlin's arrival at the parish.

The decline in the physical conditions of life for the people was accompanied by a deterioration in their spiritual life as well. Since the parish minister was both the spiritual and intellectual leader of the community, not only their religious life, but also the quality of their schooling depended largely on him. In the early years after the Reformation the ministers were regularly recruited from Montbéliard which, though French-speaking, was a Protestant county belonging to the dukes of Württemberg. For the Ban de la Roche this was a better source of supply than German-speaking Strasbourg. In 1727, however, Louis XV decreed that all state offices, including that of the clergy, were to be held only by French citizens. Thus the two parishes of the Ban were forced to turn to Strasbourg, where few theological students were capable of preaching in French. The problem of finding candidates eventually became so difficult that in 1737 the ecclesiastical authorities in Strasbourg, acting on the principle that if Mohammed will not come to the mountain, then the mountain must come to Mohammed, admonished the people to change their language from French to German. Thus these simple folk felt that they were abandoned even by those who had been, at least at times, their only comforters and consolers, namely, their ministers. At the same time, more than ever before, the Strasbourg church council looked upon the Ban de la Roche as a kind of Siberia to which they could banish clerics who had incurred their disfavor or who were, because of their way of life or for some other reason, considered unworthy of their high calling. Between 1723 and 1750, Waldersbach had four ministers who stayed only two years; two who stayed three years; one who stayed five years; and a certain Johann Rapp, a great-uncle of Oberlin's, who persevered through six years. The first hope of eventual improvement in their lot came to the people of the Waldersbach parish when Jean-Georges Stuber came there. Under his wise and devoted ministry, the foundations were laid for the great reforms accomplished by Oberlin.

Stuber was installed in the Ban de la Roche in 1750. He stayed there until 1754, when he resigned because of ill health. He returned in 1760 and stayed on until 1767. He had not chosen Waldersbach as the place to begin his ministry; an ecclesiastical decree issued shortly before his ordination that "no one who has enjoyed the benefits of the theological seminary in Strasbourg shall accept a call issued by any authority other than the ecclesiastical council" had left him no choice but to go there when he was called. In a retrospective review of his ministry, however, he wrote: "This decree was my second birth, for it brought it about that the Ban de la

Roche became my first charge."[35] He describes the condition of the parish as he found it in 1750 as follows:

> All of the inhabitants of the valley are poor; rich are only those who suffer less want. The peasants, living in thatched huts and wearing wooden shoes, eke out a bare existence by laborious, small-scale agriculture on an infertile soil and by grazing an inferior breed of cattle. Their language is a Lothringian patois; their diet consists of potatoes and sometimes a bit of rye bread; few succeed in growing enough rye to last the year, and some are in constant want, both of bread and potatoes. But there is a spirit of mutual helpfulness in the valley and nobody goes begging. There is little or no wheat, no wine, and there are many who do not taste meat all year. Sheep are unknown, even as to their appearance. Hemp is grown, some oats, and less flax. Livestock consists of a few small horses (no donkeys), a wizened breed of cattle that languish in the winter, while in the summer (which lasts but four months) they climb laboriously over steep, stony, and distant slopes to graze in pastures where there is more moss than grass. Wood for fuel and for building houses and manufacturing shoes and vehicles is almost as scarce as bread, for the forests belong to the feudal lord of the region.

Of his predecessors in Waldersbach he wrote, "From time immemorial the people have had only indifferent, if not downright vexatious, ministers; for both the parishes are scorned as poor livings; the region is remote; the way of life crude and toilsome; and any parson going there can expect from Strasbourg initial disdain and ultimate oblivion instead of sympathy, supervision, or help." Yet, looking back on his own experience there, he wrote, "The very uniqueness of the region, however, makes it possible that a good and competent man could stay there with profit for a long term, for there is so much that is unmatched in language, ideas, way of life, and in all things that a parson needs to know about that it can not be compared with any other parish in Alsace nor in all of France."

Stuber found the condition of the schools especially lamentable. There were six persons in the entire valley who were charged with school-keeping duties: two in the Rothau parish and four in the five villages served by the parson of Waldersbach. These were not trained professional educators, but just persons who had, so to speak, submitted the lowest bids for the job. More often than not the teacher turned out to be the village herdsman. Probably that seemed a logical arrangement to the peasant populace, for it gave employment and shelter to the cowherd during the winter months when neither livestock nor children could be out in the fields, and in the public mind the functions and the methods of the two vocations were comparable. The value that was ascribed to the social usefulness and services of teachers and herdsmen, respectively, is indicated in the records of the payments made to each in three of the five villages after the two functions had been separated: the average annual wages of herdsmen were forty-four francs and eight sacks of potatoes; those of teachers were forty-three francs and five sacks.[36] Of twenty pupils who had completed the entire course of instruction, only one could read at all. No two children had books of the same content. With the help of Magister Ott, a charitable friend and teacher in Strasbourg, Stuber managed to procure enough copies of a single book so that all the pupils of the same class in a given village could learn simultaneously from the same book. Each village had a different book, so that by a system of exchange each school could have the successive use of several different textbooks.

The availability of uniform textbooks made it possible for Stuber to introduce "something of the Prussian method of instruction." But though they now had textbooks, both the pupils and their teachers had only "obscure notions of the Old Testament and the New, of chapter and verse."

> If you showed the pupils the beginning of a chapter and asked them where the end of the previous chapter was, they could not find it; nor had anyone told them in school what leaf, page, line, syllable, or word was. . . . If a child had stammered his way from the top to the bottom of a page he stopped there, even if the page ended with only the first syllable or two of a polysyllabic word. One day's recitation might end with the first syllables of a word, say: *consé-*: the next day's reading would then begin with: *-cration*. The book with which the pupils were most familiar was the hymnal . . . but if another book was put in their hands they were in a strange land where faces were no longer known to them. They confused *Jesus* with *je suis*, *coeur* with *cour*, *herbeux* with *heureux*, *ardeur* with *ordure*, *honneur* with *horreur*, etc.

Stuber's long-range efforts were directed toward better training of the teachers. He chose the best of the older pupils and instructed them himself with the purpose of making teachers of them. In the hope of giving them greater prestige in the community and establishing them as professionals, he gave them the title *messieurs les régents d'écoles*. Again with the help of Magister Ott, he solicited in Strasbourg two thousand francs which he put out at interest,[37] using the income to pay premiums to the teachers over and above their paltry wages for each proficient pupil whom they turned out, giving a larger sum for the older pupils, a smaller for the younger, and an especially generous one for any pupil who, though his gifts were meager, nevertheless did good work. He brought an element of rationality into the teaching process by separating the pupils into groups or classes according to the stage of their development.

To help solve the difficult problems of teaching children in their first reading experience to read what was to them in effect a foreign language, Stuber devised and had printed a textbook which he called *L'Alphabet Méthodique pour faciliter l'art d'épeler et de lire en français*. The book was published in Strasbourg in 1762.[38]

His eventual success in teaching the children to read and write aroused the admiration of the parents, some of whom, ashamed of their own ignorance, asked him to teach them also. Thus it came about that Stuber created a school for adults.[39] Beginning in 1760 he conducted separate classes each winter for men and women. During his ministry some 150 to 200 adults learned to read and write. To supply the people with reading matter he procured from Basel a number of copies of the Bible. In order to distribute these as widely as possible, he separated each volume into several books which he bound in parchment covers. These texts were circulated among families within the parish and are said to have gone even into homes of Roman Catholics in neighboring communities. To circumvent the prohibitions of the priests, Catholics bought the Bibles secretly.

Along with teaching the reading and writing of French, Stuber also vigorously promoted instruction in singing.[40] He first taught the schoolmasters "something about notes," and eventually the school children, in groups of twenty or thirty, were singing revival hymns with the *régents* accompanying them in the bass part. "We accomplished it that the entire congregation sang familiar hymns with discant and bass. I would have a few enterprising males learn the bass part by ear; the schoolmaster would begin the singing in that voice, which all male voices would follow. In the second or third bar the women joined in, led by one or two pre-appointed voices, and so it went on merrily, the men always coming along with the bass." He speaks also of the pleasure that he found, while riding from village to village in the summer time, in hearing "now from one hilltop, now from another, our musical youth, among them some fine, clear voices, singing religious songs."

On a certain Sunday each month one of the schoolmasters had to present his scholars for public examination. The children stood around the altar and recited catechism, hymns, and Bible verses "with a noble, clear and natural French pronunciation so uniformly good that with one's eyes closed one could scarcely tell when one child ended his recitation and the next child began."

A schoolmaster once asked Stuber how he should answer a man who had remarked: "Our children are taught everything differently now; is it because we have a different God from the one we had in the past?" Stuber advised him to answer: "Yes; that one was the God of darkness; now we are seeking the God of light."

In his theological theory and his practice as a minister Stuber was an independent thinker rather than a follower of any movement, school, or creed. The Bible was at the center of his teaching, both in the schools and in the churches. He took no interest in theological disputes and opposed the prescription of ecclesiastical doctrine or dogma. His one purpose as a minister was to bring the simple message of the gospel to his people in language that they could understand and with such penetrating urgency that their personal lives would be affected by it and, in their corporate life, they would become *ein Gottesvolk,* a people of God. Religion meant nothing to him if professing it did not make a difference in the conduct of daily life.

About six years after his return to Waldersbach, Stuber was again assailed by fatigue from his labors and by frequent illnesses caused by the rigors of life in that inclement climate. Consequently, when he unexpectedly received a call to a prestigious post at St. Thomas Church in Strasbourg, he was predisposed to accept it; but he could not bring himself to do so until he could be sure in his own mind that the right kind of man had been found to be his successor. So he went to Strasbourg to make inquiries among his acquaintances and friends there. Thus it eventually came about that the young theological candidate Oberlin found Stuber knocking at his door on that cold day in January 1767.

Oberlin's initial response to the proposal that he should go to the Ban de la Roche was hesitant and tended toward the negative because of his prior commitment to the military chaplaincy. But as Stuber talked in his quiet, earnest, and persuasive way, probably using terms similar to those that we know from his written description quoted earlier in this chapter, about the primitive conditions of life in the Ban de la Roche, the poverty of the people and their need of strong, dedicated, and imaginative spiritual leadership; and especially when he told of the hardships that the minister there had to endure, the thought came to Oberlin that this might be a call from God. By the time Stuber came to the end of his presentation, the thought had become a conviction. The hitherto puzzling delay in the confirmation of his military appointment he now took to be a signal from his Master that they who most needed his services were not the godless infidels in the Most Christian King's armies, but the simple, unlettered folk in the Steintal. To test the correctness of that interpretation, he placed three conditions upon his readiness to accept a call: that the military authorities would allow him to withdraw his application for a chaplaincy; that another suitable candidate would be found for that post; and that any other candidates who might have a prior claim on the Waldersbach pastorate would forfeit their option. All these stipulations were soon met; the first with the help of friends of Stuber who had influence with the authority that appointed chaplains; the second by the circumstance that another candidate stood ready to take the chaplaincy; the third by the obvious fact that no one else among the clergy was interested in the questionable benefice of Waldersbach. So on the first day of April, 1767, John Frederic Oberlin's call, issued by the Council of Churchwardens, was approved and confirmed by Count d'Argenson, who, as the feudal lord of the Ban de la Roche, exercised the right of ecclesiastical patronage there. Since Oberlin had not yet presented a dissertation, which was requisite to the theological degree and to ordination to the ministry, he had to apply for a provisional *délégation,* which was promptly granted by the president of the ecclesiastical council at Strasbourg. The formal consecration, "according to the usage of the church of the Augsburg Confession," did not take place until the spring of 1770, three years after his installation in Waldersbach.

9 From an oil painting by Juliette Kessler. Oberlin's allée to the Perheu left of center; Mt. Donon on the horizon

10   Belmont in Morning Sun While Clouds Still Cover the Valley · From a water color painting by Marie Scheppler of Belmont

Part 2

Educational Reform, Economic Development, Spiritual Regeneration:1767-1782

4

The Children

Shortly after sunrise on a damp and chilly day in early April 1767, a heavy seigneurial coach rolled out from the center of Strasbourg. At the outskirts of the city it took the road that crosses the flat Alsatian Rhine plain in a southwesterly direction to Molsheim. From there it proceeded on the road laid out along the route of the ancient Romans, which, keeping close to the river Bruche, climbs in a long sweeping curve through the forests of the Vosges to the Donon pass and St. Die. The coach belonged to Count d'Argenson, the grand seigneur of the Ban de la Roche. It was heavily loaded with household utensils and comestibles, as well as three passengers and their luggage. The passengers were John Frederic Oberlin, his mother, Mme Marie-Madeleine Oberlin, and his sister Sophie. John Frederic was on his way to the beginning of his life's work; by way of a friendly send-off for the new pastor of a parish in his fief, d'Argenson had put the coach at Oberlin's disposal for the journey. Sophie was to be—temporarily, both she and her mother hoped—his housekeeper. Mme Oberlin was making the trip in order to see her children properly established in the new household. Late in the afternoon the coach came to the county town of Schirmeck, about thirty-five miles from Strasbourg. Above Schirmeck the road led into a narrow gorge through which the waters of the Bruche, swollen by the melting snows from the mountains, came rushing through the narrow channel, in some places lapping over the rocky ledge that accommodated the roadway in its narrow

41

passage between the torrent's edge and the wall of the gorge. A
few miles farther upstream, opposite Rothau, the walls of the
gorge fell away for a space of about a mile, admitting two small
tributary streams on the opposite bank, the Rothaine at
Rothau and the Chirgoutte at Fouday. At a point between
Rothau and Fouday the coach stopped. The travelers had not
yet reached their ultimate destination, which was Waldersbach, but the coach had come to a barrier that it could not
cross. In a drier season it might have taken the ford at this
point, though even then it would have been a precarious
passage for such a heavy vehicle because of the steepness of the
banks; but now the swiftness of the current and the depth of the
water made that prospect unthinkable. The only access to the
Ban de la Roche at this season was by a felled tree functioning
as a footbridge. The elders of Waldersbach, anticipating the
arrival, had stationed themselves with other men of the parish
at this primitive bridgehead and now escorted the travelers
across the slippery log; when the opposite bank had been
gained, each of the three was helped into a separate high-slung,
two-wheeled horsecart for the last leg of the journey. The carts
were flanked on both sides by men whose task it was to steady
the vehicles in the worst stretches and to help their passage
through the deeper mudholes. They carried poles to be used in
such situations as levers. The luggage and equipment were
carried across the stream by parishioners acting as porters and
were transported to Waldersbach in oxcarts.

The Waldersbach manse, at which the travelers were
deposited at last, seemed cheerless and forbidding. A gloomy,
low-eaved, rickety structure with a leaky thatch, Stuber had
called it "a hovel but little better than a stable." But despite its
forlorn look, it was not unoccupied now. Stuber, to be sure had
gone to Strasbourg to take up his work at St. Thomas, but
Mme Stuber had stayed on with the children, perhaps awaiting
better weather and road conditions. So the new occupants
lived for some days as guests of the old until the Stuber family
moved out. Soon thereafter Mme Oberlin also departed,
leaving her youngfolk to their own devices.

Two months later, on June 12, 1767, Oberlin also went back
to Strasbourg in order to take the final examinations for the
degree in theology, to present his thesis on the joys and trials of
the ministry, and to complete the formalities of his graduation.
Like doctoral candidates at all times and in all places, he was

without funds. When his mother asked him about his salary as minister in Waldersbach and whether he had the money to pay the university fee, he replied that he had not, and remarked: "Why should I worry, my dear mother, I am a soldier; God, my Lord, has ordered me through my superiors to go and to labor for Him in the poor Steintal. That is what I have done, and I have been so burdened with my occupation that I have not been able, nor have I wished, to think of anything else; to care for my needs I depend upon Him in whose service I stand." Many years later, Oberlin recalled that incident in a reminiscent letter to a friend, closing his account thus: "And the Lord, who guides all hearts as He controls the streams in their course, arranged all things so well that, to the great astonishment of my dear mother, I found myself at my departure for Strasbourg in possession of several six-livres."[1] It was in that spirit that, at the age of twenty-seven, he entered upon his life's work.

Oberlin's devotion to his calling was so complete that he had at times expressed his intention to live in celibacy in order to dedicate himself completely to his vocation. His parents, however, expressed their doubts about the wisdom of such a course and urged him to give it up. Now that his professional work had begun, they—especially his mother—intensified both their importunings that he marry and their search for a suitable partner, for they considered that in that primitive community he would need not only in his home life the comfort and encouragement of a sympathetic mate, but also in his work with the people the kind of help that only a capable woman fortified with the prestigious title of *Madame le Pasteur* could give. Finally, out of respect for his parents, Oberlin agreed to consider taking a wife if they could find a suitable prospect. So now, having been told in confidence that a certain daughter of a rich brewer's widow in Strasbourg would probably give John Frederic her hand, Mme Oberlin persuaded him to try his fortune. But since it was his habit to wait for some intimation from Providence whenever he faced a grave decision, he first prayed that God would reveal His will and direct him in his judgment. In due course a message from heaven was somehow conveyed that he should make a social call at the home of the young lady nominated and should take as his signal whether to advance or to retreat the manner in which the girl's mother should receive him: if she should herself propose the marriage, he would regard it as signaling divine approbation; but if not, he would abstain from mentioning the subject. He then went to the house and rang the bell. The mother received him courteously and even called down her daughter. They all sat down. His impressions of the girl were not favorable, but he joined politely enough in small talk: about the weather, about the news going around in the town, and about this and that, until all topics were exhausted. A silence fell, during which the visitor gazed at the floor and the two women looked at each other, wondering what the reason for the visit might be; then they too looked down. This state of silence continued for some minutes. Then Oberlin rose from his chair, made a polite bow, walked to the door, and amid confused and unintelligible murmurings, took his departure, leaving both mother and daughter to make their own conjectures about the purpose of the singular visit. Thereafter the marriage was never again thought of.

But Oberlin's parents, undaunted by the failure of that first attempt, soon undertook a second. Among the Strasbourg families with which they had friendly social connections was that of a colleague of father Oberlin whom Fritz had particularly liked as a teacher. There was also a daughter in the family for whom he "had long entertained a warm esteem." Oberlin's father and the girl's father drew up a marriage contract, into which both the prospective bride and groom seemed willing to enter; but before it was executed a wealthier suitor appeared who seemed more attractive to the girl's parents. Only a few weeks later, however, Oberlin received a letter from the girl's father hinting that, after all, it now seemed desirable to renew the connection. Oberlin went immediately to the father's house and politely handed his own letter back to him, saying that he was accustomed to follow the guidance of Providence and that he considered the recent occurrences as a signal that the proposed marriage would be a mistake. He assured his former teacher of his continuing affectionate gratitude and of his hope that their friendly relations would continue; thereafter the conversation went on for a while on general subjects; and finally John Frederic was able to depart without having disturbed the friendly connection between the two families.

The parents now retired from further efforts; Mme Oberlin resigned herself to the situation, even though the thought that the existing arrangement if too long continued might compromise the prospects for marriage of her daughter Sophie did not rest easy on her mind. Then, about a year later a visitor came to the parsonage in the person of Mlle Marie-Madeleine-Salomé Witter. This young woman was related to Oberlin and his family in two ways: she was Oberlin's grand-niece once removed[2] and was also the sister of his brother Jérémie-Jacques' wife. Her father had been a professor of logic and metaphysics at the university. Both her parents had died within the first year of her life, and she had been reared first by a grandmother and later by an aunt. She was handsome of figure and elegant of dress, and, as was the custom among the young women of her class and time, she cultivated the social graces and practiced as an amateur the arts of music and poetry. Early in 1768 she had been ill, and in the spring had been sent as a convalescent, escorted by Oberlin's mother, to visit her kinswoman Sophie in Waldersbach, where the pure mountain air, the quiet country life, and the wholesome fare would presumably promote her recovery.

This young lady had not been reared in a home where plain dress and sober living were closely equated with piety of heart and humility of spirit, as they were in the Oberlin family, and John Frederic did not particularly like her; her citified and worldly ways displeased him. One Sunday during her visit he preached a sermon on the subject of vanity in which he spoke of "certain young people who are too susceptible to the lure of luxury, of fine clothing, and the like."[3] Several decades after the event, Oberlin, for the benefit of a perplexed young man who sought his counsel on a matter of love and marriage, wrote an account of what transpired during that visit. "When my mother advised me to marry Madeleine-Salomé I begged her, 'Do not speak to me of that girl. . . . The very idea of marrying her is so revolting to me that I feel repugnance for her person.'" After his mother's departure, another visitor, a Mme Mueller, also advised him to marry Mlle Witter. He thought to himself, everyone torments me with this girl; but his audible response was a simple declaration that he was content and would remain as he was "until I should receive new orders." These were nearer than he thought. On the next Friday morning, when he was at his books, the thought came to him: take Mlle Witter as your wife. He dismissed it as an absurd idea, "but it returned incessantly and tortured me cruelly." He went to dig in his garden, but the idea kept returning; he went climbing in the mountains in search of herbs and insect specimens, but returned home "as sorrowful and as depressed as when I had gone out." "Oh, God," he prayed, "this is a bitter cup; if You would have me drink it, give me the necessary courage." Thereafter he found the thought "not more agreeable, but still, less painful." Saturday was much like Friday, except that his courage grew; and by Sunday he felt at peace and resolved to address himself to the young lady after church, and to take as God's will her answer to his first proposal, whether it be yes or no. "Evening having come, I asked her, in the presence of my sister, if she would be my wife; if yes, she should give me her hand. Then this woman, who had all but made a vow not to marry a minister, who had previously considered, but rejected, proposals that were favorable and attractive to her, this same person rose quickly from her chair and put her hand in mine." This happened on the fifth of June 1768; they were married on the sixth of July.

If Oberlin's way of going about the business of finding a mate seems odd to the twentieth-century reader, it should be remembered that his behavior was probably unremarkable to members of the Pietist community. The theological attitude of the Moravian Brethren, for instance, was that marriage between Christians is a symbol of the marriage between Christ and the congregation of believers and that "love is no more relevant to marriage than the appetite of the wine drinker is to Holy Communion." It is the will of God, not the affections of man, that must rule in the choice of one's mate. It was, therefore, general practice among the brethren that the elders of the congregation made the choice, and if there were any indecision as to order of preference among candidates that the final choice be made by lot. In the established churches, too, there was a tendency to consider the choice of a mate as a kind of business deal, as a means to the attainment of some vocational purpose, ecclesiastical or civil. There were well-known churchmen who showed by their example that practical considerations weighed more heavily than love in their own choice of a partner. The theologian Johann Solomon Semler, for instance, considered that he had won divine approval when he abandoned a girl whom he loved in order to marry the daughter of a rich widow in whose house he was living; the marriage made it possible for him to pay his debts and opened the way for him to become a university professor. "Only I can know," he testified, "how dejected were my spirits, until I finally learned to subject myself to the general law, the highest law, the law of God." Two of the most famous and influential authors in the Pietistic tradition, Johann Kaspar Lavater and Johann Heinrich Jung (alias Jung-Stilling), both good friends and correspondents of Oberlin, unequivocally favored the *Vernunftehe,* marriage of reason, over the *Liebesehe,* marriage for love.[4] Indeed, in the detailed description that Jung-Stilling gives in his autobiography of the anguish of his soul at the time of his own marriage there are almost verbatim echoes of Oberlin's perplexities.

Reviewing his marriage retrospectively, Oberlin could well commend to his young friend his own way of reaching a decision, for it had served him well: his feelings, having changed at the time of his marriage from distaste and antipathy to resignation thereafter developed into devoted affection, and the marriage became a happy union.

Of the wedding of John Frederic and Madeleine-Salomé not much is known. In the bibliothèque municipale de Strasbourg, however, there is a document entitled: "*Inventaria* of the Reverend J.-F. Oberlin . . . and M.-S. Oberlin née Witter."[5] It contains a list of wedding gifts (consisting mostly of housewares of various kinds) and the eighteen persons who gave them; the names of sixty persons who gave gifts of money (totalling 288 livres); and a statement of the financial resources of the two contracting parties: J.-F. Oberlin, 3,442 livres; M.-S. Oberlin née Witter, 3,200 livres. These sums presumably represent the inheritances from John Frederic's grandfather Feltz and Madeleine-Salomé's parents, respectively.

Soon after their wedding they composed a joint prayer in which they prayed, among other things, that God might bless their union with children, that He might give them grace and wisdom to rear their young in the nurture and admonition of the Lord, and that whenever either one of them should die, the survivor might soon follow after. The first of these petitions was abundantly granted: there were nine children, seven of whom survived their infancy and outlived their mother. Fulfillment of the second plea was guaranteed by the Christian devotion of the parents. But the last was denied them: Madeleine-Salomé was to die suddenly at the age of thirty-five, while John Frederic was to live on after that for forty-three more years of active and useful service.

During the first weeks of his residence in Waldersbach, Oberlin had spent much of his time exploring the field of his labor. On his very first acquaintance with his parish he observed that more than the preaching of the Gospel was needed to improve the condition of the people. His conception of his profession was that of *Seelsorger,* a custodian of souls, and every exertion of his life was therefore bent toward making the simple folk who were entrusted to him a true people of God, to use a phrase that was often on his lips after the example of Stuber. But still, like his revered predecessor and like many other religious leaders in the age of Pietism, he knew that though man lives not by bread alone, neither does he live by the Word alone. He knew that a quickening of religious life was not the "one thing needful," but only one among many things. He knew that these included such conditions of life as good housing, good sanitation, adequate crafts and industries, productive agriculture and husbandry, good communication both within the valley and with the outside world, and, most of all, a good education for every citizen.

With the long years of preparation ended at last, he threw himself into his work with reckless energy, unmindful of any limitation of human endurance. As an admirer and votary of military discipline he dragooned his people with such obdurate rigor that he aroused opposition within his parish and moved Stuber, his devoted and concerned counsellor, to lament: "Ah, but he shepherds my flock with a rod of iron."[6] But it seemed to be something more than the intimation of tyranny in Oberlin's discipline that Stuber had on his mind. In a letter of October 20, 1768, he seems to fear that his young friend might frustrate his own purposes by an imprudent dispersion of his efforts, and perhaps also that he might fall into the error of secularization of his ministry:

> You have an engaging quality that makes you really more capable than I have been, provided that you remain fearless of all except God and that you not allow yourself to be stifled or overwhelmed by a multiplicity of projects. I do want to remind you that one can be turned away from Christianity even by good works. If you are not on your guard out there, if you do not immerse yourself in God while having so much to do, so much to think about, and so many agreeable and praiseworthy projects before you, then, for lack of inspirational contacts

and other encouragements that are more readily found here than in solitude out there, you could gradually grow cold and could fall away *from* God exactly through that which you are doing *for* God.[7]

Perhaps because of this warning, but surely also because it was his natural inclination, Oberlin never wavered from the view that his first and greatest obligation was his spiritual ministry. All of his manifold projects throughout his long life were directed toward the one goal of transforming the generally deprived and sometimes depraved populace of his parish into *ein Gottesvolk*. For him the supreme institution was the church. All community projects, all corporate decisions, all social ventures, all economic or vocational enterprises were formulated and executed under its aegis: their beginning was announced from the pulpit; their progress was accompanied and guided by prayers at the altar and in the pews; their culmination was celebrated in congregation on the holy days.

Because he conceived of his mission as nothing less than a complete and lasting regeneration of the intellectual, moral, and spiritual character of the people, he saw the need of starting with the most tractable, most teachable element in the population, the one that offered the best prospect for the perpetuation of the reforms that he had in mind. He began with the children; indeed, he gave his first attention to the teaching of the infants of preschool age.

Soon after his arrival at Waldersbach, Oberlin had made a tour of the entire parish, visiting each of the five villages and three hamlets and talking to their inhabitants. He found that, despite all the improvements accomplished by Stuber, there were still conditions of wretchedness in many places. As one example among many, consider this entry in his journal: "Toward the end of May I was in Pendbois near Belmont. The little children of that place came storming around me. I could not suppress my tears when I saw these tender children and observed the terrible conditions in which they were growing up in a place where cursing, scolding, swearing, beating, and brawling are more common than daily bread."[8] Furthermore, the fact that cases of juvenile delinquency still persisted after several years of his own labor is clear from a shocking case of depravity recorded by him in a letter addressed, but not sent, to

Baron Jean de Dietrich in 1771. Eight or nine herd boys of Waldersbach, he reported, fell upon a Roman Catholic youth from Bellefosse, "a half-savage lad who scarcely knew enough to distinguish the days," and were about to emasculate him, when one Jean Caquelin, who happened to pass by, threatened them and thwarted their action. But as soon as he had gone they again attacked the boy, disrobed him, held him fast, and had gone so far as to strike two blows with a hammer when he had the good fortune to get one hand free, grasp the hammer, and with it drive away his tormentors. Oberlin learned on interrogating the boy that it was the third time he had been attacked, and that in the first assault an eleven-year-old girl had been one of the attackers. Oberlin reported the incident to the burgomaster of Bellefosse and advised the schoolmaster to exclude the miscreants from school. The burgomaster himself came on the next Sunday to interrogate them. They denied the accusations against them, but later, when confronted by their victim, they confessed. The burgomaster had them taken to Rothau, whipped by the night watchman, and confined in the tower. The next morning they were whipped again and sent home. In closing his report Oberlin wrote: "Such infamous misdemeanors are common enough here that some of the inhabitants wonder why one takes them so seriously."

There can be no doubt that this incident had aroused in Oberlin feelings of revulsion and that he had reacted to them with a flare-up of anger. Even in his early youth he had recognized a proneness to outbursts of that kind as a flaw in his character that called for stern self-control. Now, upon quieter reflection, induced perhaps by the writing of the report, he began to see that his causing the boys to be passed on to the mayor of Bellefosse, then to the mayor of Rothau, and finally to still another person for chastisement, had been quite the wrong way to deal with the problem. His first stirrings of remorse were strengthened when, just as he had finished the letter, three of the culprits' fathers came to remonstrate with him. At an unspecified time thereafter he added a postscript. "The fathers told me that the Catholic boy had committed a detestably indecent assault upon the other boys on the meadow and taught it to them and had threatened to do it also to the aforesaid girl. It was the nature of his revolting acts that had suggested emasculation as the appropriate deterrent." The men also chided Oberlin for having sent their sons to Rothau instead of to them. They were conscientious fathers, they protested, and, with the minister and the mayor as witnesses, they themselves would have punished the children even more severely than they had been punished at Rothau. Furthermore, they tried to excuse the act of savagery: "The callous hearts of the children," Oberlin reported them as saying (in words that were surely not literally transcribed from their lips) "are softened in the course of the winter by school and examinations; in the spring, however, they take up the old mischief again, at first with a bad conscience, but by midsummer evil communications have again corrupted good morals and they boldly commit any atrocity." Oberlin told the parents that he would readmit the children to school and took no further action. The responsibility for the boys, he now knew, belonged not to the mayor of Rothau, nor to the police officer, nor to the feudal overlord in Strasbourg; nor could it be entrusted to the fathers, who had neither been outraged by the whippings, nor moved by love or pity for the children, but had responded only with promises of even harder beatings. No, the responsibility belonged to him, to John Frederic Oberlin, who was now, more dramatically and urgently than ever, called to practice with patience and devotion the Christian love that he talked about in the pulpit.

He did not send the letter to Stettmeister Dietrich; but still, he did not destroy it; he kept it in his files, perhaps as an acknowledgement and a reminder to himself in the future of his responsibility. The necessity of this moment, however, was to find a way to compensate for the loveless neglect and the sometimes savage mistreatment which characterized family life in all too many homes and bred depravity and meanness in the children's hearts.

That Oberlin must have entertained the idea of establishing a place for the care of neglected children within the first year of his ministry is indicated in a letter that Stuber wrote to Oberlin on January 10, 1768, in which he warmly supported such a project, obviously in response to a letter (now lost) from Oberlin to him.[9] Furthermore, in the archives of the church at Waldersbach there is a thick notebook entitled "Réglements" that contains notes and comments on a variety of subjects. Under the heading "Strickschule 1770," there is the following undated entry, written in Oberlin's hand, in German: "During the two years of my ministry the negligent rearing of the many children in my large parish of five villages and three hamlets, lay heavy upon my heart, causing me much sorrow. I kept looking for a house, to be built or bought, that could be used as a place of nurture for these children. But it was in vain." During those two years Oberlin was also on the lookout for young women in the parish who could be recruited and trained to give the children the loving care that he considered their prime need. The breakthrough came in the late autumn of 1769 when he heard that one Sara Banzét of Belmont, who had been employed as a servant in the parsonage during the ministry of Stuber and had there learned to knit (an accomplishment that was rare in the Ban de la Roche), was in her leisure hours teaching several younger girls the skill. In the document quoted above Oberlin says, "This was delightful news to me. Quickly I went up and talked to her father. At first he made a sour face because of the fear that he would lose the girl's help in house and field, but finally I made an agreement with him according to which: 1. he would give me the services of his daughter, in the character of a housemaid, as it were, but to give knitting school lessons; 2. I would supply her meals, clothing and lodging; and 3. I would pay her wages of twenty-four francs for the year 1770. Thereupon I also rented a room in Belmont where she could teach the children tolerably undisturbed."

The agreements that Oberlin drew up and signed in January 1770, for the services of Mlle Sara Banzét and for the use of a room as a place of instruction for the year 1770, are of great importance in the history of education, for they constitute documentary evidence that Oberlin was the first person anywhere to institute a program for the training of small children in groups and away from their homes.[10] The two documents are in the Musée Alsacien in Strasbourg. Their essential contents are given in translation below.

> A. Agreement with Master Jean Banzét. I, the undersigned, Jean-Frederic Oberlin, certify that I have promised to Master Jean Banzét, Elder of Belmont, the sum of two louis d'or per year . . . for the service of his daughter Sara, who will work for me, and will have lodging . . . with her father. . . .
>
> Made at Belmont this third day of January one thousand seven hundred and seventy in the presence . . . of two citizens of Belmont.

B. Agreement with Master Nicolas Hagemann. I, the under-signed, certify that I have promised to Master Nicolas Hagemann of Belmont the sum of [illegible] for the use of his back room with stove, and for all the inconveniences that the knitting school might cause in said room. The terms of payment will extend from the first day of the new year, 1770, until the year 1771. . . .

Made at Belmont. [Here follow Oberlin's signature, Hagemann's mark, and the signatures of two witnesses to the agreement.]

After the essential requisites for making a beginning in Belmont had thus been procured, the finding of young women to serve as teachers in the other villages seems to have proceeded more quickly. The following description (also from the "Réglements") of how the second and third teachers were found affords a good example of a technique that Oberlin often used to bend the will of his people to his purposes, namely, to employ his talent for effective exhortation, both from the pulpit and in private confrontation, thus making the desired decision a matter both of public concern and of private conscience. While praying one day for divine guidance in this effort he was inspired to send for Marie Bohy of Trouchy. Although she was willing to give herself to the task, the opposition of her mother was great. He went to talk to her mother, but was "rebuffed with many humanly understand-able, everyday excuses." He then declared that he would neither trouble himself again to make that kind of request, nor, indeed, accept the services of her daughter unless she, the mother, should herself come to him asking God to forgive her and offering her daughter to His service. Therewith he went away.

This took place on a Monday. On Tuesday he sent for the wife of Jean-Martin Loux of Waldersbach and requested, in the same manner, the services of her daughter in return for proper compensation. This woman "had formerly been very worldly-minded, but on the previous Sunday at an impressive divine service, she had been deeply moved." At Oberlin's proposal she now "broke out in tears, gave her daughter to the Lord's service, and, despite her distressed circumstances, refused any compensation." To compensate her for the loss of her daughter's services, however, Oberlin did persuade her to hire a servant girl, whose wages he undertook to pay. Still more success was to come; Mme Loux had scarcely left when her husband happened to visit the presbytery on a different errand; and when Oberlin told him that he had sent for his wife, and why, and "how edifying her behavior had been, he was moved to tears at the change in his wife's attitude and was unable to speak." Furthermore, on the next day Marie Bohy herself came at the early hour of five and testified that her mother now felt deep remorse over her unchristian conduct and had gone on Tuesday to the magistrate at Solbach to tell him to use her daughter for the education of the children where Oberlin should specify.

Oberlin closed this part of the account in his journal thus: "So now we had two for one. I had long wished to have a supervisor for the children at Solbach, but had not yet had sufficient faith to seek such a person at that time, for I did not know how I would pay the wages of those whom I already had. But now that God was sending me two good young women, why would He, who feeds the ravens and clothes the lilies, not give bread and clothing for them also?"

Oberlin called these newly created institutions *écoles à tricoter* or *Strickschulen*—knitting schools—when communicating with outsiders, but when talking with his own people he called them *poêles à tricoter,* giving *poêle* the metonymical meaning "a room with a stove," a *Stube.* Perhaps his purpose was to preclude mental images of cheerless schoolrooms of the traditional mold and to evoke instead connotations of the warmth, comfort, *Gemütlichheit,* and security of a family living room dominated by the great tile stove. Similarly, in choosing a title for the women who were to preside over the *poêles,* he rejected the common designations *institutrice* or *Lehrerin* in favor of *conductrice* or *Führerin,* which evoke the image of an adult leading a child by the hand rather than one of a magisterial personage presiding over a rigidly organized institution. Connotations of gentle guidance are even more obviously present in the amplified designation *conductrice de la tendre jeunesse* and *Führerin der zarten Jugend*—leader of tender youth—that Oberlin often employed on formal or ceremonial occasions.

The most arresting feature of the educational system that Oberlin developed in the Ban de la Roche was that school attendance began at a much earlier age than in any other system existing at that time: the children entered the *poêle à tricoter* at three or four and were passed on to the *école publique* at six or seven. Thus the correctness of the surmises of earlier theorists such as Comenius and Locke that formal education could begin at an earlier age than had been generally assumed was demonstrated in actual practice in Oberlin's *poêles.*

We know both from Oberlin's own statements and from other sources what the purposes, the content, and the methods of instruction in the infant schools were. Because the physical conditions of life and the spiritual atmosphere in the peasant houses were so often unsatisfactory, Oberlin wanted to expose the children as early as feasible to more beneficial influences and happier living conditions, but without separating them completely from their families. He wanted to take the boys and girls aged three or four to six or seven years for a few hours several times each week out of the dreary, grimy, damp and chilly rooms that were their homes and gather than in bright, airy, and above all warm chambers. He wanted to separate the most pitiable among them from parents who, through hunger and despair, had become irritable, contentious, and sometimes even sadistic in the treatment of their children. He wanted to keep them busy and at the same time teach them useful skills, particularly knitting, and, for the older children, also carding and combing of flax. He wanted to make them aware of the world of nature by teaching them sketching and by directing them in identifying and collecting plants, insects, and stones. He wanted to familiarize them with the shape and contours of the land on which they lived, and to that end he showed them maps of their valley and taught them to locate their own homes and identify salient topographic features. He wanted to create in them not only the possibility of individual self-fulfillment, but also a capacity of happy community living. Not only for the good of the children themselves, but also because he was aware that the habits acquired by them would in some measure influence the way of life of their families, he attached great importance to training in cleanliness, to the forming of good habits of hygiene, to good manners and politeness, and to the tasteful, artistic attractiveness of the *poêles.* In every possible way he sought to awaken their intelligence, to stimulate their imagination, and to cause to grow in their hearts feelings of gratitude for the love of God by teaching them to pray, by making them aware of the beauty of God's earth, and by giving them a sense of identity and self-respect, of security and happiness as children of God.[11]

In a manuscript of 1770 in the parsonage at Waldersbach, Oberlin himself wrote the following notes about the purposes of the infant schools: (1) to take the children off the streets; (2) to accustom them to work; (3) to put them under good supervision; (4) to "do good work for their souls"; (5) to learn French ("speaking the patois will not be permitted, except in dire emergency; this is a most uncommonly important point"); (6) to give them opportunities to earn, not much, to be sure, but a little—"a prudent householder disdains nothing." On the last point he commented further: "If knitting should become a general thing, much money that is now spent elsewhere would remain in the community and much wasted time would be usefully employed. I have in my parish about 200 households. If one counted on only three pairs of stockings annually for each at [illegible] francs, a total of [illegible] francs would be going out of my five villages for stockings. Since little money comes into the community, it would be a great advantage if more of it could be kept there." These remarks constitute the only existing indication that Oberlin in founding the knitting schools was motivated by the prospect of some eventual economic advantage for his people. We shall see in a later chapter that this prospect was ultimately realized with the establishment of a prosperous textile industry based on the fundamental skills that were first taught in the *poêles à tricoter.*

The strong statement contained in this memorandum about the importance of teaching standard French in order to displace the patois is reiterated again and again in many documents. This concern was by no means a mere quixotic obsession of a linguistic purist. Oberlin, along with Stuber, knew that putting an end to the intellectual and social isolation of the community was an indispensable prerequisite to any effective action to wipe out the abject poverty that was the main cause of the widespread misery. He also knew that the isolation would persist as long as the speech of the people remained incomprehensible to their neighbors and their fellow countrymen. Taking the long view, he knew that the language of the children tends to become that of the whole community, and he therefore pressed hard to effect this reform, employing the pulpit and the schools as instruments of persuasion. The efforts of Stuber and Oberlin in this regard eventually came to the notice of authorities in Paris. In 1794 there came jointly to Stuber and Oberlin an unexpected accolade: on the sixteenth day of Fructidor in the year II of the Republic," the National Convention entered in its protocol of the day a commendation of the two educators for their "contributions to the universalization of the French language." Probably neither of these two German-speaking gentlemen had any idea that he was making a memorable contribution to the glory of France when he was struggling just to teach his simple peasant folk words and phrases that would be intelligible to him and to persons outside the narrow confines of the Ban de la Roche.

In a long letter acknowledging the citation, Oberlin mentions his embarrassment "because my mother tongue is German, and because I know that, though I have by reading acquired sufficient French for my beloved valley, I fall short of the French of native Frenchmen."[12] In the same letter he also describes the teaching methods of the *conductrices*. They showed "figures from history and from the kingdom of animals and plants," naming them first in patois and then in French, and finally having the children repeat them in French. They gave them knitting lessons and thereafter "amused them with games that exercise the body, stretch the limbs, and contribute to good health, and accustom them to play honorably and without quarreling." On pleasant days they took walks during which they gathered plants, telling the names and having the children repeat them several times. Oberlin continues, "I made small collections of specimens from nature, or reproductions of works of art, and of equipment to be used in preparing striking demonstrations. When the zeal of the children began to flag, a new magic trick of our kind would excite them anew and revive their desire to learn. I also mention the small maps that I engraved in wood and printed for distribution by means of which the children gradually became acquainted with all the countries of the world." When a *conductrice* told him that her pupils had mastered their exercise books, he allowed her to present the children in church, where they "displayed their progress with a joyfulness and ecstasy that brought tears to the eyes of their elders. Moreover, these public recitations enabled me to show the adults things that would be useful to them but which I had, unfortunately, not yet had the opportunity to teach them."

The allusion in this letter to natural specimens, to reproductions of works of art, and to equipment and "magic tricks" shows that Oberlin had an early and clear conception of the value and effectiveness of object lesson teaching, which Froebel later developed into a prime element of his kindergarten system at his Universal Educational Institute, founded in 1840. Also, in his recognition of spiritual training as a fundamental principle, and in his acknowledgement of the importance of pleasant surroundings, constructive activity, and physical training for the development of the child's mind, he anticipated the "founder of the first kindergarten" by two-thirds of a century.[13] The passage about the results of the public recitations is a good example of his practice of using the children to educate their parents.

The "magic tricks of our kind" may have included such demonstrations as the following, listed by Psczolla among the "games" suggested by Oberlin for the use of teachers: Making a light burn in water (by lighting a candle immersed so deep that only the wick protrudes); using water to set tinder afire (by focusing rays of sunlight on it through water contained between two watchglasses); turning a glass of water upside down without spilling it (by first covering it with paper pressed firmly around the moistened rim of the glass); melting lead in paper (by enclosing it in tissue paper and holding it over a flame); bringing water to simmering heat without putting it over a fire (by immersing hot pebbles in it); and "bending" an earthenware pipestem without breaking it (by partially immersing it in water, where it will appear to be bent).

As teachers in his infant schools, Oberlin seems to have assumed that only women would be suitable. Thus it happens that he was not only the founder of the first infant schools, but also the first to employ women as teachers in public education. As a measure of Oberlin's priority in this regard, consider, for example, how the matter was handled in England. When Robert Owen founded the first British infant school at New Lanark, some forty-six years after Oberlin's first *poêle* opened in Belmont, he employed a man, James Buchanan, as master. Buchanan, to be sure, "solicited the cooperation" of one Molly Young for the school, and when, a few years later, he had moved to London, he was "assisted" there by Mrs. Buchanan. By 1845, however, twenty-one years after Oberlin's death, the employment of women as teachers of infants in England had made great progress; in that year Mr. J. Fletcher, Her Majesty's inspector of schools, reporting on thirty-nine schools that he had visited, said that females were in charge of twenty-eight of them, and males of only eleven. But alas, this preferment of women was based not on educational theory or conviction, but on economy; it was "a result of the unvarying element of cheapness in the employment of females."[14] In Germany the first public infant schools with women as teachers were founded in 1802 by Pauline, princess regent of Lippe-Detmold.

Once the plan to establish the first of the infant schools had been implemented, Oberlin, aided and abetted by his wife, who from the beginning of her life with him was ever his confidante and sharer in the responsibilities and burdens of his office, started to work out a plan for training teachers. Following the pattern initiated in the employment of Sara Banzét, they established the practice of taking promising girls from the parish into their homes in order to teach them the necessary skills and to help them develop the attitudes, the motives, and the ideals that would be most conducive to their success as *conductrices*. Thus the Waldersbach parsonage became, in a sense, the first training school for infant-school teachers. Mme Oberlin took great pains to teach these girls the household arts, giving to each according to her needs special help in acquiring the many skills required for good housekeeping, the care of children, and the teaching of needlecrafts, drawing, writing, and singing and the telling of stories, while both father and mother Oberlin helped them to perfect such basic intellectual attributes as the mastery of standard French and conversance with the Bible and the catechism. They also held regular evening meetings with the girls in which, in a spirit of collaboration between teachers and learners, the purposes and objectives of the *poêles à tricoter* were formulated, the methods and techniques of instruction were discussed and developed, and teaching devices and realia were designed. Always the girls were treated as members of the Oberlin family, and thus they enjoyed the many advantages of living in a household of dignity and culture, where models of good behavior and manners based on Christian precepts, mutual respect, and love were constantly before them.

In a review of the founding of the *poêles à tricoter* and their early development, two questions present themselves: Where did Oberlin get the idea of creating such schools? And why, once the idea had been conceived, did the program of instruction take the particular form it did?

There is a romanticized, somewhat maudlin story of the origin of the *poêles,* repeated by several writers, that tells how on a fine spring morning the peasant maid Louise Scheppler, observing the ways of a broodhen with her chicks, suddenly conceived the idea of creating a place of shelter and nurture for infants. As an explanation of the origin of infant schools the story is unacceptable for two reasons. First, it is factually wrong: Louise Scheppler, though she eventually became the most successful and most celebrated of all the *conductrices,* was by no means the first one; indeed, she was only seven years old when Sara Banzét was installed as the first *conductrice.* Second, it is wrong in its tone: the idea of the *poêles* sprang not from any romantic caprice such as this, but from conditions as harsh and unromantic as the symptoms of poverty, hunger, and neglect that had brought tears to Oberlin's eyes on seeing those children at Pendbois. The *poêles* were soberly conceived by Oberlin as a means of meeting what he considered a practical and urgent necessity, namely, to remove the children for a few hours several times each week from the evil influences of their squalid and joyless homes into places of warmth and love and joyful activity. The impulse to action toward the realization of his plan came, to be sure, when Sara Banzét's initiative showed him that it would be possible to find young women in the parish capable of becoming *conductrices.*

"The earliest education is most important and it undoubtedly is woman's work," wrote Rousseau at the very beginning of *Emile.*[15] Was it perhaps this dictum of the greatest of all educational theorists that caused Oberlin to consider only women as prospective *conductrices? Emile* was published in 1762, just at the time that Oberlin, as a tutor, was beginning his first teaching experience. There is evidence that Oberlin not only read the book but studied it carefully; his own copy has many marginal notes in his handwriting. But it seems unlikely that it was decisively influential either in the founding of the first infant schools or in the exclusive employment of women as teachers. What is offered in *Emile* is not a model for the creation of schools; Emile's education was exclusively private, administered not by a teacher facing a group of learners, but tête-à-tête, one teacher facing one pupil. Furthermore, in its original context Rousseau's phrase "woman's work" actually means "mothers' work." I have no doubt that Oberlin would have agreed with Rousseau's proposition and would gladly have left the grave business of the "earliest education" to mothers in their homes, if he had been dealing with other mothers and other children, as for instance with those of the educated and cultivated aristocratic and upper-middle classes of Strasbourg. But it was exactly the wretched condition of his poverty-stricken and isolated parish and the consequent incompetence of both mothers and fathers to educate the children that made the founding of the *poêles* seem necessary. In the modes and methods of instruction that gradually developed both in the schools for infants and in those of older children the influence of Rousseau was present and effective, as we shall see in a more detailed discussion at the end of this chapter.

At the same time that Oberlin was developing and implementing his concept of infant schools for children aged three to seven, he was also deeply engaged in the improvement and extension of education for the children of public school age. In the Ban de la Roche, as in many peasant communities, school could be held only in the winter because the children were needed for work in the fields from seed time to harvest. Of the five villages, only Waldersbach had a schoolhouse in 1767. It was a small, mean building in bad repair; it served not only as the place of instruction but also housed the schoolmaster and the community herdsman, each in his season.[16] The children of Bellefosse attended school in Waldersbach; in Fouday, Solbach, and Belmont, lessons were given in private houses by a peripatetic schoolmaster.

Oberlin's first step toward the improvement of education was to build a new schoolhouse in Waldersbach. In this undertaking he met with opposition from the people. Biographers have ascribed this hostility to the general slothfulness that made the people content to live on in a state of ignorance and to the fear of householders that the building would entail an intolerable addition to their already heavy burden of taxes and tributes. However, the late Strasbourg schoolmaster Georg Meyer, an indigenous student of Ban de la Roche chronicles, has suggested the possibility of a different reading.[17] The civil authorities in each village, called *maire,* or in the patois *Oberchef,* were well acquainted with local conditions, and Meyer suggests that when Oberlin argued that the population had grown so large that the old schoolhouse was no longer sufficient for both Waldersbach and Bellefosse, they might not have been altogether wrong in suggesting that it would be better, for the time being, to make do with the old house in Waldersbach and to build a new one in Bellefosse, where there was none at all. That would have relieved the crowded building in Waldersbach and, at the same time, would have ended the necessity of the long daily walks for the children from Bellefosse to Waldersbach and back often through deep snow and against cold winds.

But if Oberlin did blunder in his insistence that the new schoolhouse be in Waldersbach, he did so not out of ignorance or stupidity, but out of the excess of his zeal. He was not a man of half measures, not a pusillanimous compromiser, but an idealist of strong conviction and firm decision. At the beginning of his great design of social reformation he could not be satisfied with a building that was only just adequate. He insisted from the very beginning that all schoolhouses must be commodious, light, airy, comfortable, and sufficiently imposing to symbolize the dignity of their function. By urging from the first that the inadequate old building in Waldersbach be replaced, he was proclaiming his resolve to make a new beginning in the valley, to bring in (to borrow Stuber's imagery), the reign of the new God of light in place of the old God of darkness. The new schoolhouse in the mother village was to set a new standard for all the other villages.

Whatever the distribution of praise and censure in this dispute should be, opposition to Oberlin's plan was indubitably present and strong, but he proceeded toward his project's fulfillment even against that opposition, and, indeed, with astonishing success. He was generously and effectively supported (though not without a discreet warning against immoderate exuberance) by Stuber. The two men agreed that, in order to overcome the resistance of officials and citizens and to disarm the opposition, they would have to give every assurance that the building would be constructed and equipped and the school would be operated without any new financial burden being imposed on either the feudal lord, Count d'Argenson, or on the householders.

Stuber undertook to solicit contributions in Strasbourg, where his prestige as a minister of St. Thomas Church gave him access to important personages. He began his campaign by calling on the royal praetor, Régemonte, the representative in Strasbourg of Count d'Argenson, who resided in Paris. He was not confident of winning support for the project from Régemonte, but he hoped at least to extract a promise that there would be no active opposition to it from d'Argenson nor from his deputy. On November 23, 1768, he was able to write to Oberlin: "I believe that Régemonte will not be able to forbid it, particularly in Waldersbach, where . . . there has been a schoolhouse since ancient times. The one point on which he is adamant is that he will make no contribution to it. I shall therefore tell him, of course, that we, being aware of his position, will expect no support from him. We will buy the material; not even the people of the parish will be asked to give or do anything. We will even pay for the hauling. But even so, you will have more opposition from your congregation than from Régemonte."

Knowing from his own experience that the parsonage at Waldersbach was but little better than the wretched hovel that was the old schoolhouse, Stuber suggested in the same letter the following maneuver: If Régemonte should still forbid it, Oberlin would have to build in his own name a house to serve both as school and parsonage, explaining that he could not live on his meager salary and that he was unable to supplement it because the old parsonage was too small for him to take in sufficient boarding pupils. "Be that as it may," Stuber wrote, "make a beginning in God's name; quietly procure a building site, draw up a plan, and procure the necessary material; I believe that now is the time: God will stand by us. But I commend you for not desiring anything more than is absolutely necessary. . . . *Allons,* start your training now, so that by next spring you will be a superintendent of construction who knows his business and cannot be cheated."[18]

With this encouragement, and trusting, as ever, in the aid of divine providence, Oberlin made a beginning by purchasing in his own name and with borrowed money a building site opposite the parsonage, and by sketching plans for the new structure, which, he finally decided, was to be a schoolhouse only; the building of a new parsonage would have to wait. He wrote persuasive and touching letters to friends and acquaintances who had shown interest in the progress of the Ban de la Roche and of his ministry there. One of the earliest and most generous supporters of the cause was Mme Reichart, widow of a Strasbourg senator, who had already supported Stuber during his ministry in Waldersbach with gifts for the advancement of education, and who now, after having given all the money that she could, contributed the proceeds from the sale of a pair of silver candelabra.[19] From several persons of his acquaintance Stuber received contributions in the form of loans, which he and Oberlin jointly promised to repay when due. A general solicitation of funds by Stuber brought help from various persons, including old friends of the Ban de la Roche such as Magister Ott and Dr. Ziegenhagen.

Oberlin did not leave to Stuber and Ott the entire burden of winning friends in Strasbourg for his parish and of raising funds there; he himself made many journeys to the city. In order not to lose precious daylight hours from his work at home he often mounted his horse at nightfall, rode to Strasbourg by moonlight, transacted his business there during the day, and returned to Waldersbach in the second night.

On many occasions, gratefully noted in his journals, he felt that his faith in divine providence had been justified.[20] For instance, on the morning of a day when one of his promissory notes fell due, he was in distress because he had not a sou to apply to the payment. As ever in times of stress, he resorted to prayer. Scarcely had he uttered his plea for divine assistance when there was delivered to him a letter containing five hundred francs from an anonymous donor. Oberlin, being a man of prayer par excellence, had many occasions to record similar triumphs of supplication. With every desire of his simple heart the subject of daily, sometimes hourly, orisons, he saw every propitious happening as proof of divine indulgence. When he and Stuber were finally ready to begin the actual construction of the new building, they thought it politic to make a public declaration to allay the people's suspicions that they might be taxed for the cost of the building at some time after the beginning of construction. They therefore circulated a proclamation, saying that, having procured sufficient funds as gifts from a number of benefactors, it was now possible for them to undertake the construction without requiring the slightest contribution of money or labor from the parishioners.[21]

Ground was broken on May 31, 1769; three months later the completion of the framework was celebrated in the customary topping-out ceremony, the *Richtfest*. Looking proudly over at the imposing new structure from his lowly parsonage opposite, Oberlin remarked in a letter: "I continue to live in this old house where I have to put up with constant annoyances from rats and from the rain falling through the leaking thatch; but I do not want a new residence until I have seen all the schools properly housed."

During the period of construction Oberlin had done all that he could to invite the voluntary support of the people of Waldersbach for the new enterprise. By the example of his own devotion to the cause, by the investment of his own energy and skills as planner, fund raiser, superintendent of construction, and even, on occasion, as stonemason, carpenter, and laborer he sought to engage their interest and to inspire their cooperation. Also in his sermons, in his discourse at weekly Bible study meetings, and in his private conversations he exhorted citizens and parents on the necessity of education for the improvement of their lives and the salvation of their souls. Yet, despite all his efforts, the opposition was so strong that on several occasions it found expression in acts of rowdyism that put him in danger of death, as, for instance, when a drunken mob threatened one winter night to throw him in the river Bruche.

Gradually the animosity diminished, however, and when, in 1773, he was ready to build a second schoolhouse, this time in Bellefosse, he was gratified that the first contribution of money for that cause now came not from an outside donor but from one of his parishioners. When he had found a site for this second schoolhouse, had purchased the land with his own funds and then made his first appeal to the people for help to procure the building material, the first response came from a widow of Bellefosse who contributed her mite, one franc and twenty centimes. Others followed her example and eventually a thousand francs were raised. The people bent their backs to the labor of construction, and Oberlin's chronicles note that on September 3, 1773, "almost all the men of Bellefosse were in the forest to fell trees for the roofbeams. This they did voluntarily and without orders." Oberlin closed this notation in the "Annals" with the remark that the people were "now healed of their error." But Meyer may be right in his interpretation that the general public support "shows that this time master builder Oberlin had taken hold of the matter in the right way, for he now saw his people in their true character, as capable of enthusiasm and willing to make sacrifices" when they were convinced of the necessity and the wisdom of the proposed action.[22]

The schoolhouse in Belmont was built in 1779; the material for it was donated by the new grand seigneur of the Ban de la Roche, Baron Jean de Dietrich. The one at Fouday was built in the Napoleonic period and paid for by the prefect of the *département* Bas-Rhin, M. de Lezay-Marnésia, an enlightened official and an admirer and good friend of Oberlin. The schoolhouse at Solbach, the last one to be built, was the gift of the burgomaster of that village, Martin Bernard, "who did not have the burden of a family." Thus the whole school-building project, which had begun in Waldersbach without any financial participation of the local citizens, was ultimately completed in Solbach by them alone without any outside help.

Not only in the building of the schoolhouses, but also in the development of the educational program to be carried out in them, Oberlin received invaluable help from his predecessor. Stuber had recognized the necessity of teaching the children standard French and had written his *Alphabet Méthodique* for that purpose. Oberlin found that book an effective pedagogical instrument and continued to use it as the basis for language instruction in all the schools. Stuber had also taken measures to improve the condition and professional capabilities of the schoolmasters. In France at that time the training of teachers for rural communities was not a function of institutions of higher education: just as a young physician or lawyer learned what he needed to know for his profession from a practicing master, so the aspiring teacher was "apprenticed" to a schoolmaster and "learned the trade" from him. But even if it had been the general practice to employ educated men from the cities, Oberlin would probably have sought his teachers within the rural area where they were to serve, for aside from the language problem created by the exclusive use in the valley of the patois, both Oberlin and Stuber believed that only indigenous teachers could fully understand, and therefore effectively cope with, the problems of the people. Oberlin therefore continued where Stuber had left off in raising up good and effective teachers from among the people. He also retained the prestigious title bestowed on them by Stuber: *messieurs les régents d'écoles.*

Thanks to the good work of Stuber, Oberlin did not have to start from point zero in recruiting teachers. One whom Stuber had discovered and trained was Jean-David Bohy, who supported Oberlin's efforts not only as a teacher, but also by traveling to Germany and Switzerland in 1773 to raise money for the enlargement of the church at Fouday.[23] Another was Sébastien Scheidecker. Stuber had noticed him in his second ministry in the Ban de la Roche as the most intelligent among the youths of his parish and had sent him at the age of seventeen to Barr as a worker in a sawmill in the summer and an apprentice teacher in the winter. Two years later Stuber had brought Scheidecker back to the Ban de la Roche, had employed him first as a substitute teacher wherever he was needed, and had installed him finally as *régent d'école* in Bellefosse. Oberlin, when he came to the Ban de la Roche, was so impressed with Scheidecker's excellent qualities and bright intelligence that he sent him to his own former employer and mentor, Dr. Ziegenhagen, to acquire the basic knowledge and skills of practical medicine so that he could assist Oberlin in caring for the health of the people of the valley, which had no resident physician. Thus it may be said that Scheidecker became, after Oberlin, the best educated man in the parish. As a teacher he excelled not only in skilled instruction of the children, but also in recognizing potential teachers among his pupils and in guiding, coaching, and training them as recruits in the profession. Oberlin once characterized him as a person who loved to read, especially books on medical subjects. Leenhardt credits him with the introduction of vaccination for smallpox in the Ban de la Roche.[24] He also made important contributions in later years as Oberlin's assistant in introducing the cotton spinning industry in the valley. He was a natural leader in the religious as well as in the civic life of the community. Oberlin made him his unofficial deputy as first citizen, as it were, on days when he himself was absent from the valley. Along with Louise Scheppler he was Oberlin's most valuable helper throughout his ministry. He carried on his career in the Ban de la Roche until a ripe old age, even after Oberlin's death.

Other teachers Oberlin characterized in a letter to M. Ott as follows: "Benoit Louis of Belmont: faithful, eager to serve, but does not read enough in all the books that have been given to him. J. J. Masson of Bellefosse: always displays more good will than capacity [to perform]. Vernier Masson of Waldersbach: strives to fill the gaps in his knowledge in order to make himself more capable and useful."[25]

We have seen how Oberlin went about recruiting the first *conductrices* for his *poêles à tricoter.* The care that he took in seeking a new *régent d'école* who would be pleasing to both God and man is illustrated in two documents, conveyed to me by Anne-Margrit Meyer. The first document quoted is a sermon preached at Solbach; the second, a prayer spoken at the same service. These documents offer an example of the way Oberlin tended to merge his pedagogical and ministerial functions; they also give a good idea of his lofty conception of the teaching profession. Incidentally, the first one also reveals how a quasi-secret plebiscite could be conducted in a largely illiterate community.

"My dear friends of Solbach," Oberlin said in his sermon, "because our friend and longtime teacher has asked for his release, I bid you now to pray to God that He may take the filling of this post in His hands so that the welfare and happiness of our children will be assured. . . . And after you have prayed thus, each of you come to me at the altar next Sunday after the church service and whisper in my ear the name of the person whom you would have to be a schoolmaster." And in his prayer at the close of the service he specified the qualities in the new teacher whom God was to send. "Our youth, so valuable in Thy sight, needs the very best of shepherds: . . . a man whose heart burns with the love of Thee . . . and who also holds the children within his heart. . . . A man who has wisdom and a good will, who has gentleness and goodness, but also firmness and intelligence; one who is tender without weakness; manly but not ruthless; firm but not rude; one who can be amiable, courteous, lovable, and accommodating, yet is without guile and flattery; a man with a character that inspires respect without signs of arrogance. . . ."

That Oberlin felt no pain in parting with a teacher who did not measure up to his high standard is indicated by the following notation about the same Louis Benoit whom he had criticized in his letter to Magister Ott: "Today, 17 August (1771), Benoit Louis, schoolmaster at Belmont . . . declared that, since I now had capable candidates, I would do him a favor if I would release him, for he realized that he would never be an effective teacher. He was right; and I was heartily glad. But as he talked further it became clear that the real reason for his resignation was the disappointment of his hope that he might soon be the resident of the spacious new schoolhouse.... Who would have thought that the lack of a decent schoolhouse could also have a *good* effect?"[26]

On another occasion the shortcomings of a teacher were dealt with in a less private fashion. On May 27, 1790, Oberlin said in a sermon: *"Monsieur le régent* at Waldersbach, instead of seeking his salvation with fear and trembling; instead of serving the Lord, who fervently loves children; instead of seeking solitude during these perilous holidays; instead of pleading with God to preserve his pupils from the contagion of scandal, has himself gone out and mingled with fickle folk and has thus displayed publicly a frivolity, an insouciance that is unpardonable. . . . Now to put an end to this scandal . . . I demand that he give up for four weeks the function of *présentateur* at the church services."[27]

Yet Oberlin was always concerned about the welfare of the teachers and sought in many ways to improve their condition, to increase their pay, to give them free housing in the school building, and to procure for them free fuel and food supplies. In the sermon just quoted he went on to say: "I hope that you will deliver the necessary firewood to your schoolmaster. The state of his affairs and of his health is such that it is essential for you to remember your duty in this regard. . . . Furthermore, I hope that your elder, a man who deserves praise in other respects, will make haste to set an example in this regard. Let him not be angry that I dare to name him in public; let him rather redouble the zeal and the vivacity that I know he possesses and thus show himself to be still more worthy of the high opinion that I have had of him. There are also other good citizens of Bellefosse who could join him in this work of piety." And in 1775, in a spirited defense of a senior *régent d'école,* J. J. Masson (a man of whom he was not uncritical), Oberlin said to the citizens of Bellefosse, "Your honor, your reputation, your conscience are constant concerns of your minister and pastor and true friend. But would it be right for me to be silent when I see you, my dear brothers, acting contrary to your conscience and your good name by neglecting the needs of a wise, virtuous, patriotic, and Christian man . . . your old schoolmaster? You keep him under guard, so to speak, and give him fatigue duties. . . . Thereby you are acting contrary to your duty of gratitude, to prudence, to your own reputation and interests, to the interests of your children."[28]

Oberlin did not extend the bold innovation of employing women as *conductrices de la tendre jeunesse* to installing female teachers in the public schools. There is, indeed, no evidence in any of the documents that he ever considered this as a possibility. Though it seemed only natural to him that the infant schools should be presided over by *conductrices,* not *conducteurs,* and though he entrusted other public functions, especially those of a deaconal nature, to women, the "peculiar esteem for the female sex" that he once imputed to himself did not induce him to put the schoolchildren beyond the age of seven in the care of women.

Once a teacher was chosen, either as *conductrice* or as *régent d'école,* she or he was inducted into the high office by an impressive dedicatory ceremony that was made a part of the Sunday church service. This practice throws light on several facets of Oberlin's conception of education. It symbolizes the centrality of the church in his conception of the good community and shows that his prime purpose in improving general education was to strengthen the Christian congregation; it suggests that in his mind his pastoral charge, his duties as *Seelsorger,* included the training of the intellect as well as the nurture of the soul, the discipline of the mind as well as piety of the heart, an understanding of this world as well as knowledge of the world to come; and it contributed to his purpose of improving the condition and raising the prestige of the teaching profession. Also, each of these ceremonies offered yet another occasion for Oberlin to exhort his people to give their full support to the cause of education.

Such dedicatory inaugural services were not the only occasions when the life of the schools was merged with the ceremonies of the church, for Oberlin continued to have pupils appear with their teachers at Sunday services for *récitations générales.* Just as he and Mme Oberlin met regularly with the *conductrices* for training sessions and discussions, he also required all the teachers to meet in Waldersbach every Wednesday for an exercise called *écoles générales.* At each meeting one teacher with his pupils would present a demonstration lesson, which would then be discussed and criticized by his colleagues. Occasionally Oberlin himself would take over a class in order to show how the teacher might have exploited his material to the greater profit of the pupils. These Wednesday meetings, together with the Sunday *récitations générales,* fostered a friendly and stimulating rivalry among the teachers to the improvement of their professional skill and effectiveness.

Because he knew from the beginning that the chief opposition to his efforts would come not from outside civil authorities but from the people, he tried to minimize that opposition by reducing the cost of education to the parents as much as possible. With the help of Stuber and those other generous and dedicated Strasbourg friends who helped him build the schoolhouses, he also succeeded in raising money to maintain the buildings, to pay the teachers' wages, and to distribute materials of instruction to the pupils, all without imposing intolerable financial burdens on the parents. But in the long run, adequate schools could not be financed entirely by charitable gifts from outside donors. Gradually and cautiously, therefore, he began to require that parents at least help to pay for their children's tuition. An undesirable consequence of this, however, was that parents sometimes kept their children out of school in order to reduce their liability for tuition fees.

Stuber conceived a plan that envisioned the twofold benefit of giving some financial relief to parents and, at the same time, encouraging regular school attendance by the children. His proposal was that a child who had been present in school each day without exception for one month be given a reward of two sous in the winter, four in the summer. These benefits would be given to the parents in the form of credit vouchers that could be applied to the payment of their share of the teachers' wages or the purchase of school supplies. "I know very well," he wrote, "that this will require substantial funds, but if the idea seems acceptable to you . . . I will try to find the necessary means and we can try the scheme for at least a year or two."[29] Oberlin adopted the essential features of this plan and extended it, as soon as he was able, by supplying books and other instructional materials free of charge to the children of worthy parents who were not able to pay for them. This must surely have been a very early occurrence, if not the first, of what has come to be called scholarship aid to worthy and needy students.

Compulsory education was not introduced in France until a hundred years later, and even in 1905, according to Parisot, it was by no means universally enforced. Yet Oberlin, even without the sanction and support of the law, succeeded in establishing virtually universal education in his parish by applying sanctions of his own devising. As a counterpart to the monetary compensations mentioned above, he imposed certain deprivations upon children who did not attend school regularly and upon parents who kept their children at home. One of his most potent penalties was his refusal to admit to confirmation children who had not attended school regularly each year up to the age of sixteen.[30] Another sanction became possible when he had organized his savings and loan societies, described in a later chapter: he excluded from membership in them, and therewith from certain very substantial benefits, all parents who tolerated, or perchance even abetted, the truancy of their children. In general, whenever he had dispensations, favors, or benefits of any kind at his disposal for distribution among his people, he made careful judgments concerning the worthiness of the individual recipients. Thus in 1802 he proposed a project "to correct the bad distribution of tuition fees for those who love their Lord Jesus": "Soon school books will be distributed, but only to children of parents who are not able to purchase them for all their children and who also are diligent with all their family; who let their lamps burn so that the children may work at their lessons also in the evening; who will promise, as honorable folk, to commit no theft, not even of wood from the forests, in order to make for themselves sleds, or wooden shoes, or shoulder baskets, or whatever."[31] In another place he listed as criteria for identifying the worthy poor diligence in the performance of duties; eschewal of visits to the tavern; regular attendance of children at school; and abstinence from all luxuries (which in his view included the keeping of dogs).[32]

Oberlin's conception of public education as something that benefits the whole community is illustrated by his insistence that all citizens support the schools. In the project of 1802 he introduced "in the expectation of a high solidarity" an impost on the income not only of parents, but also of those without children, whether married or celibate. Thus he anticipated something like a general income tax for the support of education. When he felt that prospects of worldly benefits or penalties were not sufficient incentives, he sometimes used the threat of dire consequences for parents who were stingy in supporting the schools and for children who were delinquent in attending them. Universal education, he repeatedly proclaimed, is an obligation laid upon man by the will of God. In one sermon he virtually added to the decalogue an eleventh commandment: Thou shalt pay thy school taxes. At the same time he promised the community escape from "those chastisements that come in the form of dissensions, disputes, and hatred," if both the rich and poor would "pay more heed to God's commandments and would give to their teachers the portion that God has ordained."

In the same sermon, alluding to the biblical metaphor of the winnow that will separate the kernels from the chaff, he says: "Oh, how much chaff there is still in our parish; how little wheat! Why was I alone charged to pay the wages of the *conductrices* and several other things besides? And who then constrained some few of my parishioners to relieve me of part of the burden of the *conductrices'* wages? It was no human law that accomplished this; no, it was the law of love, of faith in God, that brought it about. . . . It is God's ordinance that obligates all creatures endowed with reason to seek instruction in the sciences . . . and in whatsoever things are useful." And finally, he threatens to withhold "their portion of favor to all children who, instead of attending instruction regularly, prefer a kind of stupid ignorance, an ignoble clumsiness, an arrogant presumptuousness, and a brutish intractability," though they know that it is God's will that they should attend.[33]

Because the help of the older children was needed in field and pasture, the school calendar was adjusted to the demands of the seasons. But because the economy was totally agrarian there was no presssure to release the children from school to become full-time laborers at an early age. Consequently there was no strong opposition to Oberlin's requiring school attendance to age sixteen. This measure made his school district unique, for even after compulsory school attendance had, at a later time, been introduced generally in Europe, the age at which children left school was usually lower than that. The situation in England is indicated in the following, written in June 1816 by Robert Owen, reporting to Lord Brougham's

Commission on the Education of the Lower Orders: "The children generally attend the superior school until they are ten years old. . . . At this age both boys and girls are generally withdrawn from the day school, and are put into the mills, or to some regular employment."[34]

Discipline in the schools was controlled by an elaborate plan in which the pupils themselves were given the responsibility of enforcing the rules.[35] A code of behavior called *le réglement de police et de discipline,* drawn up by Oberlin in 1778, prescribed that the pupils of each village should elect wardens, squad leaders, elders, and a juror. The *gardes* were charged to inspect the pupils' hands and books for cleanliness, to keep order among the children in church, at funerals, or "wherever they appear in a body," and to report infractions of rules to the *pelotonniers.* Each *pelotonnier* was head of a *peloton* of a half-dozen pupils. It was his duty to exhort his charges to good behavior, to call them to order when necessary, and to report on their conduct either to the *ancien* or to the *régent d'école.* The *juré,* in collaboration with the *régent d'école,* presided over all the other officers and exercised judicial functions when misbehavior occurred. Just as bad conduct was severely punished, good behavior was recorded, evaluated as being of either moderate or extraordinary merit, and appropriately rewarded. The qualities that were particularly rewarded were diligence, disciplined conduct, gentleness, politeness and courtesy, quickness in the performance of duties, generosity, and extraordinary obedience.

At the head of this complex organization stood Oberlin himself, keeping a watchful eye on all the teachers and all the children. He took pleasure in acknowledging good conduct and kept his own "Catalogue of Good Children." In the first catalogue (made in 1778), he bestowed titles of royalty and nobility upon the most virtuous pupils: *empereur* for those in the most advanced schools; *prince* for the intermediate grades; *chevalier* for the little ones. He soon recognized the folly of such bizarre appellations, however, and abandoned them. But to the best pupils he gave prizes, usually consisting of such useful objects as pencils, quills, colored crayons, and books.

There is no doubt that Oberlin attached great importance to this experiment in student self-government. This is indicated not only by the care with which he designed the whole plan and supervised its implementation, but also by his insistence that all the school children should participate in it. In order to give a large number of pupils some opportunity to bear the responsibilities of holding office, he directed that the *gardes* should be changed each week, the *pelotonniers* each quarter-year. Since many of the children thus functioned as elected officers and all of them participated as electors, the whole community of youth gained experience in the processes of democracy.

Oberlin's insistence that no child should be excused from this experience is specifically documented; so too is his readiness to punish severely—not to say cruelly—anyone whose intransigence seemed to endanger the success of a community project that he considered meritorious and important. There were times when Stuber's metaphorical utterance "He shepherds my flock with a rod of iron" was indeed justified. Consider, for instance, the case of a particularly hapless miscreant named Joseph Neuvillers, who "had the effrontery to say that he would not come to school to watch over other scholars." In this case Oberlin himself acted as the court of last appeal and directed the teacher from this moment on not to consider Joseph as a scholar:

> He shall not be spoken to, shall not be permitted to read in his turn; you will not correct his copybook; his name will no longer be included in the roll call nor listed in the register of good scholars. He shall be regarded as dead and non-existent. . . .
> Also you will post a placard with the inscription: Joseph Neuvillers, *brebis galeuse* [mangy sheep]. He is to remain under this punishment until he comes and asks for forgiveness: from you for his disobedience; and from the whole school for having set a bad example. Thereafter the placard should be removed, but he will continue to be subjected to the other punishments for two more weeks.

In using the phrase *brebis galeuse* instead of either *brebis perdue* or *brebis noire* (lost sheep or black sheep), Oberlin may have had in mind the well-known proverb "il ne faut qu'une brebis galeuse pour gâter tout un tropeau"—one mangy sheep will taint a whole flock. In his mind a fault such as disobedience became a major dereliction because it set an infectious bad example for all the children and thereby endangered the solidarity of the community in the execution of a vitally important project. Thus the young citizens of that "backward" community were being schooled not only in the rights, but also—and perhaps more vigorously—in the obligations and responsibilities of communal living, albeit with the use of disciplinary techniques that would not be applauded by most educational theorists of our time.

Each year in May there was a festival for the whole parish with games and amusements for the children and the distribution of prizes. Also at the regular gatherings of the teachers in the parsonage the products of schoolwork of various kinds, including drawings and silhouettes, were inspected, compared, and judged. Sometimes prizes of money were given to the winners of competitions in writing essays on a given subject: "What advantage might a boy have who has been well instructed in arithmetic in comparison with one who has not?—A fat three-franc piece for the best answer!" Experts in pedagogics and in educational psychology may question the wisdom of offering prizes as motivation for greater learning effort; but in a primitive community with a high incidence of illiteracy, where there were few adults whom children could look up to and emulate as models demonstrating the advantages of learning, the offering of prizes must have seemed a good substitute for incentives of a more sophisticated and less material kind. Oberlin believed that his first task as an educator was to lead his young folk out of the slough of lethargy and ignorance to a higher level of existence. He saw the premiums he offered as tangible tokens of the benefits that could accrue from learning in a community where indifference or even hostility was the common attitude toward efforts to raise the general standard of education and conduct. In these circumstances Oberlin saw the prize days as "occasions to stimulate interest and excite the imagination and to give it wings." (The rhetoric of that utterance may have been suggested by the fact that the date chosen for the annual giving of prizes was Ascension Day.)

A plausible idea of what was taught in the schools can be constructed from the schedule below made by one of the *régents d'école* at Stoeber's request.[36]

The class to which this schedule applied is not specified, but since it is known that instruction in German began in the fourth year, it is presumed that this would be a typical schedule for a class in the so-called middle school, which included the

Daily Schedule for the Subjects of Instruction in the Schools of the Waldersbach Parish

Monday	Tuesday	Wednesday	Thursday	Friday	Saturday
Arithmetic	Arithmetic	Arithmetic	Arithmetic	Arithmetic	Arithmetic
French grammar	Composition on a moral tale	French reading; analysis of a paragraph	French grammar	French reading	Grammar
French reading	French grammar	Dictation and correction of composition	Dictation of German words	Grammatical analysis	Notes and singing
Geography	French reading	Catechism	Notes and singing	Geography	Religious instruction

fourth, fifth, and sixth year. The level of instruction in the other subjects also suggests that this may be for the fourth grade. Some general comments on the subjects mentioned seem in order.

The teaching of numbers began in the first class and continued year by year through the ninth. Facility in mental arithmetic was stressed. In the fourth grade, instruction included "the second course in the arithmetic of fractions to the rule of three for abstract quantities." In later classes there was instruction in such practical matters as "writing promissory notes, receipts, accounts, etc."

Language was the most intensively taught subject in all the grades. It began with the youngest children in the infant schools and was an important element in all the forms. It was also the chief subject in the classes for adults. At the beginning of his ministry Oberlin seems to have contemplated the possibility of making German the language of the schools. His letter to Stuber on this subject is lost to us, but we have Stuber's reply: "A German school is not advisable. Those who do not know German will nevermore learn it there, and the few who do know it will manage to find opportunities to learn to read, if they wish to do so. I know, the importunity of those who keep on demanding a German school impels one in that direction; but you will see that it would not give you that which you hope from it."[37] Thereafter Oberlin made the displacement of the patois by French the main objective of language instruction. The necessity of persistent teaching in this subject is clear when one remembers that for the children it was scarcely less a foreign tongue than German. The method used was the one laid down in Stuber's *Alphabet Méthodique.* The vigorous instruction, together with the strict rule against using the patois, gradually brought it about that French became the vernacular among the children, and ultimately, as they became adults, the dominant language of the community. Today there are probably less than a half-dozen residents who know the patois at all. The introduction of German, at that time the chief language of Alsace, opened the way for those who had the will to learn it to participate more fully in the rich culture of their native province, and at the same time helped to preserve the traditional bilinguality of the region.

Instruction in subjects pertaining to the earth and its products began in the infant schools and persisted throughout the whole school course. Its first objective was to give the children a sense of the beauty and bounty of God's earth; its second was to impart technical knowledge of a kind that is especially useful in an agricultural community; its ultimate aim, like that of language instruction, was to help break the bonds of narrow parochialism and isolation of the parish. Formal instruction was supplemented, especially for the younger children, by frequent excursions to gather specimens of plants and insects, of rocks and minerals and soils. Many maps were used, beginning with "blind" maps of the Ban, printed on Oberlin's little hand press from wood blocks cut by him, to which the children added the names of streams and mountains; hamlets, and farmsteads; castles, churches, and schools. Later they went on to representations of the terrestrial globe, then to charts of the solar system, and ultimately even to speculative projections of the heavenly abodes.

Stoeber describes the method of instruction in "notes and singing." The melodies of hymns were first read and memorized by a sol-fa system and were later sung with words. The hymns to be learned were presented in groups of five and each group was practiced in the weekly classes for three months. This thorough training brought it about that in the Steintal churches four-part congregational singing was the general practice. Visitors from abroad often commented on the outstanding quality of the singing. Although there is no specific mention in the records of training in instrumental music, it must have been practiced, for performances are known to have taken place. As early as 1775, for instance,

Oberlin noted in his journal, "At the first concert at Waldersbach, 12 May 1775, in honor of some persons from Strasbourg, Jean-David Bohy, Sébastien Scheidecker, and Simon and Jean-Jacques Claude of Trouchy, played the violin, Didier Neuvillers and Georges Bernard the *flûte à bec,* Vernier sang the bass and some young girls the air; M. Schweighaeuser played the *flûte traversée.* On Sunday the 18th, at the service at Belmont, another festive concert was given for the pleasure of M. Stuber, who was visiting the Steintal at that time."[38] Probably all of the participating instrumentalists had begun their musical training under Stuber.

Sketching and painting were practiced outside the regular school hours. In judging the paintings of pupils, Oberlin seems to have placed a premium on verisimilitude. "Almost all the children," he wrote in a memorandum to the *régents d'école,* "like to paint only in brilliant colors. But such colors are rare in nature: rocks and tree trunks, houses, furnishings and utensils show no shining colors. So, whenever you have a pupil who has the good sense to see nature as the proper model and therefore to choose muted colors rather than bright ones, I beg you to send the child to me with his or her sketchbook."[39] The purpose of that directive was probably to reward the child for his good sense with a prize.

The art of handwriting was taught in the upper classes and included practice in the cutting of quills. Oberlin considered good handwriting very important, and on at least one occasion even elevated it to a matter of deep social significance.[40] In a letter to a prefect he remarked that standards in the teaching of this subject are so low in France that communications "often pass indecipherable from office to office; sometimes new names are created that are quite different from the original ones, and so it happens that some poor soldiers cannot draw their pay, or even receive their papers; or, because their names are badly written, badly read, and badly copied, they may be sent to Pontoise and never seen again." He therefore begs every patriotic person to give each letter a form that will distinguish it from all others and make it impossible to be mistaken. "Promote the good; strike down confusion!" In another letter, to Mme Schauenberg, née von Berckheim, he even goes so far as to equate good handwriting with godliness: "In all things, including legible writing, the disciple of Jesus should be salt and light; he should resist corruption for all that is in him."

And, finally, he once wrote reprovingly but not without humor to a young relative: "Cutting your quills the way you do, it is not possible for you to write a single good character. Sometimes all that is needed is a slight changing of the nib and it goes very well. Don't you think that there is a connection between the 'beak' of the writer and that of a pen? Both the one and the other are in need of *un petit retranchement* [a slight curtailment]."

To Oberlin the most important school discipline of all was what he called in French *catéchisme,* in German *Kinderlehre.* It included such subjects as Bible stories, memorization of the Ten Commandments, the Lord's Prayer, the Apostles' Creed, the Lutheran doctrine of the sacraments, and the basic concepts of Christian ethics and morals. But religious instruction was by no means confined to these courses; it permeated every branch of instruction. The exercises in French composition were based on the "moral tales" and homilies of Friedrich Rochow's popular reader, *Der Kinderfreund*; passages for German dictation and for translation from German to French were taken from a book entitled *Religion- unterricht* (Instruction in Religion) by Witz; natural history, we may be sure, was not given without frequent reference to the power, love, and goodness of the Creator; and even the practical courses, given in the upper grades, dealing with commerce and trade, with agriculture and husbandry and housekeeping, surely included commentaries and preachments on the duties and obligations of Christian men and women to their neighbors. Oberlin's deep religious faith was not only the basis of his preaching and teaching; it permeated every aspect of his living and doing; its dissemination and propagation motivated all his striving for social and economic improve- ment.

Oberlin never wrote down a systematic statement of the significant pedagogical insights that he gained in building his system of education. To develop a plan on the basis of theoretical ratiocination was not his way. To those who expressed interest in the subject he gladly reported in interviews and in letters on what he had done; but to present his educational theories and his pedagogical accomplishments to the general public in print would probably have seemed presumptuous to him. His general orientation was more pragmatic than philosophical, his approach to problems was more intuitive than cognitive, his way to their solution was more inductive than deductive. There is no doubt that he read assiduously the current literature on education. The book that influenced him most was Rousseau's *Emile.* On the flyleaf of his copy, which he circulated among *régents d'école* and *conductrices,* he wrote: "An excellent book! Certainly I do not consider all the rules that [Rousseau] sets forth as the most practicable or the best; but this book contains so many valuable insights and correct observations that I wish that every parent and every teacher would read it again and again." Among the insights and observations that Oberlin probably considered as correct and valuable was the necessity of teaching not by rote, but by examples that are comprehended in the child's personal experience and observation and are presented in such a way that the child is led step by step from the concrete and simple to the abstract and complex.[41] Another is the recognition and treatment of the child as a human personality that must be shaped and guided to maturity in its entirety, that is to say, in its moral and spiritual as well as its physical and intellectual qualities. Still another is recognition of the transcendent centrality as the object of education of the person, rather than things or "subjects." Of the "rules" that Oberlin would not "consider . . . as the most practicable and the best," surely one must have been Rousseau's "incontrovertible rule, that the impulses of nature are always right; there is no original sin. . . ." Given the Christocentric quality of his unshakable faith, Oberlin could not possibly subscribe to that proposition. Nor could he have found comfort and help in the "Creed of a Savoyard Priest," which constitutes half of the fourth book of *Emile.*[42] Although Oberlin was more tolerant of Rousseau's deistic views of religion than he was of Diderot's and Holbach's atheism, Rousseau's disavowal of the divinity of Jesus and his rejection of the doctrines of original sin, atonement, and redemption, taken together with the apparent dissoluteness of his private life, impelled Oberlin to count him among the forces of the Antichrist and therefore to denounce him both in his preaching and his private conversation. There is an oft-repeated anecdote that exemplifies this ambivalence of judgment. A certain visitor at the parsonage, after broaching the subject of the influence of the *philosophes* on the life of the people, unexpectedly found himself listening to a denunciation of the immorality of Rousseau. Being somewhat shocked by the sententiousness of Oberlin's attack, his guest interposed, "But sir, has he not persuaded French mothers to revert to the breast-feeding of their babies?" to which Oberlin responded, "Ah, the dear, good man."

An important element in Oberlin's educational practices was *Anschauung*—literally, looking at things. August Hermann Francke had begun to use the technique of *Anschauungs-unterricht* (somewhat feebly translated in education textbooks as "object lesson teaching") in the paupers' school that he started in his parsonage in 1695 and continued it in the famous Francke Institutes that he later founded in Halle, where, at the time of his death, 2,200 children were being served. Oberlin knew it from reading Francke's "School Ordinances" and from the Moravian Brethren, who had been influenced by Francke in the designing and conduct of the excellent schools that they had founded in many places in Europe and in England.[43] But the ideas which excited him most and with which he found himself most in agreement were those of the Philanthropists. Johann Bernhard Basedow, the leader of that group, had published serially from 1770 to 1774 his *Elementarwerk* on reforming the schools of Germany. His program, which was strongly influenced by Locke and Rousseau, included the following imperatives: physical education and manual training should be offered; teachers and pupils should be considered as collaborators in the learning process; all formal discipline and drill should be eliminated; more emphasis should be placed on learning the mother tongue and less on Latin and Greek; more effort should be directed to *Volksbildung* (education of the people), even if it be at the expense of the elite; the teaching of religion should be interconfessional and practical; religious precepts should be based on a natural, rather than a revealed, ethic. The two points on religion aroused strong opposition from the Church; and Oberlin, too, must have rejected the preferment of natural over revealed religion, but the presence of that heresy could not damp his enthusiasm for the *Elementarwerk* as a whole. Basedow opened his school called the Philanthropinum, at Dessau in 1774. It was supported by popular subscription and was intended to be a model for national school reform. A friend and former pupil of Oberlin, Freidrich Simon, was one of Basedow's collaborators. On March 16, 1777, Oberlin wrote a long letter to thank Simon for sending him copies of the *Elementarwerk*. Both the content and the style of this letter reveal the ardor of Oberlin's devotion to the cause of education. The reading of the treatise, he says, aroused two fervent desires in him: to go to Dessau to "hear everything and to return enriched by your insights," and to give money for the furtherance of the work there. The first of these wishes he is forced regretfully to renounce for lack of both time and funds; the second he is able to fulfill with the help of his wife, who, infected by his enthusiasm for the cause, has given him a treasured pair of earrings with the request that he sell them and send the proceeds of the sale to Dessau. He closes the letter with a promise to circulate the *Elementarwerk* widely, especially in Strasbourg, and with a prayer to God to give his colleagues strength for their "enviable calling" and encourage them and give them "that which I always wish for myself: ever more fervid love for Jesus Christ and for these children who are so precious to him."[44]

The love of children is a personality trait that contributed greatly to Oberlin's success as an educator. It was disinterested, natural, instinctive, and constant; it was devoid of condescension or patronage; it was motivated by a deep respect for human personality that made no distinction between the rights, privileges, and claims to affection of children and those of adults.

This is illustrated by a sermon, discovered among Oberlin's papers by Psczolla, based on 1 Sam. 1:11: "Hannah made a vow in these words: 'O Lord of hosts, if Thou will deign to take notice of my trouble and remember me, if Thou will not forget me, but will grant me offspring, then I will give the child to the Lord for his whole life, and no razor shall ever touch his head.' " On this Oberlin commented: "Hannah surely deserves great praise because she was so grateful to God. But is her gratitude of a kind that we can truly approve and emulate? What right had she to offer her child without knowing beforehand whether such a way of life would be agreeable to him or not?" Continuing his discourse Oberlin told his congregation that it is wrong for parents to marry off a daughter in accordance with *their* wishes; or to compel a son to become, say, a physician, when because of his temperament, his talents, and his desires he might better be a merchant. "Question your children as to their wishes and talents and let them choose their own vocation, while you let them know that you stand ready to advise them. . . . One can properly fulfill his mission in life only if one stands in that position which is right for his talents."[45]

The responsibilities of parents toward their children was often the dominant theme of his preaching; but he also often reiterated similar warnings that parental responsibility for a child must stop short of domination over his life by denying him the free exercise of his will. In his view, respect for the individual human personality must include the respect of every parent for the personality of each child. The scriptural admonition, "Father, provoke not your children to wrath," was often uttered in the Steintal churches.

There remains for consideration here one more educational enterprise: the private boarding school called the *pensionnat*. After the new parsonage had been built, in 1778, Oberlin began to take in boarding pupils in order to supplement his meager income, much of which he gave to support his many projects in the parish. The *pensionnaires* were mostly adolescent boys and girls from Strasbourg and other cities and towns of Alsace, but there were also children, especially in the later years, from more distant places.[46] The pupils were housed in a building adjacent to the manse and were treated as members of the Oberlin family. The living room of the parsonage served as general gathering place and schoolroom. Ehrenfried Stoeber, who had himself been one of the *pensionnaires* in the 1780s, praises the school for the excellent religious education, love for work, and devotion to moral simplicity that it imparted, and for "the modesty, the sense of order, the strict punctuality, the devotion to the language of truth, the conscientious use of time, the frugality and charitableness that it infused in the *pensionnaires*." Oberlin, he says, "watched over their innocence and nurtured in them that tender modesty that constitutes the charm of youth, and gave them a good, sound education. Their constitution was developed and shaped amongst the mountains that isolate the Ban de la Roche, which became a peaceful habitation for them, a protective haven against the frivolity, the tempests and the depravity of the time."

Mme Roerich is more specific about the instruction the pupils received. It included reading, translation and discussion of the classics; courses in hygiene, in diseases and their treatment; and the writing of receipts, contracts, and other documents. Intellectual subjects were interspersed with practical instruction of various kinds. Every pupil had to do some kind of handwork and had to display the products of such work. Some did filet crocheting or macramé, some made gloves, others made things of horsehair and of straw. The girls received training and practice in the kitchen, the laundry, and at the spinning wheel, along with instruction in household management, while the boys made collections of plants, minerals, and insects. (Oberlin took pains to teach the children to be gentle with all living creatures. The insects, for instance, were handled with care while they were being studied, described, identified, and drawn on paper, and thereafter they were released.) French and German were used alternately as the language of instruction.

In his management of this school, Oberlin's chief purpose was, as always, the cultivation and improvement of the spiritual life of his charges. Everywhere and on all occasions the children were reminded and admonished to pray and to meditate. The walls and doors of their dormitories and of the parsonage were decorated with Bible verses printed by him; their daily tasks were begun and concluded with prayer; the program for their outings included Bible readings, hymn singing, and meditations on the glory of God in nature.

Oberlin's helpers in conducting the school were his wife and his daughter Frédérique-Bienvenue, who was later to become the wife of Pastor Rauscher, and ultimately, when her husband became Oberlin's successor, mistress of the Waldersbach manse. The chief teacher was Jean-Jacques Claude of Trouchy, son-in-law of the venerable Vernier Masson, *régent d'école* in Waldersbach. Claude gradually assumed more and more responsibility for the management of the *pensionnat* and virtually became its principal after Mme Oberlin had died and her daughter had married and left the Ban de la Roche for a time with her husband. The *pensionnat* continued operation as a private school under the ownership and management of the Claude family until 1932, when Sofie Claude, the last teacher and principal, died.

Through the 141 years of its history, the *pensionnat* not only served its primary function of education, but also played an important part in establishing and maintaining connections between the Ban de la Roche and the outside world: the *pensionnaires* brought something of the wider world into the isolated community, while Stoeber, in concluding his comments on the *pensionnat,* could aver, with the time-honored rhetoric of the old school tie, "Today [i.e., the 1820s], spread out over the whole wide world, in Alsace, in Paris, in London, and in Petersburg, Oberlin's *pensionnaires* constitute a fraternity that is sanctified by the memory of those precious days that they spent in the Steintal with that venerable man whom all of them will ever revere as their common spiritual father."

Je soussigné Jean Frederic Oberlin Ministre certifie avoir fait accord avec Maître Jean Jaques Banzet l. v. de Bellefosse; dont voici les conditions:

1. sa fille Madeleine sera à mon service trois jours de la semaine le mardi, mecredi, jeudi.

2. le rapport de tout ce qu'elle fera ces trois jours sera à moi.

3. je lui payerai vingt-quatre livres par an; et ainsi 6 ℔ par quartier.

4. son Père la nourrit et l'habille tout come jusqu'ici.

5. si quelques personnes par acconoissance des services que la fille leur rendra en enseignant leurs enfants, lui font des présens de quelque espèce qu'ils soient, les présents seront à elle.

Fait à Bellefosse ce vingt six de Mars, l'an mil septcent septante.

Jaqu. Banzet

Jean Frederic Oberlin
Ministre

1 The Contract, in Oberlin's Hand, for the Services of Sara Banzét

12 A Peasant House at Belmont

13 Oberlin as Road Builder

5

The Beautiful Life of Poverty

". . . it would be as if the spirit of Oberlin had passed over the parishes to make the life of poverty beautiful!"
—George Eliot[47]

There have been disputes about the inclemency of the Steintal weather. Some writers tend to exaggerate the severity of the winters; others assert that the climate is salubrious, citing the fact that there was once a vineyard in the vicinity of Trouchy. The disagreement can be resolved by reference to a scientific study made in Oberlin's time: in his doctoral dissertation (now in the Musée Oberlin) on the chorography and ecology of the Ban de la Roche, Oberlin's son Henri-Gottfried found that the area, small as it is, had three climatological zones. The largest of these by far, he explained, had weather comparable to that of Turku in Finland, with an average annual temperature of 5°C. (41°F.); a smaller, more temperate zone he compared with Vilna and Warsaw. Also there were a few small, favorably oriented and well-protected "islands of warmth"—like the site of that vineyard near Trouchy—with weather ranging from the northern chill of, say, Strasbourg, to a more southern ambience comparable to that of Geneva.

Scattered here and there in Oberlin's journals for 1770—the year in which the first infant school was started and the new schoolhouse at Waldersbach was completed—are the following comments on the weather. Because they had neither firewood for their hearths nor oil for their lamps, many families had to go to bed at nightfall. For more than a fortnight Jean Martin Loux was not able to heat his living room. Many householders had on hand only a few logs of firewood, though it was very cold and the deep snow made it impossible to bring in even a stick of wood. During the preceding year there had been very little fruit. In Belmont and in upper Bellefosse there had been complete crop failure. The grain had rotted, but the people had made bread of it in spite of that; some families had none left two months after the harvest. Claude Kommer had ten children, eight of them at home, nearly all infants; he could not get even wooden shoes for all of them; two were therefore barefoot all day in the cold and the rain. The mother, assisted by one of the children, had labored all day at carrying manure to the field without so much as a potato for nourishment. Bread "hasn't even been mentioned" in their house for a long time; the family was reduced to eating potato vines. Many people lived for months on grasses cooked in milk, "bread" made of tree bark, and wild fruits.

That year, to be sure, was unusual in that crops were extraordinarily poor and the winter uncommonly cold. But it was unusual in the severity, not in the kind, of its hardships; for it was a land in which even the good years yielded scarcely enough produce to nourish man and beast through the long winters. Thus it was only a slight deviation from the normal in precipitation and temperature that made 1770 a year not of ordinary scarcity, but of disastrous famine.

Oberlin was always acutely aware of the physical needs of his people and was intent on helping to alleviate them, but there were times when he was uncertain about the priority of ameliorative steps to be taken and impatient about the slowness of progress toward improvement. Near the end of the first year of his ministry, he seems to have laid before Stuber a plan of action to improve the physical conditions of life by putting the people to work at unaccustomed industrial projects. In his reply Stuber remarks that an attempt to "make the people industrious" is indeed a noble undertaking and would rank first among all the praiseworthy projects "if it only were not beyond our capabilities; we have neither the resources nor the authority and the people have neither the will nor the faith for it." He admonishes Oberlin not to force them "to submit to all sorts of preconceived ideas or to talk them into this or that," for thus he would only make himself seem troublesome, suspicious, and hateful. "Work only on their souls," he urges; "if you do that with love and with confidence in them, you will have better success. Forget about your economic schemes now; display to the people complete satisfaction with all that they are; thus you will win their confidence, and then they will come to see you as one of their own; after that nothing will seem strange or odious to them. . . . Go directly to their hearts and only to them; about economic affairs say nothing at all. . . . Let us continue with the flax spinning. As for the knitting, well, we can talk about that when next we meet."[48]

The action of founding the first *poêles à tricoter* had been in accord with the ideas expressed here by Stuber; for it had not been imposed by Oberlin, the outsider, but had begun as a voluntary action by one of the natives, Mlle Sara Banzét. Though it cannot be said that Oberlin always contained his impatience until he discovered similar spontaneous new initiatives among the people, he usually did attempt to evoke attitudes and to engender feelings among the adult citizens that would be favorable to his projects before he started to execute them.

His chief instrument for accomplishing this was the church. In the weekly prayer meetings and discussion groups for adults, in his pastoral work with individual parishioners, in his prayers at church services, and most especially in his sermons he tirelessly promulgated his ideas and made propaganda for his enterprises. Every proposal for reform, large or small, from the improvement of handwriting to the building of roads was justified and sanctified by passages from Holy Scripture; every task, no matter how menial or odious, was "spirtualized."

A sermon first preached on August 25, 1767, and repeated in 1779, 1796, and 1814 affords a good example of this. The text is Ps. 90:12: "So teach us to number our days that we may get a heart of wisdom." Leenhardt gives the following excerpt:

The hired man who sweeps together all manner of filth and carries out dung spiritualizes that work if he performs it as faithfully as he possibly can before God and out of love for his Master, Jesus Christ. The wife who is obedient to her husband and who voluntarily submits to all the inconveniences and sorrows of her sex for love of her Savior, puts her actions under the aspect of eternity and sows seeds for heaven. The farmer, patriotic and Christian, who with all the means available to him strives to improve his cultivation of the soil, . . . gives up his pernicious heedlessness and does well the work that the Eternal God has entrusted to him, spiritualizes his work and eternalizes his rustic labors.[49]

Thus, always accompanying his own labors with these and similar exhortations, Oberlin launched his campaign against poverty.

It is not true, as some writers have claimed, that the Ban de la Roche before Oberlin's time was a trackless wilderness in which the villages, the hamlets, and the single farmsteads were completely isolated from each other. From early times there had been roads of a sort from village to village, and the thoroughfare from Strasbourg to Schirmeck by which Oberlin had made the trip to Waldersbach, though by our standards a primitive one, did connect the valley with the outside world. Through the years of privation that had begun during the Thirty Years' War, however, the daily struggle for existence tended to destroy any sense of community and to engender a spirit of separateness. When each household was preoccupied with its own concerns, there was little traffic from house to house and from place to place, and consequently the roads had deteriorated from neglect. Oberlin, who knew that the assault on poverty had to be launched on a wide front and that prosperity would have to come either to the whole community or not at all, was intent upon restoring the sense of community; and because community thrives only on communication, he placed the improvement of the roads high on his list of priorities, along with such projects as language reform and the building of schools.

Long periods of virtual noncommunication within the Ban were imposed annually when the snows of winter put a stop to all movement except on foot with the aid of snowshoes. On that log thrown across the Bruche, the freezing of the enveloping spray formed a coating of ice and made any attempt to gain the highway to the outside world a flirtation with death by drowning. Countless accidents, many of them fatal, had occurred there. The coming of spring brought little relief, for the excessive accumulation of water made the primitive roads nearly impassable. But, unlike the snows, this was an evil that could be at least ameliorated by human effort, and Oberlin lost no time in starting his assault.

His early call for volunteers to begin the huge labor of improvement found little response, but keeping in mind the good advice of Stuber, he concealed his disappointment and annoyance, left off preaching about the subject for a time, and resorted to teaching by example. One fine sunny morning he marched out with pick and shovel and went to work draining and filling a mudhole at a conspicuous place on the Waldersbach-Fouday road. The next day, one or two of his more sensitive and responsible neighbors joined him, and gradually, when others saw what could be accomplished, the work force grew and at times became so large that it was possible to have several projects simultaneously under way at widely separated places. At such times Oberlin, who soon became a good horseman, took to riding from place to place, laying out plans, giving instructions, and supporting the men with words of encouragement and appreciation, along with reminders of rewards promised in the Scriptures to those who devoted themselves to advancing the common good.

It was a large undertaking, for it included such heavy labor as digging ditches for drainage; building stone retaining walls along the hillsides; giving the roadways proper contours, high in the middle and sloping off at the sides; hauling gravel from distant places and spreading it on the surface; and—most arduous of all—building bridges. In some places the adjoining fields had encroached on the right-of-way so that it was necessary to negotiate with individual peasants concerning the limits of their domain. When verbal negotiations proved unavailing, Oberlin did not hesitate to offer a financial settlement. Sometimes problems of grade or of drainage made relocation of the right of way advisable, and that also necessitated the purchase of land. All expenses, for tools and materials as well as for easements, were paid by Oberlin from funds collected by him and Stuber in small contributions from their many friends in the congregation of the faithful in Strasbourg.

As the rebuilding of the local roads approached completion, Oberlin turned his attention to the equally important objective of improved communication with the outside world. He considered this necessary not only for the cultural advantages that easier movement in and out of the valley would bring, but also for economic reasons, for he looked forward to the time when increased agricultural production would make it possible to export produce, and to the establishment of industry and the consequent bringing in of raw materials and carrying out of finished goods.

The ancient road that ran from Strasbourg westward over the Donon pass to Lorraine veered away from the Bruche Valley at Schirmeck some three miles north of Rothau, a circumstance that accounts in part for the isolation and the poverty of the Ban de la Roche. Another very old road that led from Vipucelle by way of Salm and Pleine to Senones did indeed touch the Ban de la Roche at Rothau, but it was a mountain road with grades so steep that the people shunned it in favor of the poorly drained, primitive trail along the left bank of the Bruche. The building of a road good and safe in all seasons connecting the Steintal with the highway to Strasbourg at Schirmeck seemed to Oberlin a project of such great importance that he did not hesitate to initiate it, though he was fully aware of the enormous difficulties that would have to be overcome. The first of these was the procurement of the right-of-way through a portion of the domain of the Prince de Salm. This was finally accomplished after long negotiations, personally conducted by Oberlin, and by the payment of considerable sums of money that were raised by new contributions from that faithful company of friends in Strasbourg. At several points along the Bruche the route was narrowed by boulders and by rocky cliffs rising up from the water's edge. The removal of the boulders and the cutting of a roadway out of the cliffside necessitated blasting, which required the services of skilled workers, who had to be imported. And finally, a proper bridge had to be built for the safe passage in all seasons not only of pedestrians, but also of horses and vehicles and livestock.

By the time he was ready to start the work Oberlin was not totally without experience as a bridge builder; he had already supervised the building of no less than eight wooden structures to carry the new roads over the lesser streams within the valley. This bridge, however, would have to be a much larger structure and would be more costly, not only because more building materials had to be bought, but also because an adjoining field had to be purchased for access to the site. In his efforts to recruit laborers and raise the funds for this crowning achievement that would complete the great road-building project, he talked about material advantages, but he also made copious use of the metaphorical associations with which the Scriptures and ecclesiastical rhetoric have endowed the activity of road and bridge building. In appealing to his Strasbourg friends and patrons to support the work for humanitarian reasons, he often referred to the projected structure as *ce pont de charité, diese Liebesbrücke*—this bridge of love. The name became current among the people and is used even today to designate the bridge that spans the Bruche at that place, though Oberlin's original structure has been replaced several times.

After the new roads had been completed, Oberlin observed that even when vehicles were available many of the peasants persisted in transporting their supplies and commodities on their own backs or those of their beasts of burden as they had formerly done out of necessity, instead of loading them on carts and wagons. He therefore offered a prize to anyone who used a vehicle "in which one horse can move as much as five or six men are able to carry"; and to encourage traffic with the regional market towns he offered a triple prize to the man who would transport the first wagonload of merchandise across the Champ du Feu to Barr.

Oberlin's purpose of transforming his community into a latter-day chosen people prompted him often to seek his guidelines for the management of communal affairs in the Pentateuch. In trying to persuade the civil authorities at Rothau to assume a share of the cost for building and maintaining the new bridge near there, he confronted them with a list of the casualties that had occurred because of the absence of a proper and safe crossing, at the same time citing a decree recorded in the book of Leviticus which ordained that when death occurred because of a crime, all the residents of the community in and near which it had occurred inevitably shared in the guilt for it and were obliged to do penance and to make restitution. The failure to provide a safe river crossing at Rothau, he argued, was a sin of omission and therefore, ipso facto, a crime. The Rothau officials, however, rejecting the validity of Mosaic law and citing the French civil code, which was mute on the point, denied any obligation. And so Oberlin and his parishioners, who, to be sure, made more use of the bridge than the people of Rothau, continued to pay for its maintenance, along with that of all the bridges and roads within the parish. In 1813, indeed, the mayor of Rothau wrote to Oberlin stating that he had determined that certain repairs were necessary and inquiring whether they could be paid for from capital funds existing for the maintenance of the bridge. Oberlin, perhaps heaving a long sigh, wrote: *"Monsieur le Maire:* the bridge in question, that poor orphaned bridge, is called *le pont de charité* because charity alone built it at last after several fatal accidents had occurred, and only charity has maintained it since then. This is the only 'capital fund' that exists for this cause. God be with you, *Monsieur le Maire,* and enlighten you and continue to guide you."[50] The state did not assume responsibility for roads and bridges until 1823.

While Oberlin represented the building of roads as a labor of love and supported his exhortations on that subject by references to the Bible, he considered any labor directed toward the conservation or the tilling of the soil as an outright act of worship. He often reminded his people that the words *culture, cultivateur,* and *agriculteur* are all derived from *le culte,* worship, adoration. Tomy Fallot, a former pupil in Oberlin's *pensionnat* who had become an influential industrialist and publicist and did more than any other early writer to make Oberlin's work for the advancement of agriculture known to the French people, wrote on this subject:

> Oberlin made of agriculture a sort of sacred rite: the earth, he said, is a prefiguration of heaven; its cultivation is like a heavenly sacrament. He worked out in his time, with what prophetic intuition I know not, a solution for one of the gravest problems that later confronted the post-revolutionary democracy: How to educate the ignorant peasant in such a way that his education will cause him not to regard with shame his own occupation of agriculture. It can be done, Oberlin concluded, only if one can communicate to him by the nature of the instruction that one gives him an increasing attachment to the soil, an intelligent love for its cultivation.[51]

Stuber had pointed out to his young successor what delicate tact was needed to avoid losing the people's confidence by injuring them in their sense of pride as peasants. "The basic character of my beloved Steintaler," he wrote, "is French, and it consequently demands to be treated with a kind of *noblesse* and generosity, to which they are very sensitive."[52] And in 1777, when he had heard that some of the Steintal farmers were restive under Oberlin's unrelenting goad, Stuber's friendly concern impelled him again to urge on Oberlin the necessity of patience and kindness, the desirability of showing forth his French *prévenance,* his *nature amicale,* while suppressing his tendency to importune and scold. "In German congregations," he wrote, "the minister is a machine that is always alien to the peasants as something that is of no concern to them. In the Steintal the pastor's position is, to be sure, not altogether as it should be, but yet everything is more natural. He is a friend, a father, a brother, a teacher. . . . Believe me, all the blessings of your ministry will be forfeited if they no longer take pleasure in you and are convinced that you take none in them."

To the hill folk of his parish, Oberlin, the city-bred, university-educated young clergyman, was not a prophet expected to bring useful knowledge of the earthy occupations; they had learned those from their fathers and had practiced them in daily labors beneath the sun, while the pastor had been poring over philosophical tomes and meditating on theological doctrines. The attitude in which they awaited him was more the anti-city-slicker syndrome, the universal, age-old, persistent suspicion with which the tiller of the soil regards the urban intellectual. Although Oberlin was aware of the delicacy of his situation, he could not, because of the nature both of his calling and of his personality, refrain from preaching and pleading; but he did take pains to support and supplement his verbal admonitions with demonstrations and examples. By patient endurance and persistent, toilsome effort he effected many agricultural reforms in the course of his long ministry. The scope and magnitude of those improvements are indicated in the following paragraphs.[53]

One of the emoluments of Oberlin's office was the use of an arable field adjacent to the parsonage. He used it not only as a diversified garden to supply his table, but also for purposes of demonstration and experimentation, beginning with a project to increase the yield of the shallow, sandy soil by maximal fertilization. He built the pastoral manure pit at a place where the rainwater from the roof of the house and stable would flow into it, and he dug downgrade cisterns to catch the water that seeped through the manure and emerged as liquid fertilizer. He increased the amount of solid fertilizer and humus by composting it with waste matter from the kitchen and the fields. He put children to gathering and adding to the manure piles such compostable waste as animal droppings from the village streets and small bits of used-up cloth and leather. He urged the people to build proper privies, both for hygienic reasons and for utilization of the night soil. He justified such measures by references to various passages in Leviticus and offered prizes for their emulation.

For years, as he moved about in the valley, he carried with him an earth auger with which he made test borings in the hope of finding deposits of marl that could be used to improve the soil, but this was an effort that he finally had to abandon— there was none there. He demonstrated the control of soil erosion and the conservation of moisture by contour cultivation, the strategic digging of ditches to distribute the water flowing down from the heights, and the building of dams to retard runoff. He demonstrated the effectiveness of crop rotation and of mixing sandy soil and loam with clayish or calcareous earth. He urged the people to increase production by the tillage of formerly unused areas, as along roadsides and hedgerows, and by transforming wet areas and marshes into arable fields by drainage. Stoeber testifies from personal observation that Oberlin never passed a certain sinkhole near Solbach without gathering stones along the way and throwing them into the mud there.[54]

Along with his efforts to improve the soil, Oberlin worked toward the improvement of all commodities cultivated in the Ban de la Roche, the chief of which was potatoes. The potato was apparently brought to Europe a few years before 1600 (some say by Sir Francis Drake in 1585) and soon spread through all of western Europe. For a long time it was raised only as feed for livestock, not for human consumption. It came fairly early to the Bruche Valley. There it was first listed among the crops that were subject to the tithe by a priest in Schirmeck-la Broque. It was recorded as a source of ecclesiastical income in St. Die in 1693, though it was still designated solely as fodder. It was first planted and used as food in the Ban de la Roche after the famine year of 1709, thus making this the first place in Alsace where it was consumed by human beings. From there it spread to Strasbourg and the rest of Alsace through the actions of two men, one a predecessor of Oberlin, the other his grandfather.

From 1726 to 1728 Pastor Jean-Jacques Walter, a brother-in-law of Oberlin's grandfather Feltz, was the minister at Waldersbach. In his time families still resisted using the potato as food because of widespread suspicion that it was poisonous—for was it not genetically related to the deadly nightshade? Pastor Walter sought to allay that misapprehension, to establish the good repute of the *pomme de terre*. In order to promote its use as sustenance for his undernourished people he had potatoes served regularly at his table; and so they were there also on the day of Dr. Feltz's first visit to his brother-in-law in Waldersbach. Though Feltz was not unfamiliar with potatoes, he found the local variety to be of superior quality. He took samples of the tubers back to Strasbourg from that first visit and repeatedly thereafter, and served them at his own hospitable table. Since his guests often included leading citizens of Strasbourg, the Steintaler potato became known among the cognoscenti and won the patronage of such personages as the Marchal Dubourg and the Intendant d'Angervilliers. As the demand for the new commodity grew, however, the farmers in the Alsatian Rhine plain took to planting stock from the Steintal in their own fertile fields so that ultimately nearly all of the so-called Steintaler potatoes consumed in Strasbourg came from there rather than from the Steintal itself.

Thus the potato had become a prime comestible in Alsace a good half-century before it found its way to the tables of the aristocracy at the court of Louis XVI, who made a point of wearing, in season, a potato flower as an adornment to publicize his fondness for the maligned *pomme de terre*. From the royal cuisine the potato went on to become a staple food of the bourgeoisie, of the proletariat of Paris, and ultimately of all France.

Although the Ban de la Roche thus had some part in the potato's conquest of Europe, many of the people there persisted in their prejudice against it, so that it continued to be considered chiefly as fodder for cattle and to be disdained, save in times of famine, as human food. Mme Louis Rauscher, Oberlin's daughter, wrote on the subject as follows, in a letter of uncertain date: "In 1767 the potato was still rare in the Ban de la Roche. . . . People who in the springtime ate wild grasses cooked in milk were ashamed to have potatoes on the table. If visitors came at mealtime the potatoes were quickly covered up or taken away and hidden, so that no one would know that they were being eaten."

Under these circumstances no effort was made to improve either the quality or the size of the potato crop. Thus the seed stock of the one variety that was grown in the Ban de la Roche deteriorated, so that by the time Oberlin arrived there the crop was scarcely large enough, even in the best years, to supply the needs of the local populace, while in poorer years the supply was exhausted even before the winter was over. Oberlin's first agronomic venture therefore was to increase productivity, with the ultimate goal of an abundant supply for local needs and, beyond that, a substantial exportable surplus. He started this project by experimenting with seed specimens from Lorraine, Switzerland and Holland. He had the best success with a red-skinned Swiss variety. It grew well in the Steintal soil, it had superior flavor, it was nutritiously satisfying, and it kept better in storage than the varieties grown in the Alsatian Rhine plain. The success of Oberlin's experiment was so dramatic that the people soon came to him for seed, which, of course, he gladly gave them. He showed them how to economize by cutting a whole seed potato into several pieces, each containing two or three eyes, instead of planting the whole tuber in a single hill. He also showed them how they could increase the effectiveness of the fertilizer by putting in each hill a small amount of manure, covering it with a layer of earth, and then dropping in the seed. Soon there were again enough potatoes to constitute the staff of life for the Ban de la Rochois, and by the 1780s wagonloads could be hauled over the new roads, across the *pont de charité* and on to Strasbourg, where they soon were—and remain to this day—well known and in demand under the name *Steintaler Rote.*

This was probably Oberlin's greatest single contribution to the improvement of the economy of the Ban de la Roche. While he was engaged in these efforts to improve the species, he was also haranguing the people on the dietary benefits of the potato in general and the superiority of the new variety in particular. Mme Rauscher, in the letter already quoted in part, paraphrases her father as follows:

You are devoted to your *"hach noir,"*[55] as you call your favorite dish of unpeeled, boiled potatoes, because of the good taste, especially when it is eaten with your good, fat milk. . . .

Your until recently unknown and reviled *"kmatiars"* are now going to the market in Strasbourg every autumn in fat, well-filled sacks; they are now an element in your prosperity. Not only that, they even add to your existence a touch of poetry. What a splendid scene it is when the fields are in full bloom, and again when the melancholy potato fires, at the burning of the vines in the chilly autumn, create a blue haze that envelops the hills, and fades out into silvery light as it rises higher; ah, there we have a symbol of the last impressions, the ultimate memories of the dying year.

186741

Another important product of the Ban de la Roche farms was the cow, the peasant's best friend, the supplier of meat and milk and its derivative products for his table, of leather for his feet, and, along with the horse, the drawer of his plow and harrow. Oberlin therefore was intent upon creating conditions in which cattle could flourish. His first concern was to improve the growth of grasses in pastures and meadows. To determine which species would grow best, he established several experimental plots in which he sowed various kinds of seeds, keeping a record of their growth, their progress, and their yield over periods of two to four years. One of his first findings was that the common *esparcet* or *sainfoin,* which is ubiquitous in Europe, could not attain its full growth in the Ban de la Roche because stones underlying the shallow soil there cramped its naturally deep-growing roots. Of the several specimens that he tested in the parson's glebe over a period of three or four years, he found that a species of alfalfa called lucern, which he raised from seed that he had imported from Holland, was most suitable. Gradually the farmers, as they became convinced by Oberlin's demonstrations of the superiority of the new species, reseeded their meadows, and by also following Oberlin's example in soil management, greatly increased the amount and quality of their forage crops.

As the quantity and quality of fodder increased, Oberlin urged the farmers to prolong the season of stable feeding, by which more and better beef and dairy products could be produced than by turning the stock out to graze in sparse and meager pastures. The communal grazing grounds were on lands that were unsuitable for cultivation, either because of poor drainage, as at the headwaters of the Chirgoutte, or because of the infertility of the soil, as on the Champ du Feu.

On a journey of observation and study to Köndringen in Baden in 1780,[56] Oberlin took copious notes on certain practices of soil reclamation in use there. He observed that worn-out pastures were plowed, heavily fertilized, planted to cultivated crops for several years, and thereafter reseeded with new and better grasses. He decided to introduce this system in the Steintal. There, however, the existing pastures had been relegated to their function in the first place partly because they were too stony for tillage, and the impediments to such a procedure were therefore horrendous. But Oberlin was never an irresolute sluggard who would let the mere difficulty of a project deter him in its execution. He set about it to have large, imbedded boulders broken up by blasting and removed in all but sisyphean labors, and by deploying school children to carry away the smaller stones that would impede the plow.

By such bold and drastic measures the amount of both fodder and good pasturage was enhanced, so that the land supported considerably larger herds and the meat and dairy products were improved both in quality and quantity. Within a few years the milk supply was more than sufficient for the needs of the valley; Oberlin therefore persuaded families whose cows produced a surplus to make butter, which soon joined the Steintaler potato as a readily marketable product in Strasbourg. He also undertook to improve the livestock by selective breeding and better feeding. In order to promote the adoption of the most advanced practices in animal husbandry, he offered prizes annually to the producers of the best steer and the most productive milch cow. Thus he anticipated something like the modern international institution of prize competitions among husbandmen at agricultural fairs and expositions.

Concerning livestock other than cattle there is little information in the Oberlin documents and literature. Chickens and geese and also goats are mentioned in an exhortation in which the pastor argues that it is the Christian duty of the householder to restrain such animals from damaging the gardens of neighbors. Swine are scarcely mentioned; and for all that we know from Oberlin documents, sheep seem to have remained as foreign to the Steintal as they were when Stuber arrived there. Whatever the hindrances that prevented the development of this branch of animal husbandry in Oberlin's time, they seem to have been overcome in later years, for large flocks of sheep grazing on the hillsides are now a picturesque feature of the Steintal scenery.

In order to safeguard the health of the livestock in the absence of a veterinarian, Oberlin himself acquired some rough-and-ready skills by reading standard textbooks on veterinary medicine and supplementing them with his knowledge of human anatomy and his practical skills in surgery to the extent that they were applicable.

While teaching his people how to manage their livestock, he often dwelt on the necessity of treating all domestic animals with gentleness and kindness. To him the mistreatment of an animal was a sin no less grave than wanton abuse of a fellow human being. In this respect he reminds one of that other apostolic personality, Albert Schweitzer, who was to emerge from Alsace about a century and a half later with a philosophy grounded in the concept of reverence for life.

Because of the cold climate, extensive cultivation of grain crops had never been seriously tried. Here and there some rye, barley, oats, and buckwheat were grown, but the yield was scant. Oberlin therefore sought also to improve these crops. He tried to find a variety of wheat that would thrive in that difficult terrain, but he was less successful here than in his other agricultural enterprises. Flax was being grown with moderate success. Since it was valued both for its seed and its fibers, Oberlin gave it a high priority in his experiments with seed stocks and fertilizers. He achieved moderate improvement in this commodity by importing seed from Riga.

Whether hemp was grown before Oberlin's time is not clear from available records. In any case, Oberlin took a special interest in its cultivation because it accorded with his plans for soil improvement and because its fibers were useful. He recognized the advantages of alternating hemp with potatoes for soil conservation and improvement. He taught the farmers to leave the potato vines to rot in the field through the winter, then to pick up the remaining dried stems the following spring and shake them vigorously before burning them in order to save the soil that still clung to them. Combined with the ash from the vines, this soil made a precious fertilizer for the hemp that was to be grown in the same field the next season.[57]

When Oberlin came to the Ban de la Roche he found virtually no fruit trees; the only fruits consumed there were the wild berries, apples, and pears that grew in the forests. Noting that some of the villages and hamlets were situated in folds in the mountain slopes, protected from the coldest winds and with favorable exposure to the sun, he was convinced that it would be possible to grow cultivated fruit trees in and near them. He therefore established a nursery for fruit trees soon after his arrival in Waldersbach. As the site for it he chose the front yard of the parsonage. There he planted apple, pear, and cherry trees, testing diverse varieties and experimenting with their improvement by various methods of fertilizing, pruning, and grafting. Whenever any of the many visitors to the parsonage commented on the young trees growing there, he would offer them saplings and encourage them to plant them in their dooryards. He instituted the practice of requiring each of his catechumens and each bridal couple to plant two trees as a prerequisite for confirmation and marriage, respectively, and was tireless in urging every householder in his parish to plant at least two trees for each person in his family. Furthermore, he argued that every citizen should plant a tree every two or three years in fulfillment of his continuing obligations to society after his death. In 1805 he turned over the functions of nursery-man, which he had thus far performed himself, to the community; he established a communal nursery under the management of the civil authorities. The ultimate result of all these exertions was that in the course of his ministry the Ban de la Roche passed from deprivation to relative abundance, from fruitlessness to fruitfulness.

He also cherished, and encouraged among his people, a deep appreciation of trees for the adornment of the landscape and the enjoyment of their shade. He laid out a covered walk from Waldersbach up the slope to the Perheu, the plateau which in olden times had been the scene of witch burnings and other executions and had later become a place for community gatherings, outdoor festivals, and folk divertissements of various kinds.

Although the average annual yield of agricultural produce of the Ban de la Roche increased threefold as a result of Oberlin's reforms and improvements, the inclemency of the climate still caused occasional years of crop failure and consequent famine. At such times the inhabitants were forced to revert to the practice of eating certain indigenous roots and herbs. This lent impetus and purpose to Oberlin's long-standing interest in botany, especially since members of his parish sometimes died because they had unwittingly ingested poisonous plants.[58] Also he wished to extend both his own and his people's knowledge of the curative properties of plants. He worked diligently at extending his collection of botanical specimens, identifying them by name, classifying them according to the then recently published Linnaean system, sketching the plants, their leaves and flowers, and specifying their characteristics with special reference to their nutritive, medicinal, or toxic properties.

The Musée Oberlin at Waldersbach possesses the original manuscript of the paper that Henri-Gottfried Oberlin presented on May 13, 1806, before the Association of Physicians at Strasbourg. It is based on his dissertation, which embraces a complete catalogue of the flora of the Ban de la Roche collected by his father, including two—*"le petit Pirol à ombrelle"* (*Licopodium anustinum*) and "a clover with brownish Alpine blossoms" (*Trifolium spediceum*)—which are known to grow nowhere in the Vosges except at the water's edge along the small brooks and rills running down from the Champ du Feu.[59] It also lists twenty-two plants native to the area that were commonly used as food by the inhabitants, principally in the spring, including such common weed plants as goosefoot, chickweed, dandelion, willow-herb or rosebay, buttercup, dead nettle, scarlet pimpernel, plantain, sorrel, lamb's lettuce, watercress, and corn cockle. Oberlin also taught the people how to obtain oil from beechnuts; how to make a wine (called *piquette*) from the wild cherry and from juniper; and how to distill brandy from elderberries.

In 1778 Oberlin organized the Agricultural Society of the Ban de la Roche. In doing so he hoped to create an instrument for propagating his ideas on the improvement of agriculture; to teach the *cultivateurs* the tricks of the trade that he had learned, first on visits during his childhood and youth to his grandfather's country estate, later by observation and diligent reading in the best treatises available. A secondary purpose was to instill in the farmers a spirit of solidarity and mutual helpfulness. He invited ministers and laymen of neighboring parishes to join the society and arranged for its affiliation with the Agricultural Society of Strasbourg. That association adopted a benevolent attitude toward its affiliate, sent it the desired reading materials, and put at its disposal a fund of two hundred francs for distribution as prizes.

In his introduction to a report on the regulations and the management of the new society, Jean-Luc Legrand remarks: "One can see with what care Oberlin sought to adapt this institution to the local conditions and to the modesty of the resources that were at his disposal. One also sees how, as always, he managed to give a moral and religious direction even to enterprises that served chiefly temporal purposes."[60] He also quotes Oberlin to the effect that he was first inspired to form his society by reading about similar organizations in Switzerland, where, he believed, the conditions for farming were similar to those in the Steintal.

The general design of the organization was drawn up by Oberlin in consultation with two of the *régents d'école,* David Bohy and Sébastien Scheidecker. The statutes specified that anyone who was "known as an honest man, virtuous and in agreement with the patriotic purposes of the Society, shall be granted admission, regardless of his religion, his condition, or his origin." Each new member was required to pay an initiation fee of ten sous and to pledge to "be faithful to the laws of the Society, to God, to the *seigneur du comté,* and to his country, and to strive to distinguish himself by his truly Christian conduct and by his fraternal, obliging, and kindly manners toward his neighbors." Whenever a new member was initiated, the society's emblem, with the motto "Vivons pour Dieu et la Patrie" (Let us live for God and country), was pasted in his hymnbook.[61] Thereafter he was obliged to attend the Sunday meetings of the society, to take notes there, and during the following week, as his time allowed, to make such experiments as may have been proposed in the readings. Those who had made experiments were to communicate their findings to the society at the next meeting, and each member, beginning with the president, was invited to present his own observations on them. Each meeting also included the reading, by the president, of "about eight or ten pages from a good work on rural economy," and a general discussion and exchange of opinions "in a fraternal spirit." The expenses of the society, for the purchase of books and the like, were paid from voluntary collections taken at each meeting.

The pastor's functions were laid down in the charter of the society. He would attend meetings at least once each month; receive reports on the society's work and support it with his counsel; and make a more thorough inspection every three to six months and single out for honors the three members who seemed to him to be the best informed and most capable. These were honored with prizes of books at special church ceremonies.

In founding the Agricultural Society, as in many other enterprises, Oberlin was in step with the march of progress in his time.[62] The basis for societies of that kind was created in the eighteenth century by the agricultural revolution, which brought about such signal developments as the triumph of the potato as the staple food crop of Europe; a general trend from mere subsistence farming toward commercial agriculture; great development of horticultural knowledge; a widespread application of scientific advances; and concerted efforts at selection and rotation of crops. Societies were first formed in Great Britain, then in France, and somewhat later in Germany. They were supported and abetted by a popular tendency to glorify agriculture and to romanticize rural life. Such impulses came from the philosophy of Rousseau; from the hosts of writers, poets, and essayists who were his apostles, his imitators, and his epigones; and from the economic theories of the Physiocrats. During Oberlin's childhood and student years agricultural societies had been founded in Paris, Tours, Strasbourg, and other cities.

In founding his own society, Oberlin was, as always, motivated by a desire to meet very real and practical necessities, rather than to romanticize or glorify the pastoral life. The philosophical basis for his organization he found, as always, in the Bible. Yet here, as often, when we look back on his activities in the light of social history, we see him as a social pioneer of his age, although in this instance he was not the initiator, as he had been in the founding of the infant schools. The motto of his society, "for God and country"; the stress upon "fraternal and friendly manners and kindness toward one's neighbor," as well as upon loyalty to the society and to the *seigneur du comté*—all give evidence of Oberlin's broader purpose: to create a social order based on every man's acceptance of his responsibility for his fellow men. This, together with the explicit statement of the eligibility of all citizens for membership without regard to origin, social condition, or religion shows that Oberlin's social outlook was in accord with the strong democratic views that were ultimately realized in the French Revolution.

While striving to improve agriculture in his parish, Oberlin also considered the possibility of exploiting other products of the earth for the benefit of the people. Iron, copper, and silver had all been found and mined in the Ban de la Roche at some time; mining was, indeed, the earliest industrial activity pursued there. Documentation of this is to be found in papers showing that, as early as 1558, the Ratsamhausens resisted the efforts of the emperor to develop the mineral resources of their domain.[63] There is evidence that silver was mined at Belmont in the early 1600s, while iron was mined and manufactured at Rothau. During the Thirty Years' War, however, those activities came to a halt. A letter of October 1634 from Strasbourg to an official at Rothau, inquiring whether iron ore and firewood for furnaces were available there, bears the laconic marginal note "*ist nichts.*" No attempt was made to revive the industry until 1723, when Angervilliers became the seigneur and reopened the mines and renovated the furnaces. His successor, Baron de Dietrich, developed the industry to its greatest efficiency and its product to its highest quality. In his journals Oberlin notes the fact that the shaft of an old, abandoned iron mine was accidentally discovered by a peasant near Waldersbach in 1785. A project to reopen it, however, was abandoned because of the high cost of sinking the necessary shafts for ventilation down to the deep vein of ore, and because Dietrich himself determined that the crumbly rock mass (*rocher pourri*) would make mining there dangerous. The mining of silver at Belmont and of copper on the Perheu was never resumed because of the low quality of the ore.

Inferring that there might be sandstone deposits in the valley or reasonably near it, and knowing what a boon sandstone would be to the community, where legal restrictions created a scarcity of timber for building, Oberlin commissioned his versatile helper Sébastien Scheidecker to search for such deposits. Scheidecker's diligence was rewarded when, following hints from old men of the region, he discovered a quarry of good building-quality stone near Colroy-la-Roche in 1775. Oberlin himself scouted out several bogs and directed a program for the exploitation of sphagnum and peat as soil conditioners and fuel.

When Oberlin arrived in the Ban de la Roche, virtually none of the skilled trades were being practiced there.[64] Thus a farmer who had the misfortune of breaking a tool was burdened not only with the cost of repair or replacement, but also with loss of working time because of the necessity of making a trip to Schirmeck or Barr. For want of skilled workers, damage to buildings often went unrepaired. Quite early, therefore, Oberlin selected intelligent, reliable, and ambitious young men and sent each to an appropriate community outside the Ban to learn one of the trades essential to an agricultural community. He also established and equipped a workshop for himself where he practiced as an amateur, both for recreation and to arouse the interest of his young friends, such arts and crafts as woodworking, engraving and printing, and all kinds of pottering and mending. Within a few years local citizens had established themselves as blacksmiths and wheelwrights, carpenters, masons and joiners, harness makers, shoemakers and cobblers, thatchers and glaziers. This development brought the further advantage that money formerly spent for such services imported from other places now remained in the parish.

To safeguard and promote public health, Oberlin also sent young women to Strasbourg to acquire the skills of midwifery and nursing. With a view to supplementing his own services as physician and surgeon, he sent Sébastien Scheidecker as an apprentice to Dr. Ziegenhagen.

From the beginning he saw the necessity of creating opportunities for employment of the peasant population in the seasons when there was no work to be done in the fields, for at such times the young men, and some not so young, were in the habit of roaming from place to place in the valley creating mischief, and whole families succumbed to the debilitating effects of idleness and boredom.

Early in the 1770s one M. Reber of Saint-Marie-aux-Mines, who had already established spinning and weaving operations in that place and also in Münster, Orbé, and the Villé Valley, considered establishing a new branch of his business in the Ban de la Roche. Oberlin gave him every encouragement and, after he had started a new operation in Waldersbach, helped him to recruit the necessary workers.

Oberlin soon learned, however, that it was not enough simply to make the possibility of employment available to the people; it was also necessary to persuade them to seize the opportunity. The men considered the doing of handwork for wages degrading for such as themselves, men of the soil and of husbandry; and the thought of their womenfolk doing such work elicited the question, *"On veut en faire des demoiselles?"* —Do you want to make ladies of them?

In order to disarm such opposition, Mme Oberlin herself had a spinning wheel installed in her living room and worked at it to the extent that family and parochial duties allowed. To lure men, women, and children to the distaff, the loom, and the needle, or to the learning of any other trade, Oberlin used every means of persuasion at his disposal. As always, when his flock was to be enticed into new and greener, albeit unfamiliar, pastures, the inducements that he used included the promise of concrete material rewards in the form of prizes: three sous for a pair of small stockings, four for a large pair; a special prize for the first person who would undertake to become a saddler, a mason, a joiner, or a metal worker. For learning these trades and any others approved by him and not yet adequately represented in the community, he offered an annual prize for every year spent in apprenticeship, provided that the prospective recipient could present a certificate of good conduct from his master.

All such awards, like those given to school children, were bestowed with ceremony on public occasions, thus making the recipient aware of the value of his effort not only by a monetary award, but also by the honor and respect of his fellow citizens. To stir up the people Oberlin gave his powers of persuasion full play at church services and gatherings of various kinds, and in broadsides distributed in the villages. In one sermon, for instance, he set forth six motives for taking on new kinds of employment:

La motif de piété: Do this for the love of God who demands that we should all be usefully employed, for idleness is the bed of repose of the devil and of all impure spirits.

La motif d'économie: However slight your wage may be, it will still be better than doing nothing.

La motif de gratitude: You will be better able to support your parents; you will be able, with foresight, to lay up funds with which eventually to establish your own household.

La motif de charité: You will be better able to succor the sick and the poor, and to contribute generously to useful public works of mercy.

La motif d'honneur: To be a sluggard and an idler is to be a contemptible creature; among animals it is only the swine that enjoys the privilege of being idle.

La motif d'honnêteté: Even heathen people have recognized that an idler is not an honest man; he steals not only from himself, but also from his neighbor, from the commonwealth, and from his God and creator. In some heathen tribes the law requires that the sluggard and idler be prosecuted as relentlessly and punished as severely as the thief.[65]

Gradually the people accommodated themselves to the new way of life. Visitors testified that the hum of the spinning wheel and the clack and clang of the loom were village sounds that remained long in their memories. In the year from May 1785 to May 1786, M. Reber paid out wages of 32,000 francs for the weaving, spinning, and knitting that had been done in the parish. Whatever the value of that sum may have been in terms of present-day currency, there is no doubt that it was a large sum at that time and in that place. It made possible a considerable escalation in the standard of living.

On his arrival in Waldersbach, Oberlin found that many of his parishioners, among both the very poorest and the relatively prosperous, were in debt. Recognizing it as an important cause of the discouragement, anxiety, and despair that oppressed the people, he vigorously launched an assault on this scourge. His first effort was directed toward preventing any further spreading of the affliction. His motto for this campaign he took from Rom. 1:8: "Owe no man anything, save to love one another." In countless sermons and in his daily pastoral counselling he advanced the argument that borrowing and lending fostered suspicion and distrust, anguish and misery, while mutual helpfulness tendered with brotherly love harvested both the favor of God and the reciprocal charity of man. His homilies were copiously illustrated with anecdotes and parables from Bible stories, from folk literature, and from local family histories, showing that borrowing, lending, and litigation all led to misery, both in this life and hereafter, while frugality, generosity, and forgiveness brought both earthly happiness and heavenly bliss.[66]

Here, as always, Oberlin backed his exhortations with practical measures. The first of these was the creation of a loan fund. The first "investment" in this fund was his own contribution; others he solicited from Strasbourg friends and from those of his own parishioners who were able to contribute their mite. He himself kept the books and made the decisions on granting or withholding loans, according to general rules set down and interpreted by him according to his own best judgment. These rules were (1) loans shall be free of interest and shall not be secured "save in the memory of God"; (2) the note of indebtedness shall be signed by the debtor and every payment made shall be recorded on it; (3) the sum shall be repaid, at a rate within the debtor's means, within the space of six years. If at the end of that term there is still an unpaid balance, the debt shall be expunged, for thus God decreed it for His people according to Deut. 15:1.[67]

Contemplating the circumstance that in all the years of the fund's existence very few of its users defaulted in their payments or took unfair advantage of the feature of forgiveness in the "sabbatical year," one wonders, with Leenhardt, who should be honored the more: the people who thus displayed such a high standard of morality, or the man who, by moral suasion, by his own example, and, in some cases, by the skillful application of the powers of his ministerial office, was able to educate them to a mode of moral and social behavior of such a high order.

To be sure, the rules that Oberlin applied in judging the worthiness of applicants to make use of the fund were both numerous and strict.[68] The general requirement was that the borrower had to be a man of honor, of good repute and conduct, gainfully employed, and able to furnish impeccable credentials. Many of the questions that were asked of a prospective debtor would surely seem irrelevant to ordinary bankers, either of Oberlin's time or of ours. They included: Do your children attend school regularly? Do your girls dress modestly, decently, and simply? Do your boys refrain from roaming the streets at night and from playing cards? Are your male and female children separated in your house in a way that creates no scandal? (See Lev. 18:9). Do you maintain a proper privy on your premises? Are your stove and chimney properly maintained? Have you laid out an orchard and planted trees along the wayside and beside brooks? Are you frugal in the use of firewood? Do you keep the roads adjacent to your fields in good order and make no encroachment on the right-of-way? Are your impulses on all occasions patriotic? In summing up the regulations, Oberlin says that those who can truthfully answer acceptably such questions as these will be served;

others will be considered, each in his turn, whenever he has risen to these standards of probity.

This operation was certainly not an exercise in high finance, but still, it solved problems of temporary pecuniary embarrassment for many families, saved them the cost of interest, and for creditors it obviated the embarrassment and expense of calling on the bailiff to collect payments in case of default. In a report that Oberlin made in reply to certain criticisms made by "several persons," he said that in a single year the total amount of debts that had been liquidated was 1,975 livres,[69] a figure that suggests that Oberlin's pride in the rate at which the fund revolved in the community and "worked for the poor" was justified. It seldom happened that the balance sheet showed cash on hand: moneys received in payment of loans were immediately disbursed to applicants whose names were on the waiting list. Sometimes it happened that Oberlin heard reports of distressing need at moments when there were no funds on hand; perhaps a family was in danger of ruin because of its inability to meet an obligation incurred before the creation of the fund, or a householder was threatened with legal action that would only increase the amount he would ultimately have to pay to retire a defaulted note. In such cases Oberlin was known more than once to have mounted his horse for one of those nocturnal rides to Strasbourg to call once more on his generous friends there, and to have returned with the necessary funds in his purse.

On November 27, 1815, Oberlin wrote a letter to one Dr. Reiffeisen, thanking him for the gracious reception accorded to his son on a recent visit, and for a gift of thirty francs for the relief of victims of a fire in Belmont. Leenhardt identifies this Dr. Reiffeisen with Dr. Friedrich Wilhelm Raiffeisen, the celebrated founder of the system of credit cooperatives that bear his name and persist to this day as a ubiquitous and important feature of the rural economic scene in Germany. But here the usually reliable Leenhardt must be mistaken, for Dr. F. W. Raiffeisen was born more than a year after Oberlin's letter was written, and he founded his first credit cooperative in 1846, twenty years after Oberlin's death. The fact is that in founding his own cooperative loan fund, Oberlin had anticipated the Raiffeisen system by several decades.[70]

The great achievement of the revolving loan fund was that it transformed a community in which most of the householders were in debt and many were deeply involved in litigation to one where nearly all were financially solvent. In a place where poverty had previously been universal, and at a time when millions of mendicants swarmed on the streets and highways of Europe, creating one of the continent's most serious social problems, pauperism in the Ban de la Roche became a rare condition, and beggary was totally eradicated. It would be oversimplifying the case to say that this was, or could have been, accomplished simply by opening a bank or a savings and loan fund on the traditional model. The effective ingredient was Oberlin's skillful use of the fund in his campaign for general moral improvement, as an instrument and an incentive to individual integrity, probity, fidelity, self-respect, and good management. It represents yet another triumph of the sagacity in his unique system of sanctions and awards.

But the personal solvency of each of his parishioners was not the only goal that Oberlin envisioned for his program of economic reform. Large sums of money had come into the community in the early years as donations from friends. Now, as money began to be available and to circulate within the community, he undertook to educate the people to their responsibility not only to pay the total costs of their religious and social institutions and projects themselves, but also to "repay" the benevolences received from abroad by sending money and goods out from the community to relieve distress and to promote and support worthy projects for religious, educational, and social improvement elsewhere. "He gave them to understand that God's purpose in giving men greater means is not to satisfy their own egoism but to enable them to serve Him by succoring their brothers. Their learning about the uses of credit and the advantages of cooperation, as well as all their other projects, had to be, if they were to attain their full effects, permeated with the spirit of brotherhood."[71] Sermons on the evils of avarice and stinginess were numerous, discursive, and insistent. Repeatedly he stressed the point that the ultimate purpose of frugality is to expand the individual's capability for benevolence.

A friend once asked Oberlin to explain to him the matter of giving tithes. Oberlin responded with a long letter in which he explicitly described how he managed his own benevolences.[72] Of all his income, whatever its nature or its source may be, he said, he strove to put aside "three tithes (*dîmes*), or more exactly, two tenths plus one thirtieth" of his total income. This odd calculation was based on his interpretation of what he read in the Pentateuch. He considered that the basis, the irreducible minimum, for his annual giving was the fixed amount of two tithes, or a total of 20 percent of his income. In Deuteronomy, chapter fourteen, however, he read: "At the end of every third year you shall bring out all the tithe of your produce for that year and leave it in your settlements so that the Levites, who have no holding or patrimony among you, and the aliens, orphans, and widows in your settlements may come and eat their fill." He took this to mean that in every third year he was required to pay an additional tithe, thus bringing his total obligation in every third year to a staggering 30 percent of his income.

In order to ease that shock, he decided that he could pay the extraordinary obligation on a three-installment plan by adding a third of it to each of his annual payments. Thus his total annual obligation came to two full tithes, plus one-third of another, or 23.33 percent of his income. This figure he rounded out in the formulation "three tithes, or more exactly, two-tenths plus one-thirtieth." He commended his own practice in this as an example to all the householders of his parish. Each of the three "tithes" was to be kept in its separate cash box, each box containing a paper on which were written the purposes for which that particular fund was to be used, each purpose being documented by reference to the appropriate passages from the Scriptures.

Thus the first box was marked "for divine worship," with Bible references to Lev. 27:30; Mal. 3:10; Tob. 1:17; Matt. 33:23. Specific purposes to which Oberlin applied this fund in his own practice included maintenance of "the sacred buildings," which in his usage meant the schoolhouses as well as the churches; payment of the *conductrices* and the *régents d'école;* the purchase of books; in short, "all things having to do with the service of God and the dissemination of His holy word." The second box, with references to Deut. 14:22-27 and 16:16, and to Tob. 1:18, was used for many things, for example: for offerings in church; for work on the roads; for school prizes; for all public works; "the small expenses that one has," for instance, as godfather, or when inviting to meals the poor from other villages who come to church on Sundays; churchwarden's fees, "both the required contribution and that which one gives for the love of God." The third box was marked "for the poor," with references to Deut. 14:28-29 and Tob. 1:19. Oberlin used it "for various charities that seem suitable; for help to the poor and the victims of fires."

Oberlin urged each person, young and old, rich and poor, to give the three tithes: in money if the person's income was in that form, in kind if it was not. He promised them that they would reap a rich reward in the pleasure that they would find in giving, and "in the love that God returns to those who give out of love for Him." He advised them to use the system of the three boxes, warning them that if they were unsystematic or casual in calculating what they should save, they would likely put too little aside and would therefore suffer the vexation of finding insufficient funds on hand when occasions for giving presented themselves.

He granted no exemptions from the moral obligation of charity. In 1817, when funds were needed to help a family in Solbach rebuild their burnt-out house, he said, "Let no man excuse himself with the plea that he is too poor to give, for that would be a lie and black ingratitude toward God. Why, the poorest of persons could not live if he did not have *some* income. And remember: the three tithes of all that you have do not belong to you at all. But let us speak now only of one tithe. If every person in our parish would give only one tenth, or even an equitable portion thereof, for this cause, the thing could be done, with God's blessing."[73]

In order to obviate fakery and parasitism, Oberlin set forth very specific declarations on what he meant when he spoke of the worthy poor. A poor man (as distinguished from an idler or a faker), he says, is one whom adverse circumstances have placed momentarily in a state of inability to earn his living. In judging his worthiness to receive aid the following criteria should be applied: he has a family; he takes care of his money; he is content with the simplest clothing; his family has no bonnets, no handkerchiefs, no silk collars; he shuns the tavern; he is content with the simplest and most necessary food; his whole family works to help earn the daily bread; he works even into the evening; he cooperates, if possible, with other families to save oil for lamps, and to share the warmth from the hearth; he rises early in the morning; he seeks honorable and profitable employment not only in the summer, but in all seasons; he is always ready to help a neighbor who needs extra hands to finish his work; he commends himself by his noble and patriotic sentiments and by contributing, wherever possible, to good order and the public good; he does not excuse himself from labors performed for the community, for example, building and maintaining roads, on the pretext that he has no cart of his own; he does not withhold evidence of his gratitude to those who labor for his children and therefore pays, to the extent that he is able, the *régents d'école* and the elders.

One particular impulsion to charity resulted from an unusual incident that is known to us through Jean-Luc Legrand's report of it. The dead body of an itinerant Jew was found on the Champ du Feu, a short distance from Belmont; the man had been robbed and murdered by persons unknown. Oberlin, guided as so often by the Old Testament, believed that the individual citizens should expiate the curse that was visited upon a place where a crime had been committed. He therefore sent a substantial gift to the widow of the deceased, and thereafter for several years made additional annual payments of fifty francs each.

Another incident which, in Oberlin's conception, imposed a moral obligation on the community occurred in 1791 or 1792.[74] A company of volunteers from the Ban de la Roche was commanded to report for duty in Strasbourg with the stipulation that the men would be allowed to return home soon and that they would receive a per diem of three sous en route. On the march to Strasbourg the men stopped for the night in the town of Dorlisheim. For supper, lodging, and breakfast they requisitioned all the inns of the town. When they departed in the morning, one group of about thirty men did not pay their bills, but promised to pay on their return journey, when they would have their expense money in their pockets. But instead of being sent home again, they were reassigned to the garrison at Strasbourg and eventually sent from there to the field.

Some six or seven years later, Oberlin learned from the aggrieved innkeeper that he had not been paid. Oberlin made an investigation and satisfied himself that the claim was true and just. Thereupon he circulated a broadside in which he committed the matter to the conscience of the community. He pledged that every Sunday he would give for this cause all funds from his tithes not previously committed, and he urged all others to join him in this as an act of corporate atonement.

Documentation of the final issue of this affair is missing, but we can safely assume that here, too, Oberlin attained the purpose that he often stated in his sermons, namely, fulfillment of "the wish and the will of Jesus Christ that His church should stand pure and without blemish before the world."

Another incident of a similar kind again involved an itinerant Jewish merchant. This man was well known in the Ban de la Roche, for he came often, offering his goods for sale in all the houses. Sometimes, when a customer was in need of necessities, such as clothing and shoes, but had no money, he accommodated him by selling on credit. Thus it happened that many householders were in debt to him. Now there came a time when the peddler did not appear in his customary season, and inquiry revealed that he had been taken ill and died. Many of his debtors felt relieved, for they considered that therewith their obligation had been extinguished. Not so, said Oberlin. He found out the name and address of the peddler's widow, inspected the account books of her deceased husband, and thereafter called upon each of the debtors, advising them to pay all that they owed. In cases where families were so destitute that they could not possibly pay, he assumed the debt himself and paid it out of his "third tithe."

In his unremitting effort to inculcate the habit of charity in his people, Oberlin often, and particularly at communion services, took his text from the fifty-eighth chapter of Isaiah: "Is not this what I require of you as a fast: to loose the fetters of injustice, to untie the knots of the yoke, to snap every yoke and set free those who have been crushed? Is it not sharing your food with the hungry, taking the homeless into your house, clothing the naked when you meet them and never evading a duty to your kinfolk? Then shall your light break forth like the dawn and soon you will grow healthy like a wound newly healed; your own righteousness shall be your vanguard and the glory of the Lord your rearguard. Then, if you call, the Lord will say, 'Here I am.' "[75]

Oberlin's teaching and example inspired a layman of his congregation to make restitution through an act of charity for a long-standing family debt of honor.[76] On May 15, 1814, Jean-Jacques Neuvillers, a bachelor of Bellefosse, handed Oberlin three hundred francs to be spent for charitable purposes in the name of the late Jean-Philippe Reinhold, who had been the pastor at Waldersbach for five years. When

Reinhold had moved away in 1742, he had left behind an uncollected debt of five louis d'or owed to him by the grandfather of Jean-Jacques. Now, seventy-two years later, the pious grandson had come to pay the debt of honor in behalf of the delinquent deceased grandfather. Oberlin's journal records that Neuvillers ultimately paid a total of 558 francs; 120 francs to cover the capital sum of five louis d'or, and 438 francs for interest. In closing his account of this incident, Stoeber remarks: "Honor to the memory of Jean-Jacques Neuvillers; honor and glory to the man of God who imbued his parishioners with such ways of thinking!"

Oberlin applied the principle of cooperative societies, on which his credit association was based, to other community enterprises also.[77] A frequent occurrence in any agricultural community is the breakage of the simple, primitive implements that are essential to the farmer's trade, such as spades, hoes, picks, rakes, forks, axes, plows and harrows. Oberlin was most distressed whenever such an accident happened to one of the poorer families, for their crops might then suffer from neglect because there was no cash in hand to purchase a new tool; and even a man who had money might lose as much as a day's work because he had to make the journey to the market town to fetch a new implement. Oberlin therefore kept a stock of implements which he sold at cost, allowing the buyer, when necessary, to postpone payment for it. He later extended the credit trade in implements to include seeds and plants, and other items indispensable to farmers and householders. Thus he created a model organization for the distribution of consumer goods, with a social motive of mutual helpfulness replacing the conventional motive of financial profit.

Once each week on Saturday, which was by ancient tradition baking day in peasant households, each housewife was accustomed to fire up her outdoor oven. Oberlin considered this as egregious wastefulness. He therefore circulated a notice in the parish in which he proposed a new system in the interests of good management and of Christian virtue. Thrift in the use of ovens, he said, was mandatory, for firewood was becoming harder to get all the time, and besides, every Christian ought to use it sparingly, even if he had plenty of it. The customary way of baking was the chief cause of waste, because everyone heated up his own oven, while "in places where such things are managed better," one oven served many families: once an oven was heated it could be kept hot with but little wood. "Try to introduce this good custom among yourselves. At first you will find difficulties, but little by little, with persistence, you will succeed. Let six or eight families combine to work together. Arrange it in such a way that all may bake their bread in turn, using one single oven. Each family shall use its own wood to heat the oven for its own bread, but since the one that heats the oven first will use more wood than the rest, you must take turns in being the first."

To encourage such cooperative action, he offered a pound of wool for each family that would join in a society of four sharers, and a pound and a half each for a society of six. Another cause of waste was the fact that the ovens were much larger than they needed to be for baking, because they were also used for drying hemp. If one of the societies would decide to build a smaller oven for baking only, he offered a certain sum of money to help pay for it.[78] At the end of the document he delivered the usual exhortation. "My dear parishioners! If you approve this plan, let not those hard feelings and jealousies which divide so many households, so many families, keep you from this undertaking. Sacrifice your jealousies. Be Christians. When you have formed your societies, be persevering, gentle, ready to yield. Overcome roughness, insolence, and ill temper by patience, gentleness and kindliness." Soon all families were peacefully joined in *sociétés des fours* and enjoying the fruits of Christian cooperation.

Other contributions made by Oberlin to the common good not mentioned elsewhere included the purchase of a pumping machine and organization of a volunteer fire-fighting organization; the making and setting up of sundials throughout the community; introduction of the metric system of weights and measures; the preparation, publication, and free distribution to all parishioners of an annual almanac containing useful information and practical hints for farmers and husbandmen, as well as good and edifying reading material for families.[79]

The best measure of the success of his religious and social ministry is that he transformed a settlement in which most families had been living in degrading and hopeless poverty, and many in discord and ruinous litigation with their neighbors, into a harmonious community, where none lived in luxury, but all in modest sufficiency; where even those who, because of some special disability, could not attain competence were at least spared the degradation of beggary by the charity and the spirit of mutual helpfulness that pervaded the congregation. Before Oberlin's arrival, the Ban de la Roche had aroused either pity or contempt among its Alsatian neighbors, if, indeed, it was known to them at all. By the time of Oberlin's death, his work there was renowned, not only in France and in Germany, but in all of Europe and England and America as well. During his last years many visitors came from afar to observe the life of that simple folk and returned home to write reports and essays in praise of the vision of a new social order that they had seen.

In July 1771 there occurred an event that constitutes an important milestone in the history of the Ban de la Roche, for it created a new political situation that greatly increased the effectiveness of Oberlin's exertions for economic and social improvement. Count d'Argenson, finding himself in need of cash, had persuaded Louis XV to allow him to sell the Ban de la Roche to anyone who was eligible for feudal tenure. D'Argenson soon found a buyer in the person of Baron Jean de Dietrich, who purchased it for 330,000 francs. Dietrich was the scion of a rich and distinguished Strasbourg family, one of the four *Stettmeisters,* the elected officials who presided over the government of the city, and one of the largest landowners in Alsace.[80] When the news of his accession came to the Steintal, there was great rejoicing among the people, who felt that he would do better by them than the rapacious d'Argenson, who lived in Paris, rarely visited his distant fief in the Vosges, and was interested in it only for the profits that he could extract from it. Among the reasons for the people's optimism about Baron de Dietrich were these: as an Alsatian, he shared their provincial patriotism; as a Lutheran, he confessed the same faith; as a leader of men, he was generally known and respected for his warm, though dignified, bonhomie and his natural, instinctive kindness, generosity, and democracy.

The six-day festival celebrating the new overlord's first visit, when he came to receive the usual oaths of fealty of his new subjects, was described by Oberlin in a four-thousand-word German manuscript that was first published soon after its discovery in 1933, and reprinted by Heinsius.[81] It shows the Ban de la Roche, as Heinsius says, in a different light from that in which we usually see it; it shows, for a change, "not just poverty and the cares of the long, dreary winter months, but the festive mood of a high summer's day, with men on horseback, the soldierly order in which the tenants of the several villages draw near to pay their homage to their new lord." It is a primitive genre piece depicting a rustic idyll of the age of sentiment, "a last luminous image of the old feudal sovereign power, shining once more in its most favorable light, shortly before the storm of the great Revolution was to sweep away, in the Steintal as elsewhere, the last privileges of the nobility."

During the six-day festival, lasting from Sunday, June 14, 1771, to the following Friday, there was a gala reception of the *Stettmeister* and his numerous party, with cries of *"Vive le roi!"* and *"Vive notre seigneur!"* by the entire populace; with swearings of fealty by the elders of each village; with homages paid by maidens in traditional folk dress, bearing flowers; with triumphal processions from village to village, in which the seigneur was escorted by sword-bearing youths, with musical accompaniment by marching bands and by choirs of school-children hidden in wayside hedges; with feastings and speech-makings and the distribution of largesse by the seigneur, who was many times moved to tears by expressions of respect and affection from that simple but warmhearted folk. Oberlin, who had planned and managed every detail of the celebration, was gratified to learn, after the *Herr Stettmeister* had returned to Strasbourg, that all expenses incurred on this occasion would be paid by the seigneur, and that he had also left behind "a considerable fund as a gift from which each family . . . was to receive its portion, . . . and all this without counting the money that had been . . . distributed in other ways."

Thus, under the most favorable aspect imaginable, began the tenure of the last feudal lord of the Ban de la Roche. The optimistic hopes of the people were fulfilled, at least in part, during the eighteen years of his tenure: tributes were substantially reduced; the iron works at Rothau were reopened and afforded new possibilities of employment; the church at Fouday was enlarged; the salaries of the ministers of both parishes were increased. The baron also announced his readiness to build a new parsonage at Waldersbach, but Oberlin declared that until each of the five villages had a new schoolhouse, he would prefer to put up with the dilapidated old thatchroofed "rat's nest," and thus the building of the new manse was postponed for fifteen years.

The exalted level of magniloquent communication that marked the early letters that passed between the seigneur and his minister, however, could not always be maintained without occasional lapses. Thus we find the seigneur, in a letter of October 5, 1772, reassuring the pastor of his continuing regard and affection, but expressing his disapproval of the "airs of superiority that you have assumed" and the "passionate zeal" that has caused him to "commit three acts of indiscretion."[82] The basic cause of the contretemps, as of many of the hostilities that developed against Oberlin through the years, lay in his unbending opposition to the tavernkeepers, both those within his parish and those in nearby villages, who in his opinion corrupted the morals of the young by promoting Saturday night dances in their taverns. The immediate occasion for the letter alluded to here was a particularly vigorous campaign that Oberlin had mounted against the innkeepers, who had taken their complaints against the crusading reformer of their morals directly to the grand seigneur. Farther on in his letter Dietrich regrets that his remarks will distress Oberlin, but finds it necessary to demand that the pastor reflect more earnestly before flying into action. In closing, he begs to remind his minister that he, after all, is himself "a man of religion, of good morals, and of experience." To this letter Oberlin responded, politely and respectfully, that the distress that he had felt while reading it was "principally for the pain and embarrassment that I have caused you by my imprudence."

Sixteen years later, when, under the influence of Rousseau's *Social Contract* and other writings of the *philosophes,* the position of the aristocrats in France was being subjected to new questioning, and the great transformations of 1789 were approaching, there was another, more acrimonious exchange between the grand seigneur and his dissident pastor. Even aside from any immediate provocations, such disputes were probably inevitable between two men who were more accustomed to ordain, each in his own way and in his own sphere, than to submit. And yet, the orotund assurances of mutual amity, respect, and esteem were somewhat more than the empty bombast dictated by the epistolary fashion of the time. That became clear a few years later, when Dietrich came for the last time to the Ban de la Roche, not as a grand seigneur, but as a deeply humbled man, a victim of the Reign of Terror.

14

15 Flora of the Ban de la Roche; Oberlin's Mark-ings

16   Oberlin's Homemade Printing Press

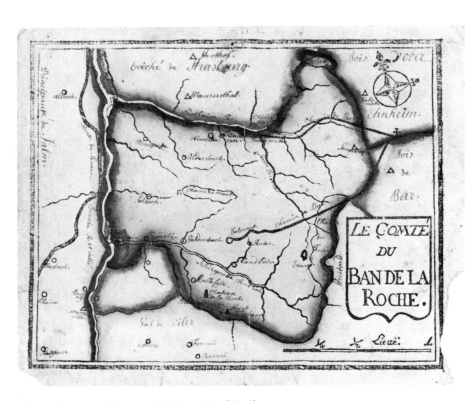

17   A Woodcut Made and Printed by Oberlin

6

The Preacher and Pastor

"If we do well here, we shall do well there:
I can tell you no more, though I preach a whole year."
—*John Edwin Smith (1749-1823)*

In his religious views Oberlin was liberal in the sense that he always maintained his independence of any commitment to the dogma of a particular sect. It was that liberalism that made it possible for him to deviate from the behavior patterns of his Lutheran brethren in his friendliness toward other sects. His ecumenism is evidenced, for instance, by his close connections with the Moravian Brethren and his adherence to many of their tenets and precepts, and by his tolerance toward, and friendly relations with, his Roman Catholic neighbors: at his altar both Protestants and Catholics were invited to take communion, and among his closest friends he counted many Catholic clergymen, from the village priest in Rothau to the Abbé Grégoire in Paris.

The ability to maintain his stance of liberalism and independence he owed in considerable measure to the remoteness and isolation of his parish. Elsewhere in Alsace the ecclesiastical hierarchy of Protestantism would not have countenanced such apostasy as offering Holy Communion to Protestants and Catholics alike; it would not have allowed such deviations from canonical practice as withholding the sacraments from parishioners who neglected the education of their children; it would not have approved of many heterodox ideas that were preached from the pulpits of the Waldersbach parish. But the lords spiritual of Alsace had more important fiefdoms to govern and therefore had but little time to expend on censuring the obscure minister of the Steintal for leading his starveling backwoodsmen down the paths of heterodoxy. Later, to be sure, when Oberlin's fame had begun to spread abroad, the Strasbourg consistory—influenced, perhaps, by the testy complaints of Baron de Dietrich—did call Oberlin to account for his deviations from acceptable dogma, but chose, in the end, not to prosecute him for them.

It is not my intention to imply that Oberlin was an active rebel, or even a militant, against ecclesiastical authority. His heterodoxy, if it may be called that, did not stem from any desire to reform the church or to stir up theological disputes. He was no more a systematic theoretician in theology than he was in education or in economics. He simply was not interested in theological systems, in disputes about dogma, or in the clash of creeds. His Christian faith was based on the Apostles' Creed, quite literally interpreted; to that extent he was conservative and orthodox.[83] He deviated from the strict Lutheran doctrine of the Strasbourg consistory not in his views about the relations between God and men, but in his beliefs about the relations of man with his fellow men and with the world.

He deviated from Pietistic doctrine, with which he was generally sympathetic, in that he did not see life as a passage through a vale of tears, but as a journey through a landscape made beautiful by the gifts of divine grace. He believed that it was man's duty, in the course of his striving toward eschatological fulfillment in the new estate that awaited the redeemed after death, to exploit in a life of mundane labor all his creative capabilities. Man's earthly life seemed to him a precious opportunity to approach, through the practice of virtue, the ideal of God-likeness.[84] He saw the attainment of such perfection through devoted labor in the love of God and of his neighbor as God's imperative to man. This becomes clear from the reading of a variety of communications from the minister to his people. The remarks on the spiritualization of labor referred to near the beginning of chapter five are one example of this. As another I cite the preamble to a proclamation concerning soil improvement by flood control and drainage. Though it is a call to an action of a literally earthy kind, it is couched in exalted theological rhetoric: the digging of a ditch becomes a part of God's design. "The love of

God and of one's neighbor is the first and principal one of God's commandments. . . . It is to establish the reign of His virtues on earth . . . that we should with all our powers aid Him in His designs."[85] Martha Buch sums up the significance of Oberlin's religious beliefs in shaping his way of life thus: "His religion, the Christianity that he preached, was not just a Sunday and holiday affair, not just an ornament of life, a shield and defense against its hostilities and threats, . . . nor was it something that one remembers only in the best moments of life with a comforting feeling that one is more than mere matter. For him religion and life were identical. . . . It is impossible to distinguish where his religion ends and his life (meaning his vocational activity in the schools, the homes, the fields, his involvement in the social order and his obligations as a citizen of the state) begins."

This identification of religion with the everyday activities and concerns of life caused Oberlin to consider any subject, no matter how mundane, suitable for the religious discourses that he delivered from the pulpit on Sundays and also in the schools and at the weekday prayer and Bible study meetings for adults. It also separated him from those fanatically pietistic pharisees who turned away from the world, thanking God that they were not like other men. Far from rejecting the world as an unredeemable place of evil, he accepted it as a product of God's creative will, and as a place where man could attain both happiness and holiness by subjecting his own will to God's, thus becoming God's collaborator in working out His plan of salvation, both for individual men and for mankind. This synergistic situation demands of man not only that he accept the world, but also that he utilize whatever gifts of mind and spirit God has given him to acquaint himself with it in all its manifold complexity.

The first thing Oberlin wanted his people to see and acknowledge about the earth, and specifically about their own little part of it, was that it is beautiful. This was a frequently recurring theme in his preaching. As an example, consider the following panegyric of 1791, couched in the rhetoric of the romantic poets of his time.[86]

God speaks to us in nature. . . . Behold the delights of this earthly paradise, the rapturous beauty of a mountain land-scape, gleaming under the sun . . . the fields covered with grain and other lovely and useful crops; the meadows adorned with flowers and verdure; trees, endlessly varied in color, height, growth. . . . Feel the beneficent breezes that play about us. Hear the murmuring and babbling of the lovely brooks that wind through our meadows, making them fruitful. . . . Consider the insects . . . the birds . . . and countless thousands, even millions of other things that are lovely to see, to taste, and to smell—all these the Creator has spread from the fullness of His hands over the earth, the dwelling place of men . . . to invite them to make themselves worthy of the heavenly paradise.

Yet such anthropocentric reveries on the beauty of the world, useful as they may have been in making the people conscious of God's favors to man, were not enough. A sufficient appreciation of God the Creator required not only an emotional response to the beauty of the world, but technical knowledge of the nature and structure of the earth and the solar system as well. The teaching of geography and geology, of plant and animal ecology, of physics and astronomy, to people of all ages, from children of three to adults at the outer limits of old age, was in Oberlin's view as much an act of religious ministry as preaching, praying, and administering the sacraments.

Collaboration with God in working out the salvation and sanctification of the world also makes it necessary for each person to be informed about the affairs of men in the world. History, politics, and economics were therefore joined with the sciences as subjects of frequent allusion and explication. In Oberlin's system of values, to lose the desire to learn was to lose one's right to participate in God's plan of salvation. But learning to know the world was not in itself enough. Man's collaborative situation demands, above all else, action, engagement, participation.

The predisposition of the people to idleness was the trait that disturbed him most during his first weeks at Waldersbach. He abominated the habit of indolent loafing around the house by day and in the taverns by night. Every moment that a man or woman spent in idleness meant, in his view, the loss of an opportunity to do something for the improvement of the idler's own situation or that of other persons. He saw the habit of slothful inactivity as causing not only individuals, but whole families to pass their days in a state of stupor, and the society to sink into a disastrous anomie.

Against these dangers Oberlin fought with every resource, including his preaching and his own tireless activity, which he hoped would stir the people to creative emulation. In many a sermon he inveighed against idleness of body and mind as an invitation to Satan to occupy and possess the souls that rightfully belonged to God. He did not even concede the propriety of inactivity on the Sabbath. "Go now after the service to your homes," he preached in September 1767,

> review in your soul what you have heard here; pray to God to help you translate it into action; write down in a notebook whatever seems most important of what you have heard. Continue to use the sabbath for spiritual labor. Read the Scriptures and other good books that are kept here for your use. Sing a hymn with other children of God. But whatever you do, flee, flee as from the plague from that miserable indolence, that criminal sloth that reigns in all your houses on Sundays. If it is a sin to neglect your daily worldly tasks out of laziness, it is a doubly greater sin to neglect your spiritual labors. Why? Because your concern for your souls must be infinitely more important than your concern for your bodies.

In another sermon he warns that God will not fail to punish those who pass the Sabbath "in idle conversation or other foolishness," in drinking, dancing, playing cards, quarreling or fighting or other such "indecent activities." And at another time he questions whether one can truly honor the Sabbath without performing some labor for one's fellow men. Preaching on the text, "For I tell you this: anything you did for one of my brothers here, however humble, you did for me," he urged the people to employ the Sabbath to knit garments for the poor, to assist a helpless neighbor in gathering wood and stones to repair his dilapidated house, to work the field of one who is sick, or to collect food and clothing for poor widows and orphans, and similar charitable labors.

In one of his diatribes against sloth we find him resorting to a sarcastic wit that is not often found in his preaching. "Do you tell me," he asks, "that you were never trained to work? Poor man, poor woman, how sensible I am of your unhappy state! What good fortune that you were trained to put yourself to bed, for otherwise you wouldn't ever stand up and go there. What luck that you were taught to eat, for else you, such a useful member of the human race, would long ago have died of starvation, to the deep chagrin of all good people. And how glad I am that you were taught to peel potatoes, for lacking that, you would eat the potato, the peel, the dirt and all."

Oberlin's synergistic theology was relatively simplistic. This can be documented by references to many sermons. As good an example as any is the following: "It is the duty of man to make use of everything that God has given him, lest he become guilty of the sin of sloth; or more explicitly: a Christian must let himself be guided by Christ's spirit of love. Sanctification consists in an unceasing battle against one's selfishness, in indefatigable exertion for the common good. It is the duty of all Christians, working together, to build the city of God. Their lives must be completely permeated by the spirit of Christ; service to one's neighbor must be exalted to a veritable cult."[87]

Among the young people, idleness led not only to tedium and slothful stupidity, but also to a kind of antisocial behavior that was peculiar to the Ban de la Roche. Stoeber gives an account of an incident of this kind. The report also affords a unique insight into the way that Oberlin's religious views could be altered, at least on one occasion, by the influence of another person. One of the Waldersbach elders, Jean-Georges Claude, was disturbed that some of the annual festivals seemed to offer occasion for disorder because the young people believed that they could then take unlimited liberties. As one of these festivals was approaching, M. Claude came to Oberlin and suggested that he preach once more about divine punishment. He used the colloquial German phrase "make hell right hot for them." Oberlin gladly accepted the challenge. In his sermon he described all the frightening and horrible torments of that abode of the damned, and stressed the point that the tortures would never end. In the evening following the sermon, he was surprised and also pleased that all seemed to be quiet, for it was well known that the young people, according to an old custom, spent their Saturday and Sunday nights wandering from hilltop to hilltop, shouting and bellowing like wild savages. He rode to where they were gathered, for he wanted to be quite sure that they would indeed be deflected from such customary behavior. He spoke to them in a friendly way, without making a long speech: "My friends," he said, "it is late and time to go to bed."

But that night, which he had thought would be so quiet, turned out later to be one of the most horrible of all; in the end there was at least twice the usual racket. On Monday the good elder came to see him again. "Ah, my dear sir," he said, "did you hear the great noise last night?"

"Yes," Oberlin replied, "but from what you heard in church yesterday, you know that I did my best to prevent it."

"It is not your fault," he said, "there is a new preacher who is the cause of it all."

"A new preacher? Tell me more."

Thereupon M. Claude gave Oberlin the following account:

Instead of going home after you had left them, the young people went to the tavern and there met Niclas, whom you probably know; Niclas who never goes to church and is nearly always drunk. "Hello, Niclas," they said, "for heaven's sake, are you forever in the tavern? Won't you ever repent? Didn't you hear this morning what our minister said about hell? Some day, you'll be burning down there too."

"Me listen to the preacher? Me go to church?" said Niclas. "My church is the tavern. That's the only church I go to."

So they told him about the torments of hell as you described them and warned him that they would go on forever. Thereupon Niclas gave them a long, scornful look, and then said: "And you believe that nonsense, you fools? Listen to me! You know that I'm a no-good fellow. I never go to church. I never try to do good for anybody. I've spent all my money, poured it down my gullet. . . . But you also know, I've got a son. He's a good boy. He does what I say and I love him. . . . But maybe someday he won't do what I say. Maybe he'll promise to be good but will break all his promises and make me turn him out of the house, make me say I'll never think of him as my son again. And then maybe, a long time later, I hear that he feels sorry. He cries and wants me to forgive him. And then maybe he comes to me himself and says, 'Father, I have sinned against you. Forgive me.' Now, do you think I would not forgive him? Ah, I would say, come to me my son, I forgive you. . . . Now, if I, old Niclas, the village bum as everybody knows, could forgive him, do you think God couldn't do it? What did preacher Oberlin say? God will keep us sinners forever in hell? Why you know He couldn't do that. He couldn't even think of doing it!"

"You're right, Niclas!" said the young men, "of course you're right. Hey *garçon!* Bring wine! We'll drink to Niclas . . . to preacher Niclas!"

And so, they went on drinking, and when all of them were drunk they left the tavern at last and went out and from then until dawn made the infernal racket that you heard.

Reflecting on this incident and considering again the sometimes ambiguous evidence of the Scriptures on the infinite duration of God's wrath, he resolved, in the end, never again to preach of the torments of hell as lasting eternally.[88]

All too often as one reads the documents of Oberlin's day-to-day interactions with his people, one catches the image of a religious zealot, opinionated and obdurate in his conviction of the indefeasibility of his own moral code. Amid that evidence of self-righteous intractability, one hails this story of preacher Niclas with relief and delight. All honor to Oberlin at last: a man capable after all of being influenced by the opinions of others; one who can bear to have his views on eternal damnation as the wages of sin put to rights, even though it be by the casuistry of the village drunk reminding him that the Scriptures do not inevitably and unequivocally support pietistic dogmas of divine inexorability.

But still, he was not ready to believe that the repentant prodigal son would be completely excused from any chastisement, nor even that the discomforts of his remorseful wretchedness would end with his earthly life. No, he continued to preach of hellfire, as before, compromising only on the point of its duration. In his campaign against sin, he was not yet ready to sacrifice completely the deterrent of fear of the wrath to come. He would have agreed with the sentiment that "to appreciate heaven well, 'tis good for a man to have some fifteen minutes in hell." In a discussion with the young folk of the parish that took place soon after the Niclas affair, he said: "I don't want to quarrel with you about matters of taste; but let me tell you this: no matter how short you calculate the time will be that you will have to spend in hell, I for myself would find it much too long. But if hell should be according to your desire, you should begin now to accustom yourself gradually to the bearing of its torments. . . . Start by holding your little finger in a flame. . . . Begin with the first joint, and when that is consumed, proceed with the second. . . ." This homily was well remembered; thereafter, whenever he met one of his young folk drunk at the tavern or in the street, all he needed to do to cause the sinner to cast down his eyes in shame was to hold up to him the first joint of his little finger.

Soon after the Niclas incident, Oberlin was accused of heterodoxy. The particulars of indictment and defense are not known; all we have is Oberlin's brief statement: "I was called before the president of the Strasbourg consistory to answer charges that I had preached against the doctrine of eternal punishment in hell; but when I had finished telling him the true facts about the Niclas affair as I have related them here, he remarked, 'Indeed, you could not have done otherwise. *Mein Gott,* do you have such people in your parish? Sir, you have acted wisely.' " Here again is evidence that Oberlin could take liberties in his "Alsatian Siberia" that might not have been allowed elsewhere: the churchman had inverted the sense of the old adage "Quod licet Jovi non licet bovi," and was allowing to the ox that which was denied to Jupiter.

The service of worship was held each week in a different church in the sequence Waldersbach-Belmont-Waldersbach-Fouday-Waldersbach. Thus Waldersbach had a service every two weeks, Belmont and Fouday every four. In Belmont some of the services were in German; in the other churches all were in French. In the later years, when old age made walking difficult for the pastor, families of the outlying congregations enjoyed in turn the honor of lending a horse for the journey from the parsonage and back and of having the minister as a guest at table. The master of the host family would bring the horse to the manse and a spontaneous procession would form with the minister riding at its head, the owner of the horse walking alongside carrying a satchel containing the pastor's cope and his Bible and prayer books, and worshippers from Waldersbach following after. Before the return trip Oberlin would dine with the chosen family, which basked in the honor of his presence. He always insisted, however, on paying for his meal.[89]

In Waldersbach the order of worship went as follows: Early in the morning the church bell sounded the angelus to call the villagers to prayer in their homes, as it called them to vespers in the fields on weekdays. As church time approached, it began to ring again and there was traffic on the footpaths all through the valley, with worshippers coming down the slopes from lofty Belmont and la Hutte and Pendbois, from Bellefosse and from the isolated farmsteads of the Champ du Feu, upward along the Chirgoutte from Fouday and Trouchy, and across the Perheu from the forests of Solbach. In fine weather these last were often joined by outside visitors (including both Protestants and Catholics) coming across the Perheu from distant Rothau and Wildersbach. All the people were arrayed in their Sunday best, the women and girls in the folk costumes of the region, with small black bonnets trailing ribbons down their backs and the somber black of their dresses relieved by white pinafores. "Inwardly," Leenhardt says, "they were prepared and disposed to take part in the service and to attend to the counsels of their pastor," for Oberlin insistently urged his parishioners to spend early Sunday hours in meditation and prayer and in memorizing Bible verses and hymns, which, he admonished them, "will serve you also in other situations of life."[90]

After the people had entered the church, the bell fell silent; Oberlin entered; the congregation rose. The service then followed the order initiated by Stuber, with few changes. One of the schoolmasters in a loud voice read the first stanza of the opening hymn; the best female voices struck up the air, the schoolmasters fell in with the bass, and "soon the whole congregation is singing as a melodious choir." The hymns were always sung in parts, though without instrumental accompaniment in the early years. The hymnal edited by Stuber was used.[91]

The care that Oberlin took in planning the musical portion of festival occasions is suggested by notations made by him in connection with a special service of unknown date.

It is a great festival day; distinguished guests are expected from far and near. A choir has rehearsed the music for a special order of service. A favorite hymn of the congregation, "Non, non, non, nul ne vaincra Gédéon" is to open the service. Three girls, singing in unison and called *soli* intone the first line; the choir responds from the other side with the second; the *soli* sing the third and fourth lines. They are accompanied by a single tambourine, the choir by several. Thereafter each stanza, intoned by the *soli*, is sung not only by the choir, but by the whole congregation. Thus the hymn is sung as by a great choir through all its stanzas with the tambourines marking the rhythm to the last line of the final couplet: "C'est sans savoir périr."

One can imagine that the worshippers were sometimes overexuberant in their rendition of this rousing hymn, a kind of eighteenth-century "We shall overcome," for Oberlin at some time added to his program notes a parenthetical caution: *"Mais N.B.:* some of the tambourines should be more muted, more subdued." In later years, the tambourines were joined by other accompanying instruments, including lutes, recorders, and clarinets.

The opening hymn was followed by a pastoral prayer. Oberlin's prayers were generally freely composed, rather than read from the officially approved rubrics. In later years he collected in a book his prayers for special occasions, ceremonies, and festivals of the church year. After the prayer came the Scripture readings from both the Old and the New Testament. This part of the service Oberlin also prepared and executed with great care, for he considered the Bible not only as the basis for all worship, but also as the sole and inerrant guide to religious faith and practice. In order to be sure that the congregation understood what it heard, he often interrupted the reading to paraphrase difficult passages or to interpolate words of explanation. Often such commentaries constituted an introduction to the sermon.

After the sermon, announcements and public notices were read from the pulpit. These were sometimes numerous and long, for they purveyed the news of the week, including happenings within the parish and those of the great world outside, often with a pastoral commentary. After that there was again a general prayer which usually included special intercessions for particular persons who were in anguish or distress, as well as prayers for the nation and its rulers, and for the seigneur and the community, especially when these were confronted with unusual problems, as in times of war and revolution, or of extraordinary local happenings. Thus, for instance, when new deputies to the National Convention had been elected, Oberlin commended them to God's grace and mercy; or in a time of drought he offered special prayers, pleading not only for rain, but also for the enlightenment of the people so that they would "recognize the withering of their crops as a chastisement ordained by the God of retribution for the dessication and sterility of our own fruits of justice and charity." At another time he spoke of unseasonable frost as retribution for coldness of heart and of spirit.[92]

Contrary to the Lutheran tradition of standing during prayer, Oberlin's congregations prayed on their knees. At the end of the pastoral prayer the congregation joined in the Lord's Prayer, accompanied by the ringing of the church bell as an invitation to the sick and the infirm in their homes to join in their devotions with the praying congregation. As the people filed out of the church they performed their worship of sacrifice, leaving their offering in the collection box at the door. Stoeber testifies that, though this was only part of their tithe, the collections were astonishingly large.

Oberlin, who loved festivals, often held services outdoors. He was particularly fond of the meadow on the plateau of the Perheu as the site for the great summer *fête champêtre* dedicated to the youth of the parish, at which school promotions were celebrated and prizes were awarded. On such occasions the villagers of Waldersbach, Fouday, and Bellefosse would march up the long tree-lined walk to that temple under the open sky, where they were joined by the worshippers from Solbach and Belmont.

Though Oberlin considered preaching the very heart and soul of his pastoral calling, he never did it easily. During the preparation of a sermon he spent much time in anguish on his knees, and as he mounted the pulpit he was generally full of tension and apprehension. In the early years he sometimes poured out his heart on this subject to Stuber, and there are also evidences of his anxieties at other times during his ministry. Thus, on a Sunday evening in the second year he wrote in his journal:

> Oh my God, what a fearful day was yesterday! Despite all my efforts, studies, and meditations, I was not capable of preparing my sermon for today. My heart was torn and over-whelmed with chagrin. From all sides vexations pressed in upon me: great debts . . . the loss of various things that sustain the economy; the ingratitude of a goodly number of parishioners; abandonment of the building of the schoolhouse for a whole week by the workers; a host of distressing occupations

and affairs. . . . All these afflicted and enraged my heart. Oh God, forgive me for the despair and anger that I displayed yesterday evening. Your intention was good; my arrogance was in need of a remedy; You have given it a bitter medicine indeed; but its effect has been good. This morning, as I went up to preach, I was deeply distressed, but soon I was conscious of a newly contented soul, humbled and filled with a sweet and agreeable tranquility, for I had the experience that God himself opened my lips. . . . Oh, how miserable I am that my too vivacious, too impetuous temperament again and again impels me to act rashly. Oh God, moderate my excessive vivacity; give me at last a calm spirit and an even temper.

Nine years later, in commenting on the fact that a visiting theological student had offered to occupy his pulpit one Sunday, Oberlin wrote the following somewhat petulant parenthetical remarks about his failure to establish rapport in his preaching between himself and the people whose hearts he is trying to reach.[93]

I have come to know the limitations of these good people and their extreme ignorance in all things, and especially in the very language in which one preaches to them and I have therefore descended as much as possible to their level and have taken pains to preach in a style that is in accord with the needs of my auditors. The only result of this has been that my preaching is incessantly criticized. Some people say that I am too acerbic, some that "anybody can preach that well," and some intimate that my sermons are written by my housemaids. Thus preaching has given me more vexation than all the rest of my official duties taken together, and I am therefore glad when occasionally someone is willing to preach for me.

And again eleven years later, he wrote in his journal: "Today, after table, I had a talk in Waldersbach with Pastor Stuber about the evangelical gentleness that he has not always found in my preaching. . . . May God bless this conversation to all eternity for me and for my congregation. God bless Pastor Stuber, now and forever, for reproving me on this point with such inexpressible patience."

Three or four months later he again searched his heart, asked himself if the unctions of the Holy Spirit were observable, not only in his preaching, but in his whole life, and thereupon wrote: "Yesterday and today I have become aware that the spirit that inspires my life, my actions, and my words, especially in society, is still not the same that speaks in my preaching." He names three parishioners, Catherine Gagnière, Madeleine Banzét, and Sophie Bernard, as persons who do live and act in the spirit of his sermons, and concludes, with remorse, that his sanctification is inferior to theirs.

That Oberlin expended much time and labor in the preparation of his weekly discourses, despite the multifarious concerns and activities that filled his days, there can be no doubt.[94] That he was concerned about his pulpit style is indicated by the fact that his papers contain notes on a book called *Eloquence in the Pulpit,* and excerpts from one entitled *Theodor, or the Art of Preaching* (1765). Also, a glance at the manuscript of any one of the many outlines of sermons that are still to be seen in the archives at Strasbourg and Waldersbach shows what pains Oberlin took in preparing them: most of them are written on four sheets of twenty to twenty-six lines each; the main divisions and subdivisions are clearly marked and usually numbered; important passages are underlined, sometimes in varying colors. Once in the pulpit he filled in these outlines in free, spontaneous discourse. As he spoke he was always more intent on the clarity of his utterance than on brilliance and profundity. In order to render the abstract concrete, the mysterious palpable, the inconceivable comprehensible, he made use of various rhetorical devices. Several examples are given here.[95]

To inspire the people to charity he says, "The cheerful giver gleams and sparkles like the newly fallen snow, while the stingy egotist is as black as the soot in your chimney; the one is as bright as the sun itself, the other is but a stinking wick." He is particularly eloquent in expressing the enormity of the wages of sin and the amplitude of the rewards of righteousness. "The leaves of the quaking aspen hang still and immovable by comparison with the terrible and endless trembling that will hereafter come over you who fail to tremble now." The images that he evokes of the life of the blessed redeemed in heaven are equally vigorous and impressive. Or shall one say even more extravagant and rhapsodic? The example given here is reminiscent of Lavater's writings. "In the moment when I have put off my earthy garment I shall traverse thousands of miles.

Then I shall be as the light of the sun; shall visit planets, shall hasten from comet to comet, from sun to sun; thousands of stars will follow me like flying sparks. Though endless distances will separate us, my friends, I shall yet be near to you."

As a final example of Oberlin's style, consider now an incident that shows his ability to edify and to enchant in a less formal setting by the combination of his deep sincerity and the eloquence of his utterance. The occasion is an evening stroll on a hill overlooking Waldersbach; the time is after the Revolution; Oberlin's companions are several of the provincial literati of Alsace who were living in the Ban de la Roche as refugees (all of them members of the circle around the poet Konrad Pfeffel of Colmar, who had the habit of bestowing special, mostly arboreal, names on members of his coterie, as, for instance, Cedar for Oberlin, Laurel for August Perrier). The narrator is Mlle de Berckheim.

> The day was ending, but the moon was mounting its silver throne and it illuminated our path. The Cedar spoke to us of the beauty of nature and of the beauty of the firmament hymning its praise of the eternal Creator. . . . He also spoke to us of piety and of the enduring happiness of the truly believing soul, which, despite the most terrible happenings, rests secure in God. After he had finished, there was silence. Then the Laurel said, "Sir, whatever may befall, I hope that you will be one of those who will possess that happiness." "Oh, *ja, ja,*" Oberlin replied, "I *am* happy." Then he said it again: "I *am* happy!" and his luminous countenance, his persuasive tone made me feel happy, too, deep in my soul.

Always, whether in conversation or in public speaking, Oberlin's tone, his gestures, and his posture made it clear that he was confronting each of his hearers personally. He constantly searched their faces to measure the effectiveness of his discourse by their expressions. Sometimes, when he felt, as he preached, that he was not *en rapport* with the people he would suddenly stop, fall to his knees in the pulpit, and cry out to God to put the right words in his mouth and to open the ears and the hearts of his hearers to receive them. With the instinct of the revivalist he was intent upon evoking a definite response, a yes or no, from each one.

Often, like Lorenz, the mentor of his student days, he addressed his admonitions to a particular group within the congregation. To the fathers he would say, "Where are you ... who, like Aaron, as priests within your families ought to carry the eternal welfare of the members of your household in your hearts and bring it to the Lord in prayer?" To the parents: "You weep when your children die at an early age though they are thereby translated to a better world; but you feel no tormenting anguish when you see them, as young men and women, rushing down to their eternal spiritual death. Your cattle, your swine are not created in the image of God, nor ransomed by the blood of Jesus; but your children are. Yet at night you carefully lock your stables to keep marauders from entering; but you take no steps to protect your children from the snares of Satan." To the young people: "Remember your Creator when you hear the bell calling to worship; remember: it tolls for you, too. . . . Do not tarry; never absent yourself from the Lord's service."

Oberlin took his texts from various sources: from the Old Testament or the New, from the Apocrypha, or from a hymn or a religious poem, so long as it afforded an opportunity to treat a subject that was relevant to some event in the parish, or to anything that chanced momentarily to occupy the mind of the people. His preaching was always relevant to their daily lives and concerns; in Leenhardt's words, he always sought to "spice his preaching with the salt of actuality." A striking difference between his preaching and that of most Lutheran ministers of his time is that he more often took his texts from the Old Testament, and particularly from the Pentateuch. He admired the culture of Judah and many of his social and economic dispositions in the Ban de la Roche were modeled on the Mosaic law.

He was not above borrowing from published collections of sermons. Wohlfahrt lists sixteen publications that he used in that way, three of them written by his friend and mentor, Lorenz. One of the sixteen books was in French, the others were in German. Whenever he had made use of such help in preparing a sermon, he conscientiously documented it at the head of his manuscript, using a code that gave the author and title in Greek characters. Such identifications have been found by Wohlfahrt on thirty-five of the one hundred thirty-eight funeral sermons preached between 1769 and 1817.[96]

In pursuing his pastoral duties Oberlin spent a large portion of his working days en route from place to place within his far-flung parish. In fine weather he could ride his good horse Content and could enjoy the beauty of the landscape, the pleasant sights and sounds of productive labor and industry in the fields and the villages, and the friendly shouts of *"Bonjour papa"* that accompanied his passing among the people. But on stormy days in the long cruel winters he was exposed on his travels to extraordinary fatigues and dangers. Just the day's walking up and down the steep footpaths was in itself exhausting even when the ground was clear of snow, and when the paths were under drifts, a house call could be a monumental undertaking. In a letter to his mother, for instance, he wrote in a humorous vein about an errand on which the ten men who had escorted him had had difficulty clearing a path for him through the storm. On many a winter journey, dangers to life and limb were present at every step: bone fractures could result from falls while clambering over icy rocks, and suffocation from breakthroughs into hidden sinkholes and crevasses; injury and destruction threatened from above in avalanches, landslides, and falling rocks and trees; danger of drowning lurked at every crossing over rushing, swollen streams by rude log footbridges made slippery by spray and frost; death by freezing could ensue from losing one's way in fog or darkness. Indeed, so frequent were such perils and often so narrow his escapes from them that Oberlin himself was moved to wonder again and again and to praise the faithfulness of his guardian angel, in whom he believed with childlike naiveté. Here is a part of the record:

15 October 1770: God graciously protected us from a great, destructive fire. 28 October 1773: Throughout an entire week God preserved me from a catastrophe that threatened sometimes my family, sometimes me. 13 February 1782: Two of my *pensionnaires* and I, travelling together, sank in the snow, but were saved by an upholding arm. The next day, an unseen hand held me in equilibrium as I walked the log across the Bruche. 6 July 1787: God so directed the course of a great rock that came hurtling down the mountain that it passed between two of my students and me as we were walking together without touching any of us. On 13 May 1818 [after a serious

illness]: Several times I was near death, but was saved by the prayers of my congregation.[97]

Yet, despite such comforting awareness of special divine intervention, Oberlin must on many occasions have repondered the question of just where the crucial point of balance lay between the comforts and discomforts of the ministry that he had weighed in the academic thesis of his youth. All too often the scales seemed too heavily loaded on the negative side. Thus, in response to yet another request from church authorities for an accounting of his stewardship he wrote:

> The parson of the Steintal, trying to do all that is expected of him in this widely scattered, difficult parish, which can in no way be compared with any community in the Rhine plain, is really a poor dog, a workhorse, a beast of burden. He is expected to do everything. From early morning until late at night I am busy, driven, overburdened, incapable of doing half—nay even a tenth—of all that ought to be done. . . . Everything depends on the minister, who is everywhere delayed and frustrated by hindrances, obstruction, delays and formalities, and who never can satisfy anyone, never can fulfill all the contradictory and incompatible demands and, even while trying to do so, must labor against malevolent opposition.[98]

On a winter's day, in a year of famine, as Oberlin was riding along in a contemplative mood, he felt suddenly so overwhelmed by the multiplicity of his cares that he leaped from his horse, knelt on the frozen ground and prayed, "Lord God, have mercy . . . on my poor parish! . . . You must see that we are perishing."

In one respect his pastoral life was unique: he was not only the custodian of the people's spiritual welfare, he was also the guardian of the good health of their bodies. Indeed, the daily calls for help that came to the parsonage were perhaps more often directed to Oberlin the physician than to Oberlin the parson.

Before Oberlin came to the Ban de la Roche the panacea for ailments and complaints of every kind had been olive oil mixed in water or brandy. By diligent research on *materia medica* and pharmacology, by reading about, and collecting specimens of, herbs and plants, he gained knowledge that enabled him not only to prescribe medicines but also to compound some and to keep a stock of them in the pharmaceutical cabinet that he maintained in the parsonage for the people's use. There is no record or list of the specific medicines he used, but it is safe to assume that most of those that were available in Strasbourg were kept on his shelves also. Indeed, it is possible that his stock exceeded that of some urban apothecary shops, especially under the rubric of teas and tonics extracted from indigenous flora, for there was probably no one in Alsace who knew them better than Oberlin. As for surgical, orthopedic, and therapeutic procedures, he practiced those he had learned from Dr. Ziegenhagen. They probably included all the standard procedures in general medical practice of the time.

Just as important for the health of the people as his services as a general practitioner of medical therapy were his contributions to public health and preventive medicine. At the very beginning of his ministry he initiated a campaign for the improvement of sanitation in dwellings and barnyards and village streets. In order to reduce the incidence of infectious diseases, he employed every facility for education and communication at his disposal to promote cleanness and good ventilation in homes and schools and to establish good habits of bodily cleanliness and personal hygiene. Perhaps his most notable accomplishment was that in his parish, through his persistent efforts, vaccination became virtually compulsory and universal. The Ban de la Roche was one of the first communities anywhere in which pockmarked faces, at that time so numerous in all Europe, disappeared from the local scene.

For the health and protection of mothers and their newborn infants Oberlin made properly trained and skilled midwives available to all families and carried on an educational campaign for good prenatal and postnatal care, often against considerable popular opposition. A woman who visited the community only a few years before Oberlin's death heard a citizen express the judgment that the minister was generally loved "in spite of serious mistakes."[99] When she asked about the nature of the mistakes, she was told that he encouraged laziness. "What do you mean by that?" she asked. Well, he had laid down rules requiring that after parturition a mother should have the previously unknown privilege of childbed, and that, while nursing her infant, she should be relieved of some of her ordinary labors. Indeed, sometimes he had gone so far as to pay from his own funds for hired help under such circumstances in households that could not otherwise afford to lose the mother's services. These were unprecedented measures in that backwoods community, where a woman's ability to give birth without losing a day's work in the fields was traditionally considered—at least by the menfolk—as evidence of good health and a sturdy character, while the new measures were denigrated as pampering that would in the long run debilitate and demoralize the race.

The most important fact about Oberlin's medical practice is that it was an integral part of his ministry; his functions as pastor and as medical practitioner cannot be separated. Having arrived at a home to which he had been called as physician, his invariable first move was to call the family and any other persons present in the house together at the patient's bedside, where he led them in prayers in which he implored: for the patient, faith and courage to endure the ordeal of illness and pain, and faith in God's mercy, whatever the outcome might be; for the family and friends, comfort in their sorrow; for himself, wisdom and skill for his hands. And finally, when he had set and splinted the broken bone, or washed or cauterized and dressed the infected wound, or lanced the abscess, or let the poisoned blood, or applied and prescribed the indicated poultices, purgatives, emetics, anodynes, stimulants, or sedatives, and had done all else that was within his power and competence, he would again sink to his knees and lead whatever persons were present in intercessory prayer for the patient's temporal and eternal salvation. If death seemed imminent he would administer the sacrament of communion. On arriving at home after a visit, he would add the patient's name to the list that he kept on his study door of people whom he particularly wished to remember in his daily orisons.

As a pastor, Oberlin was a professional; as a physician he was an amateur, albeit an unusually practiced one. So great, however, was the faith of the people in the capabilities of their *papa* as a healer that they imputed to him the power to restore life to the dead. Three instances are traditionally cited. All three of the patients were girls, and all were presumed to be dead—one by freezing, two by drowning—before Oberlin's arrival on the scene of the accident.

The date of the earliest was February of the unusually cold winter of 1776. An orphan child who was living with an aunt and uncle got up in the night to go to the outdoor privy. On returning she found that the wind had closed the door and she was able neither to regain entry to the house nor to awaken the sleepers within. She was said to have lain naked in the snow for two hours. When she was found, "her flesh was frozen as hard as a rock and her body was as stiff as a board." Oberlin's treatment was to thaw the body slowly by first immersing it in cold water, then by applying warmth and massage to stimulate heart action and breathing. The child "gradually regained consciousness."

In January 1786 an eleven-year-old girl was pulled out of a millpond after having lain immersed under a raft of floating logs for a quarter hour. Oberlin and his helper Sébastien Scheidecker applied artificial respiration and "after days of exertion and constant, fervent prayers the child regained consciousness, after having cried out pitifully, meanwhile, often for hours at a time." The only explanation that we have of the crying is Oberlin's enigmatic statement that "her soul had continued long in the water; hence her anguish."

The other near drowning happened to a child of two. She was brought to the parsonage, apparently dead, and was revived there, with the help of prayers by Mme Oberlin and the other women of the household. Oberlin is said to have made a report on these cases to a Strasbourg physician. Mme Roerich gives information which may be based on that report—and therewith incidentally also gives us an unconventional image of eccentric behavior by the usually courtly Oberlin. She relates that people often gathered in the place where the victim of such an accident lay and engaged in loud whining and wailing, "but without taking any positive action," and quotes Oberlin as writing about a particular instance: "I arrive on the scene, in haste and feigning anger; I stamp my foot heavily and bellow like a sailor; I quarrel with the howling women and threaten to whip them all if they do not deliver to me instantly everything that I need." By thus asserting his authority, he creates quiet and order among the hysterical company, "and by applying heavy woolen stockings and vigorous massage I succeed in bringing back the fleeting breath of life."[100] It is difficult to explain a display of rude vehemence such as the one described here unless one assumes that the whinings and wailings were believed by Oberlin to be heathenish incantations inspired not by anguish or grief, but by superstitions implanted by the wiles of Satan.[101]

The circulation of rumors about his resuscitations and his consequent notoriety as a restorer of life embarrassed Oberlin, for his own estimation of his medical skills and of medicine in general was certainly modest enough. In a sermon he said,

> To turn to a physician in a spirit of obedience and subjection to God's ordinance is meet and right. He has created the vocation of physicians and it is His will that the people should make use of their skills. But to call a physician in the belief that one cannot be healed without medical help signifies a transgression of the first commandment: thou shalt have no other Gods before me. Furthermore: to persist in one's reliance on doctors and on medication even when God has demonstrated by their ineffectiveness that one should give them up and begin to look to Him is to persist in error and to prolong one's suffering. . . . There are sicknesses and sufferings that are consequences of transgressions against and resistance to God's will. For such cases prayer is not sufficient; confession and repentance are indicated.[102]

Illness and injuries, however, were by no means the only occasions for Oberlin's house calls. In order to be their pastor in the fullest sense of the German word *Seelsorger*, he believed that he had to know all his parishioners, to know them, indeed, with a kind of knowledge that could come only from observing their habits; from estimating their spiritual, mental, and physical strengths and weaknesses; from being privy to their enthusiasms and aversions; from intimate acquaintance with their family situations and their private affairs; and from penetrating their psyches and analyzing their personalities.

To accomplish such deep and intimate familiarity he sought as many contacts with each one of his charges as possible and supplemented his casual observations with physiognomic studies and other anthroposcopic "tests" based on such things as their choice of colors, their gestures, postures, and mannerisms. But above all, he seized every opportunity to engage them in intimate conversations, to listen earnestly to every word that they spoke. One of his parishioners said,

Since he wanted to know personally all the people, including their thoughts and their endeavors, he often visited them in their homes in order to inform himself about everything. On such visits there were always things to be done: sicknesses and infirmities to be healed; sorrows to be alleviated; conversions to be made from arrogance to humility, from ignorance to enlightenment, from negligence to good order; the discipline of children to be improved and supplemented; peace to be kept or restored within families and between neighbors; litigations to be quashed or brought to an end; perseverance and industry to be encouraged. In all things Oberlin was friend, adviser, and guardian angel to all his parishioners.[103]

On first acquaintance with his parish, Oberlin saw it only as a place of poverty, ignorance, demoralization, and depravity. As he came to know the people better, however, he recognized among them a considerable number of men and women who had both a large capacity for dedicated Christian living and a high potential for social leadership.[104] Some of these had been discovered, and their talents nourished and developed, by Stuber, others by Oberlin himself. Yet Oberlin felt that he was not doing all that could be done to give people of that kind special opportunities to develop their capacities for spirituality and for exemplary Christian living and leadership. In the early 1780s, he was reading the religious writings of the French philosopher Fénelon, *The Rise and Progress of Religion in the Soul* by the English clergyman Philip Doddridge, and *The Marvels of Heaven and Earth* by the Swedish seer Emanuel Swedenborg; he was studying the life of Count von Zinzendorf and corresponding with the Moravian Preachers' Conference at Herrnhut. He was poring over the eschatological dreamings of Lavater and exchanging fraternal letters with him. He was contemplating the messianic epics of Milton and of Klopstock.[105] In the light of such lofty models, his own efforts toward the spiritual regeneration of his people seemed to him feeble and his accomplishments paltry. "Woe," he wrote in the margin of one of his manuscripts, "woe is me! I have not converted a single soul!"

In the contemplation of the great task that he still saw before him of attaining the perfection that God seemed to demand both of him and of his people, his revivalistic fervor grew to an intensity that impelled him to bold and aggressive action. He conceived a plan to found a Christian Society on the model of organizations existing in congregations of the Moravian Brethren in many countries, often called *ecclesiola in ecclesia,* the little church within the church.[106] His purpose was to bring together in a formal organization the spiritual elite of the parish for the intensive practice of prayer and all the other disciplines of righteousness and holiness, in the expectation of a proliferation of good works in the community, eventually a more bounteous outpouring of divine grace, and ultimately participation in the life eternal for its members.

The best men and women of the parish were to be charter members of the society, which was to be open to all who seemed capable of conforming their lives to the stern imperatives of its statutes, the first of which required the writing of an "act of consecration" similar to the one that Oberlin himself had written on his twentieth birthday and periodically renewed thereafter. By the beginning of 1782, he was ready to proclaim the founding of the society. The pulpit notes that he used in making the announcement are in the form of cue words and phrases and are dated January 30, 1782:

> Rebirth—sanctification—both in Jesus Christ . . . not to follow the world; not evil spirit of the times . . . to nourish inner man through Word of God, persistent prayer, frequent use of Holy Communion—all members mutually to watch over, exhort, and instruct each other—gentleness, love, humility, and patience—unity in same objective . . . all members collaborators of their pastor and of Jesus . . . good housekeeping—good rearing of children . . . diligent searching of the Scriptures— industry with skill and thoughtfulness—no anxious cares for temporal things, no wasting of time, no negligence or sloth . . . honest and prompt payment of debts . . . brotherly love for all . . . offering to God . . . a part of one's labors for the common good.

Because he knew that the cares of poverty hindered the growth of religion in the soul, Oberlin mounted a special effort to give this select group early and effective economic relief: with money raised expressly for this purpose, he created a special loan fund for the exclusive use of members of the society and thereafter required from each prospective member a complete inventory of all his or her debts, exacting from each one a pledge that no new debts would be incurred and no extraordinary expenditures would be made without his knowledge and consent.

Stuber applauded the founding of the society, but at the same time, knowing better perhaps than anyone else his young friend's tendency toward overexuberance in his evangelistic zeal, he issued a warning on March 25, 1782, admonishing him to "take great care to be cautious, gentle, circumspect, and wise toward those who are not included, so that hatefulness, bitterness, *esprit de parti* (the only evil forces that I have always feared in such projects) will not cause damage as great as, or even greater than, the good that the *Société* will do."

There were many parishioners who had, if not a potential for, at least an urge toward, extraordinary spiritual discipline: during the Christian Society's short life, some 130 men and women joined it. Stuber's fears, however, proved to be more than justified, and Oberlin would have been well advised to heed his cautionings more explicitly and assiduously than he did. Jealousy and a sense of injury soon developed among those who did not possess sufficient spiritual maturity to qualify for membership, for they felt resentment that the insiders would, by the quick liquidation of their debts, reap a material advantage not available to them. Animosities and hostilities that thus developed within the community were magnified by evil rumors that circulated in Strasbourg, where the society was condemned by Baron de Dietrich, who now mounted a formidable attack on the hitherto revered keeper of the faith in his fief. Like other large property owners in Europe at that time, Dietrich felt that the security of his holdings was threatened by the many secret fraternal orders that were springing up everywhere and seemed to him to be working, behind false façades of philanthropic enterprise, to undermine the authority and the rights of the propertied classes. Thus his reading of the constitution of the Christian Society, with its stress on solidarity and its tone of all for one and one for all, may have aroused in his mind a suspicion that an incipient rebellion might be brewing against him. In any case, he felt impelled to act.

For reasons unknown, however, he did not address himself directly to Oberlin—perhaps it was because he did not want to get embroiled in yet another contretemps with the magisterial and outspoken manager of spiritual affairs in his realm.

Instead he requested the presence of Professor Jérémie-Jacques Oberlin in his chambers, and laid before him a variety of rumors that he had heard to the effect that his younger brother was neglecting the proper instruction of the young, along with other duties of his office, because he was playing fantastic mystical and visionary games with an especially favored coterie of religious fanatics. The baron therefore asked the professor kindly to use his influence to bring his misguided brother to his senses. Jérémie-Jacques in turn called on his mother, and it was through a worried and admonitory letter from her that John Frederic was first apprised of the seigneurial displeasure.

Stuber, too, must have made an inquiry about similar rumors, for on April 30, 1783, Oberlin sent him, apparently in response to a request, a statement in his own defense. It was eight pages long and listed nineteen "accusations and calumnies" leveled against him by his adversaries. The old familiar canards about Oberlin "enjoying the company of his concubines" were revived and spiced with new ingredients of piquancy, especially after Mme Oberlin's death in January 1783. To them were added exaggerated statements about the exclusion of the poor from the Christian Society and allegations of sectarianism and the fomenting of schisms.

It is no doubt true that Oberlin had been in some measure indiscreet. He had probably pressed too hard in his effort to get the society off to a strong and early start. Perhaps he had himself given cause for the accusations of sectarianism by overstating the special qualifications necessary for admission to membership. He may, in the blindness of his perfectionistic zeal, not have sensed the invidiousness in the metaphor of "the good grain and the chaff" that he had used in explaining the new project. And finally—and most probable of all—once opposition had been overtly expressed, the intemperate vehemence of his personality again kept him from displaying the gentleness that Stuber commended to him on many occasions, including this one, and from exercising those very qualities of "gentleness, love, humility, and patience" that he himself had set down as conditions prerequisite to membership in the society.

But he did have the good sense to acknowledge his errors of judgment, to recognize the fact that the society was not essential to the attainment of his ultimate purposes, and then to take the decisive action of dissolving it. On May 11, 1783, sixteen months after he had proclaimed it, he announced its dissolution in an address to all the people entitled, significantly: "Abrogation of the Name and of the External Form of the Christian Society." For biblical documentation—which was never absent from any of his public utterances—he took from the farewell discourses of Jesus the passage recorded in John 17:21-23, which he always considered to be the great testamentary gift of the Redeemer to His people, and in which the ideas of unity and solidarity are iterated and reiterated: "But it is not for these alone that I pray, but for those also who through their words put their faith in me; may they all be one: as Thou, Father, art in me, and I in Thee, so also may they be in us. . . . The glory which Thou hast given me I have given to them that they may be one, as we are one. . . ." In the ensuing discourse Oberlin declared that now, in taking this action, he was just as sure that he was complying with God's will as he had been two years earlier, when he had made the decision to found the society. He said that he had seen it as one means among many to make all the people true Christians, for he had cherished the hope that eventually the society would encompass the whole parish; but in order to put an end to the "atrocious calumnies" and the animosities, he was now abrogating the name and outward forms of the society. That, he affirmed, he could do with a clear conscience, for true Christianity consists neither in names nor external forms, which are always subject to change.

In the eighth year of Oberlin's ministry there occurred an incident that has been strangely misrepresented in the Oberlin literature. The earliest document about it is a letter dated "Autumn 1774" from Oberlin to his brother Jérémie-Jacques.[107] It is a long, argumentative letter, giving in detail Oberlin's reasons for his decision to accept a call to the congregation at "Ebenezer in America." One gathers that his purpose in writing was to give Jérémie-Jacques information for his use in dealing with critical gossip circulating in Strasbourg that he intended to forsake his parish in the Ban de la Roche in order to indulge in a quixotic transatlantic adventure. "You will ask," he writes in closing, "why I have written in such detail; I have done it more for my own sake than for yours . . . for I know how useful you can be to me in this matter by communicating the contents of this letter to all those who look upon my decision from a false point of view." The heart of his long argument is that it was God's will that he should go. He had, as was his wont, laid the burden of decision on his Lord and Master by asking Him in prayer to give him a sign whether to accept or reject the call. Then he had passed the letter containing the call to his wife "without adding a single word." Thereupon she, too, went to pray in seclusion, and when she returned to him, each of them had been given to know that it was God's will that they should go to Ebenezer.

Ebenezer was a settlement that had been founded in 1733, in a marshy wilderness near Savannah in the newly founded colony of Georgia, by a company of Protestants who had been expelled from their homeland in Austria by Leopold Anton Firmian, Prince-Bishop of Salzburg. They had gone there under the care and at the expense of the British Trustees for the Colony of Georgia, assisted by the British Society for the Promotion of Christian Knowledge. The first transport of seventy-eight persons was followed by two more and, by 1774, the Ebenezer colony had four churches and two ministers.

What was there about the prospect of going there that made it attractive to Oberlin? In the letter to his mother he adds to what he has written to Jérémie-Jacques the following reasons for his desire to go to Ebenezer: (1) since his childhood he has had "an inexpressible urge to travel"; (2) ever since he first dedicated himself to the Lord's service, he has also felt a yearning to be a missionary to heathen peoples and he sees this call as an opportunity to fulfill that desire, for "though Ebenezer is a German Lutheran congregation, there are heathen Indian tribes nearby"; (3) there are also in that region "many unfortunate African slaves, and I should be able to accomplish infinitely much good if I could create schools and institutes for the young Negroes"; and (4) the schools at Ebenezer are in need of reform, "a matter in which I could make good use of the insights that I have gained here in the Steintal." As for the fate of his Alsatian parish, now soon to be orphaned, he argues that "it is in a much happier situation than that of Ebenezer, for it has at its head a Protestant seigneur who applauds the improvements that have been made and will further advance them," while in M. Stuber, "its first and excellent reformer," it will continue to have a devoted fatherly adviser.

Of specific details about Ebenezer, its climate and topography, its economy and its history, he seems to have been innocent; so innocent, indeed, that in the letter to his mother he erroneously identifies it as being in Pennsylvania.[108] Furthermore, about the occasion for his being called he must also have been misinformed, for he says the parish "has been orphaned by the death of the worthy pastor Bolzius," although Bolzius, the colony's first pastor, had been dead since 1765 and his post had been continuously occupied by his successors in the nine-year interim.

But the greatest anomaly of all seems to be the uncertainty whether or not he had actually received a call. In the letter to his brother dated "Autumn 1774," he speaks of "the letter in which this call came to me"; but "at the beginning of 1775" he tells his mother that he has "not yet received the official call" and explains that in his earlier letter to Jérémie-Jacques he was only trying to "prove whether in my position as an honest man and as a Christian I would be able to respond affirmatively *if I should be asked* if I *would be disposed* [emphasis added] to accept a call to Ebenezer in Pennsylvania." And further on in the same letter he says, ". . . at the present moment it is therefore a question of knowing what my intention will be when the official call, as opposed to the merely preliminary inquiry, is forthcoming."

All we know about how the inquiry came to Oberlin is what we read in Stoeber's account, namely that a certain Pastor Johannes Urlsperger of Augsburg, after reading an article about Oberlin and the Steintal in the *Leipziger Intelligenzblatt* "cast his eyes on Oberlin" and asked a friend, a Mr. Hebeisen, a pious Christian of Strasbourg, to sound out Oberlin's receptiveness to an eventual call.[109] But why was the preliminary inquiry never followed by an actual call? A search of all available evidence on the history of Ebenezer in the turbulent 1770s yields no answer to this question. By 1774 the little colony was already deeply embroiled in events that led to the War of Independence. The second minister, Pastor Triebner, unlike the first minister and most of the people, had strong loyalist sympathies. His proselyting activities were creating a disturbance in the parish as early as 1773. It seems likely that Urlsperger, who represented the British Society for the Promotion of Christian Knowledge as custodian of the spiritual affairs of the colony, being informed about these excitements and anticipating the necessity of eventually replacing Triebner, proceeded to his strictly private and unofficial inquiry; so private and unofficial was it, indeed, that he had Hebeisen act for him, apparently in order to keep his own name from appearing in the record of negotiations.[110] Meanwhile, the onrushing events of history engulfed the embattled community and precluded any further thought of recruiting a new minister in Europe.[111]

Gradually, one assumes, as the days of waiting for the call stretched into weeks and the weeks into months, Oberlin came to the conclusion that it was not God's will that he should leave his post in the Ban de la Roche. Indeed, this conviction became so strong that, though many enticing opportunities came to him, he never again considered any suggestion that he should change the scene of his labors. In later years, after his wife had died, any suggestion made to him either that he marry again or that he change congregations seems to have evoked in his mind a favorite image in the rhetoric of Pietism, namely, the relationship of the minister to his congregation as a reflection of the church as the bride of Christ. In each case he is said customarily to have replied: *Une seule femme, une seule paroisse"*—one wife, one parish.

In writing finis to the Ebenezer affair, Oberlin, alluding to I Sam. 7:12, composed a quatrain—the only piece of verse that he is known to have written—to celebrate, as it were, the end of the ordeal of indecision and his acceptance of the proposition that he would find his own Ebenezer in the place where God had placed him, namely, in the Valley of the Rock.

Ich will dir einen Altar bauen,
Der Ebenezer heissen soll;
Drauf soll man diese Worte schauen:
Gott führet seine Kinder wohl.

I will build Thee an altar
Which shall be called Ebenezer;
On it shall be seen the words:
God leads his children well.

18   The Waldersbach Parsonage

19   The Waldersbach Church

20 Madame Madeleine Solomé Obédic

Part 3

The Lonely Years: 1782-1788

7

A Man with His Contradictions[1]

Ever the teacher, the persuader, the exhorter, Oberlin converted the presbytery, save only the family sitting room and bedrooms, into a museum for the instruction and edification of the parishioners and, in the later years, of the many visitors who came to Waldersbach from faraway places.[2] In rooms and passageways there were vitrines displaying collections of insects, of rocks and minerals, and of flowers, herbs, and grasses, as well as open shelves containing books, pamphlets, and periodicals. The walls everywhere were hung with pictures: portraits of historic personages, drawings and paintings of landscapes, religious figures, and Biblical scenes and incidents. There were geographical maps, charts representing speculations on the abodes of the dead, and placards displaying Bible verses and maxims. The door to the study served as a bulletin board on which were written in chalk various memoranda, including the names of persons to be remembered in prayer. Within the room there were "small ornaments pertaining to physics" and various scientific instruments. Tables and a sofa were piled high with books and other objects. On a commode there was a human skull with cranial areas delineated and labeled according to the system of Gall; in a vitrine there was a collection of precious stones, with Biblical explanations of their symbolic properties; on the walls were protraits of Luther, of Gustavus Adolphus, of the prefect Lezay-Marnésia, of Jérémie-Jacques. Oberlin took great pleasure in conducting his guests through the house and explaining the exhibits. He liked especially to linger over an optical illusion that he often used as a visual aid in his pastoral function as a marriage counsellor. The picture is painted on an accordion-folded panel in such a way that it shows different images when seen from different angles. When a disaffected or contentious couple came to Oberlin, he would station the partners several feet apart and facing the wall; then he would hang the picture before them and ask, "Etienne, what do you see?"

"I see a bird."

"And Suzanne, what do you see?"

"I see a flower!"

"What, you disagree even when you are both looking at the same thing? Well now, change places; Etienne on the left, Suzanne on the right. Now Etienne, what do you see?"

"Why, now I see a flower!"

"And Suzanne?"

"Aha, now I see a bird!"

One can imagine that this little exercise rendered its obvious point, and therewith the pastor's counsel, more trenchant and therefore more memorable. It is a good example of Oberlin's vivid and dramatic way of teaching.

Whenever a visitor was announced, Oberlin responded immediately. Whether the caller was a humble peasant neighbor, a distinguished personage from Strasbourg, or a scholarly traveller from a foreign land, he approached the guest with outstretched hand and warm words of greeting. If it happened to be a friend whom he had not seen for some time— a former pupil, say, or someone whom he had known only by correspondence—he was wont to approach him eagerly, and, whether the visitor was a speaker of French or German, or even English, he would utter his favorite German expletive, *"Potzhunderttausend"* (approximate equivalent: good gracious), accompanied by a snapping of the fingers and followed by *"Nein, ist's möglich? Quoi! est-il possible?"* and a warm, firm handclasp. As a souvenir of the visit he often gave a departing guest one or more of the three-by-four-inch etiquettes imprinted with Bible verses that he turned out by the hundreds on his little homemade wooden hand press.

Although Oberlin had an abundance of friends, there were also people who considered him their enemy, for like any man who has ever set out to reform his fellow men or to improve their condition, Oberlin met with opposition from many of those he was trying to help. As a man of stern self-discipline, a perfectionist seeking to eradicate every fault from his own character, he could not desist from imposing on others his own standards of self-control and improvement. Deeply convinced of the unassailable rightness of the Scriptures, which constituted his model for judging all human conduct, and secure in his own long-practiced habits of austere self-possession, he sometimes displayed a self-righteous censoriousness, an impatient, fretful intolerance of even the minor frailties, the innocuous imperfections of others. His reproofs for such peccadilloes were usually delivered in good humor, but sometimes with sarcastic or captious phrases. If, for instance, one of his boarding pupils, having taken more than he could eat, left food on his plate, thus violating the strict rule of the house that nothing should be allowed to go to waste, Oberlin would take his cap and throw it at the young delinquent, who would then be obliged to do penance by bringing it back to him, and, in doing so, looking into his sad, censorious eyes. Or if someone came to him in what he considered vain, ostentatious, or frivolous dress, his censure could be biting. There was a time when the dandies of Strasbourg affected small green waistcoats and very tight nankeen breeches. Theology students who perchance came to Waldersbach thus attired aroused his greatest displeasure. To a particularly foppish one who happened also to be wearing his hair fashionably low over forehead and eyebrows, he remarked: "Well, what have we here? Is this a new fashion that you bring us, or are the Strasbourgeois now at last too timorous to face up to the world?" (The German phrase is *mit offener Stirn einhergehen,* to walk about with open brow.)

In his mode of dress, as in all his habits, he was conservative and frugal. Stoeber says that during the thirty years of his acquaintance with him, he always found Oberlin dressed in the same way: indoors, in a long coat with buttoned-up lapels and wearing a little round leather cap; outdoors, always in black and wearing a peruke "such as one sees in portraits of Jean-Jacques Rousseau," topped by a hat covered with oilcloth and with the rim turned up on both sides. One portrait shows him wearing a knitted stocking cap. A passport issued to him at the age of sixty-three gives the following data: waist, 32 inches; hair, gray; eyebrows, black; eyes, brown; nose, long; mouth, medium; chin, pointed; face, long.[3] He carried himself very straight. His stature was neither tall nor broad. He impressed people not so much by his physical presence as by his manners, the expressiveness of his countenance, the warmth and vividness of his personality.

In regard to cleanliness he was scrupulous, even dainty. Dust or crumbs on the floor or filth on roadways or footpaths disgusted him; he urged his pupils to remove any offal that they found in the streets or around the houses, or at least to cover it with leaves, supporting his remonstrances with quotations from Deuteronomy. In eating and drinking he was frugal and abstemious; on his table only plain but wholesome foods were served, even when the most distinguished guests were present.

One luxury, however, he did allow himself: he was fond of taking an occasional pinch of snuff. Indeed, at intimate gatherings of small groups—as, for instance, at the Bible study meetings in the manse—he sometimes passed the snuffbox around, according to his habit of sharing everything with anyone who happened to be in his presence. Yet this self-indulgence, too, was under the surveillance of his minatory conscience; when he felt that it threatened to become compulsive, he sternly imposed moderation upon himself, as in the following scene witnessed by a house guest: Just as he was about to take a pinch he looked at the box with a scowl and said, "Ah, my snuffbox, you think you can give me orders? I'll show you which one of us has to obey the other; off to prison with you!" Thereupon he carried the box down the stairs, through the hall, and across the dining room, and locked it up in a cupboard, knowing that thereafter he would not often be tempted to make the long trip to reach for it. Thus even he, the austere disciplinarian, like any other mortal, sometimes had to resort to subterfuges to overcome the temptations of appetite.

While his efforts to improve private habits were generally confined to friendly remonstrance and gentle persuasion, in his unending war against public indulgences, such as dancing and noisy merrymaking, he was invariably aggressive, harsh, and relentless. By his incessant denunciations of dancing, he incurred the ill will of the innkeepers and their clientele, which even in that poor and somber community was numerous, and gained the reputation among them of being a meddlesome intruder, a detestable busybody, while by his diatribes against the saturnalian revelries of the village roisterers, he aroused overt ferocity among the roughneck element. But he never relented in his hostility toward unrepentant sinners; never abated his attack; never winced, even in the face of their direst threats. There are several incidents, often retold, in which, by showing his courage, he faced down threats of mayhem against his own person or against others. Three such stories will serve as examples.

One day, quite early in his ministry, rowdies planned to waylay him on a trip to a remote part of his parish and to throw him into the waters of the Bruche "to cool his ardor." Getting wind of the plot, he started out somewhat earlier than planned, made a detour to the place where the men were gathering, and, dismounting from his horse, surrendered himself to them "to save you the trouble of an ambush." The men shamefacedly dispersed.

Another time, when he was walking through the forest, he came face to face in a remote and lonely place with a man whom he recognized as one of a gang of brawlers whom he had recently excoriated from the pulpit. He was a rough and shaggy fellow of frightening visage and was carrying an axe. "Aha," the ruffian said as he advanced toward him, "now I've got you, you scoundrel." "But no," said Oberlin, holding up his hand in a restraining gesture, "you are quite mistaken; my name is not Scoundrel; I am John Frederic Oberlin." Therewith he took off his hat, made a low bow, walked past the man with straight back and firm tread, and continued on his way, leaving his adversary immobilized and speechless with surprise and wonder.

The third instance gives evidence not only of his courage and the cleverness of his strategy in dealing with wrongdoers, but also of his ecumenical tolerance.[4] It happened that a Catholic family moved into the community. Though they were good and upright people, many of their neighbors were full of hostility toward them, a hostility compounded of religious bigotry, jealousy (for the man was not in debt and was therefore said to be "rich"), and the ancient, persistent xenophobia of isolated and impoverished folk. As the newcomers were preparing to journey to Schirmeck *en famille* for the baptism of a new baby, they heard rumors that a band of self-appointed defenders of the Protestant faith planned to waylay and harass them. When the family appealed to Oberlin for counsel, he offered to escort them; the offer was gladly accepted. As the little company, walking through the woods, approached the spot that seemed most dangerous, Oberlin fell on his knees and prayed to God to turn away the threat of danger, or, failing that, to give his companions strength and courage for the ordeal. Then he took the infant from its mother and advanced carrying it in his arms. Soon a wild and noisy mob broke out of the thicket, but stopped in surprise at the sight of Oberlin; they had not anticipated that their Protestant minister would escort a Roman Catholic family to the performance of its popish rites. Standing thus face to face with the belligerent tormentors, Oberlin held the baby up before them and said, "See here, this is the object of your wrath, the tiny creature who is causing you so much sorrow and trouble, the dangerous threat to your peaceful existence." As they, one by one, turned their eyes away from his steadfast gaze, he gave the child back to its mother saying, "Go in peace, and God be with you," and the family passed unmolested through the mob and on to Schirmeck.

But Oberlin stayed behind with the men and talked to them in his quiet, persuasive way about the duty of a Christian to love his neighbor and about religious tolerance; ultimately he walked home with them, taking his leave with the admonition, "Children, remember this day if you would that I should forget it." On the next day a delegation from the now chastened posse of Protestant vigilantes went to the parents of the newly christened child and begged pardon for their hostile behavior.

Such crass assaults as these could be dealt with simply and effectively, given the courage in the face of physical danger that Oberlin possessed, for their perpetrators were visible, identifiable, and present, and could therefore be confronted and faced down by a man of strong character; and gradually, as it became generally known that the young parson could not be intimidated, the attacks were abandoned. But other assaults were made that could not be turned back so easily, because they were insidious and the aggressors were faceless and anonymous; their media were insinuation and innuendo. Such attacks began quite early in Oberlin's ministry, probably reached their greatest intensity in the second and third decades, continued, though less virulently, into the 1800s, and receded only when their target's advance toward elderly venerability evoked virtually unanimous benevolence. It cannot be said that Oberlin ever learned simply to ignore such attackers, which might have been the best way to deal with them; instead, he often wrangled with them in closely argued briefs in his own defense. The calumnies were mostly aimed at his good name in regard to two of the several virtues that he was wont to stress most insistently in his preaching and exhortations, namely, financial responsibility and moral probity.

Among the Oberlin manuscripts in the Strasbourg archives, there is a long list entitled "Calumnies Leveled Against Me." The first four items will suffice as examples: "1. For one louis d'or that I gave to a poor man I took up to three francs interest annually; 2. I enjoy always my bedmates or concubines; 3. I requested funds for repair of roads, but did not use the money by half and put the rest in my pocket; 4. I am the richest man in the land. . . ."[5]

Rather than quote Oberlin's reply to the first of these specific allegations, I cite here an incident related in a manuscript of 1783, which exemplifies his attitude regarding creditors and debtors generally. In 1767 or 1768, Oberlin lent a man one louis d'or. The debtor put off repayment "as everyone did here at that time." Oberlin gave him much charitable assistance in order to enable him to pay all his debts, but the man accepted all that he got from him and from others as if it were owed to him and did not pay his bills. Finally Oberlin turned the promissory note over to the bailiff for collection. But that official succeeded in getting as payment only one and a half bushels of rotting potatoes. Oberlin was willing to cancel the debt, but the bailiff would not waive the court costs. "Now, fifteen or sixteen years later," Oberlin wrote, "the man is again being sued. To keep him and his family from ruin, I must help him by paying his debt for him: three livres for the creditor, four for the court. It is best to do as the Lord says: If someone takes what is yours, do not require it back; if he takes your coat, give him your shirt also; only do not go to court."

As for the calumny regarding concubines and bedmates, there is no record of Oberlin's making specific responses to allegations of moral turpitude except by the diaphanous rectitude of his private life.

That he sometimes grew weary of continuous welldoing in the face of endless opposition is indicated in a letter of 1779 to a friend (probably Stuber), commenting on miseries at Belmont because of a flood, and on the necessity of boarding (at his expense) masons who were working on the new school building. "If one forever labors as a serf—and what is pastoral service here if not unremitting serfdom—how can one help others? I withdraw, I weep, I try to keep from being choked; I go forth, I remonstrate, I plead; I advise everyone to sow love, compatibility, conciliation, submissiveness, consolation against despair, as long as I can drag my weary body, consumed by ever present cares, concern, and tormenting sorrows."[6] And in 1782 he wrote in a letter to his mother about a trip by horse to Barr. "Arriving at the crest of the Champ du Feu and seeing the village of Waldersbach, so poor, so small far down in the stony valley, all the misery and all the burdens of my difficult charge fell so heavily on my heart that I threw myself down from my horse and lay on the ground and wrestled with God and pleaded with Him to have mercy on me in my anguish. Thereafter I continued on my way encouraged, consoled, and revived." He closed this letter in a whimsical vein: "And so, my dear Mama, I am, at forty-one years, Your obedient Fritz."

Oberlin was sometimes aware that his austere discipline and constant insistence on the primacy of the life of the spirit could have bad results along with the good: it could, for instance, foster in the young a tendency to mopishness or melancholia. This awareness is indicated in two documents. The first is a memorandum that he circulated among the *pensionnaires* in January, 1782.

> My dear pupils: I fear that you do not understand me. You think that you may no longer laugh nor have fun; and yet, none have so much right to be merry as the children of God, and St. Paul admonishes us: rejoice, rejoice! That you are not doing, and therein you are very wrong. All things have their time; even prayer and singing the glory of God could be displeasing to God, indeed, they could be sinful, if doing them should diminish our zeal for the tasks that are assigned to us.... Everything that hinders you in this is wrong, whether it be joking or singing, laughing or praying, joyfulness or sadness... and will be punished with poverty and misery.... Draw from this the following conclusions and make the following distinction: 1. Prayer and piety that would keep us from the zeal that is necessary for our work would surely be displeasing to God; 2. jesting and laughter, if it be in the presence of God and of a

kind that does not hinder us in the zeal necessary for our work, can be pleasing to God.[7]

The second document shows that Oberlin, for all his sternness and austerity, was capable of joining his pupils in their play. It is a diary kept by one Mlle Sofie Diemer from the Alsatian town of Oberbronn. Telling of her experiences as a *pensionnaire* in 1805, she writes about various school outings, including one led by Oberlin.[8] It began with an evening *promenade* to Belmont, which often enjoys several hours of morning sunshine while Waldersbach, far down in the valley, is still under its blanket of fog. At five o'clock the next morning the participants rose from their beds in the cottages of Belmont friends, had a breakfast of bread and wine, and started out on the day's hike. It was raining, alas, but the drizzle did not dampen the spirits of the company, which, amid laughter, singing, and jesting, proceeded to the Sommerhof on the Champ du Feu. There they were served a meal of milk soup and potatoes, with fresh butter. Since it had meanwhile become too windy and chilly to be outdoors, they repaired to the empty hayloft, where they sang "Il pleut, il pleut, bergère," and played various party games and charades with mock-pastoral roles, after the fashion of the more sophisticated urban youth in the age of sentimentalism. On the way home one of the girls climbed up among the branches of a tree and imitated the singing of a bird. "The rest of the company caught the spirit of the game and soon the grove was echoing with the songs of various birds." Papa Oberlin assumed the voice of the cuckoo. "Thereafter Papa distributed bonbons, for the singing had made our throats dry. And so we returned to Waldersbach at eight o'clock."

Such divertissements as these could be approved by Oberlin because they were of his kind; they involved neither noisy merrymaking nor extraordinary expense. There were other, traditional festivities, however, some of them deeply rooted in the folkways of the region, that he overtly and stubbornly opposed, chiefly because they were costly and tended to raise the level of indebtedness of many families, but also because they sometimes deteriorated into wanton and lewd debaucheries. Among them were the traditional wedding celebrations, which went somewhat as follows: The bans were published in church on Sunday. On Monday the bride and groom went through all the valley delivering invitations. On Tuesday the wedding garments of bride and groom and all attendants were prepared. The bride's dress was black with a wide silken sash and was richly bedizened with gilded and silver leaves and sprays of rosemary; the groom's black suit was similarly decorated. The bride's bonnet was festooned with long, colorful ribbons falling over her shoulders and down her back and with a crown of flowers. At the climax of the ceremony this was to be exchanged for a brightly colored wreath bordered with tinsel. Her stockings were of scarlet cotton or wool.

On Wednesday, the actual wedding day, the fathers of the bride and groom waited for the minister and escorted him to the church at the head of a procession composed of the families of the couple, their guard of honor, and all the guests. All carried branches of rosemary; the groom also carried a branch of laurel. After the matrimonial sermon, the minister performed the marriage ceremony and spoke the blessing. Thereupon the first man of honor stepped forward and led the bride to the bridegroom in front of the altar. As the bridal couple walked out of the church they found their passage blocked by a barrier of ribbons held by little girls, which was lowered only after the bridegroom had given each girl a coin.

At the home of the bride's parents a great feast was spread. It included various meats, black bread, and cabbage in several forms, particularly sauerkraut, ever favored by Alsatians. There were also spiced patés, especially the Alsatian delicacy paté de foie gras. Dessert consisted of a regional specialty, a three-cornered French pastry called *coinnates,* and, as a final delicacy, a cake made with wheat flour, topped with a cooked cheese and served with whipped cream. The matrimonial bed was enclosed in curtains of white linen decorated with colored ribbons. The festivities were considered ended for the day when one of the men of honor drew the curtains. In relatively well off households, wedding festivities continued thereafter for several more days.[9] Virtually all families, prosperous or poor, found themselves deeper in debt at the end of such celebrations.

One can understand that Oberlin, who hated ostentation and prodigality and who considered indebtedness the bane of husbandry, abominated such mummeries and feastings. A household generally considered itself honored to have the minister present at any family festival, but it was an honor that

Oberlin withheld if the festival did not conform to acceptable standards of moderation and dignity. At those weddings that he did grace with his presence, he instituted a new practice intended to encourage uxorial responsibility and competence in place of irresponsible frivolity: the bride would lay before him for his inspection and approval three things of her own making: a loaf of bread, a homemade camisole or chemise, and a pair of knitted stockings. Thereupon the pastor, finding the products of her hands praiseworthy, would deliver an encomium on her accomplishments and offer a pretty toast to the bridal couple. Gradually the great wedding feasts went out of fashion, giving way to a practice by which the bridal couple, after the civil ceremony performed by the mayor, would repair to the church, where the minister would talk to them in simple terms about the religious significance of marriage and family life and give their marriage the sanctification and blessing of the church, whereafter the cup of honor was passed around among relatives and witnesses, and the celebration ended.

Should such changes as these in the indigenous folkways of the region be celebrated as indispensable prerequisites to social stability, moral probity, and economic prosperity? Or should they be deplored as an unjustified suppression of a natural, rustic, and harmless exuberance in the name of a pietistic sobriety and a stuffy conformism imposed by a strong, domineering, puritanical personality? Folklorists and other admirers of ethnic diversity will lament the eradication of the unique indigenous language of the Ban de la Roche and the transforming of merry rustic festivals into sober ceremonies; others, who see social unification and standardization as steps toward a better world, will applaud them. Still, the record invites speculation whether the severity of discipline applied by Oberlin was really necessary for the attainment of his ends, or if it was rather a projection, above and beyond the necessities of the case, of his own personal crotchets and idiosyncrasies.

A visitor once asked Oberlin's daughter, Mme Rauscher, "Doesn't your father have any faults at all?" She reflected a moment and then said, *"Il se fâche"* —He gets angry. This trait was remarked also by Stuber and acknowledged by Oberlin himself. His impatience with anything less than perfection in human behavior and accomplishment created tensions within himself and between him and others that sometimes constituted a serious threat to the effectiveness of his ministry. His implacable wrath was more understandable and excusable when it was directed against such fundamental moral issues as parental neglect or mistreatment of children, cruelty to fellow human beings and animals, and transgressions against the laws of God as they are summarized in the Decalogue. It seemed less comprehensible when its object was any of the small and innocuous human foibles. His insistent preachments, in some cases reinforced by the imposition of sanctions, on such diverse private matters as habits of dress and grooming, the disposal of excrement and the management of the manure pile, the keeping of dogs, devotional exercises within the family circle, and even the frame of mind of married couples at the moment of the conception of a new life, often struck the people as unwarranted interference in their personal and private lives and were the cause of much of the hostility directed against Oberlin.

Fortunately there were influences that worked against this tendency toward unreasonable impatience and irascibility. One of these was the faithful counselling of Stuber; another was the tranquilizing influence of Mme Oberlin, whose common sense and gentle, soothing presence often moderated his wrathfulness and calmed his vehement temper. But the strongest force toward temperateness was his own predominating trait of amiability. His fundamental world view was based on submission to God's will and love of his fellow men. The same deponent quoted above, Mme Rauscher wrote: "He had a special talent for approaching everyone in such a way that one felt at ease with him. He knew how to receive persons of high rank and station with just the right and proper *politesse,* and treated plain and simple folk with such tenderness and sweet cordiality and even deference, that they, too, felt instantly at ease in his presence. His familiarity was never patronizing, but always amiable, affable." And Mlle de Berckheim, who knew him well, both as a student and later as a member of his congregation, wrote:

> What an excellent figure! A great coat covering his body from his shoulders to his heels, his posture so straight, the lofty brow . . . proclaim the lively and sublime imagination that characterizes him. In his eyes, when one talks with him, there is an extraordinary look of individuality and expressiveness. His nose, long, perpendicular, with but a slight elevation in the

middle, proclaims his profound character, and also gives an intimation of the spirit of repartee, of those sparks of humor that flash forth suddenly and make his company so charming. His speech, above all, is distinguished from that of other people. . . . It is not that he is more fluent (especially not in French), yet he has a very unusual power to convince people. It is a quality that is peculiar to his person. . . . The lofty quality of his soul is visible in a remarkable and fascinating way in his facial expression and gives his most simple words an aura of the extraordinary. . . . It is simply a fact that for him heaven and the hereafter inform and sanctify all that is here and now.[10]

In the presence of such contradictory evidence, with allegations of stern severity conflicting with testimonials of amiability, one feels impelled to turn to an analysis of his own personality that Oberlin wrote in 1820. There one finds him describing himself with such paradoxical phrases as "firm, yet complaisant; generous and grateful, yet irritable and formidable; responsive to generosity, yet (in matters of conscience) firm in opposition; willing to be convinced, but when unpersuaded never yielding."[11] He was indeed, as he says at the beginning of the self-analysis quoted above, "a strange compound of contradictory qualities," which made it difficult for him to "know what I am to make of myself." Is he perhaps closer to the root of his quandary than he knows when, a few lines farther on, he lists among his "contradictory qualities" the fact that he is both a German and a Frenchman?

Much of Oberlin's private time was given to reading. He was accustomed to rise with the dawn in the summer, and long before it in the winter. After his morning prayer he went to his study, which was adjacent to his bedroom, and there devoted himself to his books. The one that most persistently engaged his attention was the Bible. Through many attentive and prayerful readings in German and French and comparisons with the original Hebrew and Greek texts, he became thoroughly familiar with all its books, both canonical and apocryphal. Unlike most other Bible students and clergymen of his time, he ascribed great importance to the Old Testament, especially to the five books of Moses, as a guide and standard for both Christian living and for civic responsibility.

His secular interests as a reader were broad and varied. According to his own testimony his favorite studies were technology and natural history. The questions with which he approached these studies were practical rather than theoretical or philosophical. We have seen that his interest in botany and ecology, which more than any of the other sciences engaged his attention, was motivated by the necessity of finding solutions to nutritional and toxicological problems. His readings and experiments in chemistry and geology were directed toward extending his knowledge of the nature and improvement of the soil on which the life of his people depended. His experiments in physics and mechanics were aimed at the solution of practical problems that he encountered in his workshop, where he prepared apparatus and devices for pedagogical demonstrations, laid out plans for drainage and irrigation, road making, bridge building and flood control, and practiced the crafts of the carpenter and joiner, the blacksmith, the wheelwright, the printer, and the bookbinder.

In none of the fields of learning to which he devoted himself in his readings and meditations, including theology, can he be said to have become an expert or a scholar. In the end, one must take him at his word when he says, in the previously quoted self-analysis: "I habitually work my way through my studies till I obtain clear ideas; but if I wish to penetrate deeper, everything vanishes before me. . . . I am given to planning and scheming, and yet endeavor, in my peculiar way, to do things in the best [i.e., the most practicable] manner."

Another motivation for his intellectual activities was his desire to find in all things evidences of the grace and glory of God. This determined and directed in large part his readings and observations in astronomy, geology, and geography, and in the history of exploration and discovery. In fragments of his journals now in the city archives of Strasbourg, there is evidence that he was greatly excited by the news of the balloon experiments of the brothers Montgolfier in the late 1770s and early 1780s. He read with avid interest about the various ascensions that followed in close succession: by de Rozier in 1783, by Charles in the same year, and the English Channel crossing by Blanchard and Jeffries in 1784. These events beguiled him into musings and speculations about eventual travel in outer space and about the probable existence of living things on the moon. (If there were such, he believed that they would be of the species man.)

As a self-made physician and pharmacist he regularly read books and articles on those subjects. He took a special interest in Franz Anton Mesmer, whose theories of animal magnetism were very much in vogue. There is no evidence, however, that Oberlin ever applied the techniques of mesmerism to his medical practice. His compulsive desire to know and to understand the personality of each one of his spiritual charges led him to readings on other recondite subjects that were also in vogue in his time. These included essays on graphology, the writings on phrenology of Franz Joseph Gall, and the *Physiognomische Fragmente* of his friend Johann Kaspar Lavater. A human skull with the alleged seats of the several mental faculties delineated, as well as numerous silhouettes for use in his physiognomic character analyses, were conspicuous among the furnishings of his study.

He supplemented his studies on cranial and facial contours with observations of such characteristics as tone of voice, posture in standing and sitting, gait, gestures, style of dress, taste in food and drink, manners and mannerisms. Another, even more esoteric, source of inspiration and guidance for personality studies was the mystic symbolism ascribed in the Book of Revelations to precious stones.[12] Starting with St. John's vision of the holy city of Jerusalem and its twelve gates made of twelve different precious stones and their symbolic association with the twelve tribes of Israel and the twelve apostles, and using various commentaries to supplement his own imagination, he developed an elaborate theory of colors as symbols of human character. The apparatus that he used is on display in the Waldersbach museum. It is a glass-covered box in which small specimens of stones are arranged in concentric circles according to the color gradations of the spectrum. The analyses were made on the basis of the subjects' designations of their favorite colors.

The record of the curiosa that captured Oberlin's attention would not be complete without some mention of his preoccupation with such supernatural manifestations as divination, premonition, extrasensory perception, somnambulism, and apparitions. In manuscript four of the Oberlin collection in the bibliothèque municipale de Strasbourg, under the heading *Spektra,* there are more than thirty detailed reports of incidents, each told to Oberlin in 1774 by the person who claimed to have had the experience. These include twelve apparitions in human form, some vaguely recognizable as deceased acquaintances, but mostly not, eleven identified as male, one as female; thirteen manifestations of an invisible human presence, seven of them perceived by harsh blows on shoulders, cheeks, or chest, three as violent nocturnal attacks (followed by an hour-long wrestling match and ending at the stroke of midnight), one as a disembodied voice (speaking patois), two by cracking of branches and a roaring wind in the forest; and eight apparitions of animals, three "great" cats, three "long" dogs, one "large" pig, and one "huge" ox, all with fiery eyes.

These stories were probably brought to Oberlin on his invitation. He recorded each one in exact detail, but without comment or value judgment. He did not reject them out of hand as sheer fantasies, else he would not have taken the pains to collect them and write them down. If questioned about his interest in them, he might have responded with the quotation from Terence that had become a rallying cry of the *philosophes* and that he cited on occasion: "Homo sum: humani nihil a me alienum puto"—I am a man, therefore nothing that concerns man do I deem alien to me. But eventually it came to pass, as we shall see, that he had his own tale to tell about apparitions.

Oberlin also kept up with new developments in the arts and read the works of contemporary authors. Among the writers of his age, his favorite was probably Klopstock, with his odes celebrating love and friendship, God and nature, freedom and fatherland, and his long epic poem *Messias,* in which were expressed in exalted words and dithyrambic periods beliefs and feelings that were familiar to Oberlin's own heart. That he was himself responsive to the beauty of nature and capable, when beholding it, of emotions similar to those that it inspired in Klopstock, is suggested by the following passage from his journal of 1773, in which he describes an experience during a trip to Barr on a winter's day.

On the summit of the Champ du Feu nature was incomparably beautiful. A solemn stillness reigned all around, there was no wind—a rare phenomenon. The valleys and the mountains were covered, as in a garment of luminous white; the fir trees were as if sprinkled with hoarfrost, and the frozen snow everywhere reflected and intensified the rays of the sun. The apparent nearness of heaven inspired my heart with strength and courage.

More than ever before, I resolved to dedicate my life to the welfare of my fellow men, in order to fulfill the purpose of my Creator and in this way to follow the precepts of our Savior. Everywhere nature revealed beauties such as no summer's day ever offers. And yet, the weariness of the body pressed all the more heavily upon my limbs and dangers increased with every step. Now there were old, half-decayed tree trunks that suddenly made me fall down because they were hidden under the snow; now there were great boulders covered with ice that nevertheless had to be scaled at the very edge of terrifying chasms.[13]

On this journey as on many others, he felt, on the one hand, the protective arm of the Lord supporting him in moments of danger, and was reminded, on the other, of the necessity of man to accommodate himself to nature's whims: he had intended to return home on the next day, but during the night the wind changed and a great thaw set in and made the roads impassable so that "for several days I was a prisoner of snow and storms."

22 Louise Scheppler

23 The Oberlin Family: John Frederic, Madeleine-Salomé, Jacques Wolf, Fidélité-Caroline Wolf née Oberlin, Charles-Conservé, Henri-Gottfried, Henriette-Charité, Frédérique-Bienvenue

24 The Man in the Gallery Contemplating
the Resurrection

25 The Pillar of Doom in Strasbourg
Cathedral

8

"You Have Taken My Wife from Me"

Of the nine children born to Madeleine-Salomé and John Frederic Oberlin, the first and the third died as infants: Emmanuel-Frédéric, December 24, 1769-February 6, 1771, and Frédérique-Salomé, February 6, 1773-November 6, 1776.[14] The surviving children were:

Frédéric-Jérémie: born January 2, 1772; studied medicine; volunteered as a soldier; died in the battle of Bergzabern, August 27, 1793.

Fidélité-Caroline: born September 11, 1775; in 1795 married Pastor Jean-Jacques Wolf; died May 15, 1809.

Charles-Conservé: born December 27, 1776, studied medicine and theology; lived in Rothau, first as minister and physician, later as physician only; died May 28, 1853.

Henri-Gottfried: born May 11, 1778; studied natural sciences and theology; wrote a significant work on ecology;[15] *Hofmeister* in Riga; prolonged illness in Waldersbach; colporteur for the French Bible Society; died November 15, 1817.

Henriette-Charité: born October 27, 1779; married Josué Graf, who was a missionary in Asiatic Russia, and later (1818-1824) Oberlin's assistant; died February 18, 1839.

Louise-Charité: born April 5, 1781; in 1803 married Peter Witz, minister at Mühlausen, Bienne, and Colmar; died August 23, 1836.

Frédérique-Bienvenue: born November 14, 1782; married
Louis Rauscher, minister at Harskirch and Barr, in 1825
Oberlin's vicar, thereafter his successor; died February 18,
1854.

The married life of Madeleine-Salomé Oberlin extended
over fourteen and a half years, a total of 174 months. During 81
months she was pregnant. For all but two of her accouche-
ments she went to Strasbourg, usually arriving early and
extending her postpartum recovery to weeks, even months,
thus taking respite from the physical rigors of life in the Ban de
la Roche and the tedium of the intellectually and culturally
limited backwoods community. Furthermore, she was frequently ill and several times took prolonged cures at
Niederbronn-les-Bains. Considering all those absences from
home, along with the delicate state of health that necessitated
the cures, Georg Meyer has questioned the justification of the
title "Mother of the Steintal," which some writers have
bestowed on Mme Oberlin, and which, indeed, Oberlin himself
used upon occasion.[16]
That she was a good mother to her own family there can be
no doubt. Testimony on this point comes not so much from her
own children—their ages ranged, when she died, from eleven
years down to eight weeks—as from several more mature
persons who were almost as closely associated with the family
as the Oberlin children themselves; from such persons as Anne-
Catherine Gagnière and Louise Scheppler. These two, assisted
by other young women who lived with the family while they
were learning the household arts and acquiring the knowledge
and skills they would need as *conductrices,* nurses, and
nursemaids, shared with Mme Oberlin the physical care of the
infants and took charge of the household when she was absent.
As the babies grew into childhood and school age their
mother and father together watched over the learning of their
school lessons, their sketching and coloring, their collecting of
plant and insect specimens; Mme Oberlin taught the girls
knitting, spinning, and weaving, while Oberlin took the boys
into his workshop, which was equipped for carpentry, joinery,
masonry, and metal and leather work.
Despite her many separations from the Ban de la Roche, her
frailty, and all the fatigues of motherhood and of managing a
large household, Mme Oberlin still helped with the pastoral

work of her husband, sharing with him not only the training of teachers, but also the conducting of many devotional and educational meetings. She made visits to peasant cottages, particularly when illness or other misfortunes created need for help and for special words of peace and comfort; she performed emergency medical and first-aid services in her husband's absence; she presided over a large table, serving not only her own family but also the boarding pupils, as well as the many visitors who came to the parsonage, all of whom, from the lowliest mendicant to the most distinguished personage, she received with generous hospitality and unaffected social grace. When her husband encountered difficulty in convincing the people that working for wages was not dishonorable, Mme Oberlin found the time and the energy to set an example by herself taking on work in knitting, spinning, and weaving. All in all, it seems to me that writers who have called this remarkable woman the mother of the Steintal had good reason to do so, in spite of her frequent absences. If her memory shines less brightly than her husband's, the explanation lies not so much in faults or deficiencies of her services as in the tragic brevity of their duration.

In addition to her maternal and household labors, Mme Oberlin made invaluable contributions to her husband's work in her private capacity as wife, helpmeet, and counselor. The balanced combination in her personality of submissiveness and devotion, of modesty and self-assurance, of compliance and firmness made it possible for her to strengthen Oberlin at his weakest points. It seems probable that her influence often moderated his impetuosity, restrained his vehemence, and tempered the occasional harshness of his moral judgments. Oberlin's own summary of her contribution reads: "She helped me wonderfully and untiringly backed all my ideas, all my labors; she was the mother of my parish."[17] Probably he uttered more than once the prayer that appears in his diary: "Lord give me nothing but potato peelings to eat and water from puddles to drink, only do not take my beloved wife from me."

Somber thoughts about the possibility of her early death often came to him. He seems to have hidden them from her, but to have shared with her the happier forebodings that he seems also to have had in times when his spirits were less depressed. Consider, for instance, a letter (without date) addressed to her at Niederbronn. "Last evening, at 9:15 o'clock, I had a feeling of great joy about you and was impelled to thank God and to bless Him; I would be very curious to know if anything special happened to you at that same moment. If you did not notice anything, it is none the less certain that something concerning you happened, or was decided upon, in heaven." The letter is composed in unusually tender terms and closes: *"Adieu, mon chère enfant."*

Although Oberlin was totally free of any fear of death as far as his own person was concerned—indeed, he often gave overt expression to a strong death wish—the thought of his wife's demise filled him with an anguish that sometimes mounted to terror, particularly during times when she was absent. When his first child was born (on Christmas Eve, 1769) he was overjoyed; but three weeks later he wrote in his journal: "How terribly long this week seems to me. I ought to be patient, I ought to be thanking the good Lord that He is allowing me to go to fetch my beloved wife next week; and yet, I do not have a moment's peace, though I do not know the cause of my disquietude. In vain I ask my heart: what do you want of me? it does not answer. . . . No matter what I do, whether I read or pray, or sigh, or weep, alas, it is always the same. Could it be true that my wife has died, as I imagined last Saturday that she had? . . ."

Many writers on Oberlin have ascribed to him certain extraordinary powers of prescience. Some say that it was inherited from his grandfather Feltz, whose possession of a similar gift is based on reports that he correctly predicted the exact day—some claim even the very hour—of his death. Also cited as evidence is the fact that Oberlin often noted instances when sudden, mysterious revelations came to him concerning something that had happened or was about to happen at some place far away. Usually the notation of January 1770 quoted above is cited as an example of his "premonitions." It seems to me, however, that this is not in the nature of a premonition, but of just normally gloomy thoughts, induced, perhaps, by lonesomeness, compounded by anxieties about the possibility of his "losing" his wife, to which he often gave expression without specific reference to any particular date or event. It was one way of expressing his devotion to her and his appreciation of her; it was an acknowledgment of his dependence on her.

In any case, if those anxieties of January 1770 were a premonition of impending death, it was a very inaccurate one, for its subject lived on for thirteen more years; and if it was a telepathic message that she had already died, as Oberlin himself suggests, it was, of course, totally wrong. Furthermore, if there was indeed an inner voice that conveyed messages of impending events to his conscious mind, it was strangely silent at the time that his wife's death was actually approaching; so silent, indeed, that he had to be wakened out of a deep sleep, apparently innocent of any premonitory uneasiness.

Oberlin himself wrote two accounts of the events of January 18, 1783, and the preceding evening. One of them, written on that very day, has been printed directly from Oberlin's manuscript by Leenhardt; the other, without date and apparently written later, is quoted by Stoeber. The following account is excerpted from these two documents.[18]

In the evening, after the rest of the household had retired, master and mistress tarried a while in intimate and pleasant conversation, "in perfect health and very happy." Being in a reminiscent mood that evening, Mme Oberlin remarked that when as a young maiden she was being urged to marry and was herself concerned about the choice of a husband, she had found assurance in the words, "I will show you my salvation." "And so it has been," she said to her husband on the eve of her death, "the Lord has kept his promise. ... To you I owe all that I know of the happy life that awaits us after death." They parted with a kiss, he going to his room upstairs, she to a lower room that she shared with her child of two months and the child's nursemaid, Louise Scheppler.

Toward six in the morning another helper, Sara Caquelin, came to wake Oberlin with the words, "Madame le Pasteur is ill." Here the two reports diverge: Leenhardt's says that Oberlin got up, but seems to have been in no hurry, for Louise Scheppler came while he was still dressing and said, "Madame is *very* ill"; Stoeber quotes Oberlin as saying: "I was extraordinarily sleepy, and since I had known her to be more often sick than well, I fell asleep again; then the second maid came."

When he entered the room at last, he found her sitting on the bed, her feet in a footbath, her body bent forward, her head supported by Sara Caquelin. "She was writhing piteously and crying out: 'Oh God, have mercy . . . help me in my awful agony.' Her face was blue, her eyes fixed toward heaven, and I don't know whether she was aware of my presence (but I think she was)." There were convulsions and frothing at the mouth; she struggled for breath; there was "a wild kicking of the feet, then a slight crackling sound in her throat or her chest." Twice she straightened up, her face bluer than before, her eyes closed. "I felt first for her pulse, but could not find it; then for her heart, but it was beating no longer." Sébastien Scheidecker had arrived; he too could find no pulse; just the same, they had the girls massage her gently; but her body soon stiffened. "I stayed with her until about 11:30 in the morning, Oberlin wrote; "she had gone quite rigid. I don't believe I had held her alive in my arms more than a few minutes. For a long time I took her condition for a coma."

As the news of Mme Oberlin's death spread, the whole parish was "as if thunderstruck." Yet in the days following her death many reports came to Oberlin from people who claimed to have had mysterious feelings of disquietude during the day and the night preceding the death. Only the Oberlin household seems to have been at peace—except, perhaps, Mme Oberlin herself, for in retrospect the maids thought that she had been unusually active in the last weeks with such work as laying in larger stores than usual in the larder and making extra clothing for the children; and Louise Scheppler reported that in the fatal night Madame had stayed up nearly two hours after Oberlin had retired, going over the whole house, making doubly sure that everything was in good order, and finally, just before midnight, going to the beds of her children, laying her hand on the head of each one as if in blessing—something that she had never been observed to do before. Still later, Oberlin learned that some weeks before Madeleine-Salomé's death she had confided to a friend that her deceased sister, the late wife of Jérémie-Jacques Oberlin, had appeared to her in a dream and told her the day of her death.

The following account of Oberlin's actions after leaving his wife's bedside, still hopefully thinking that she was only in a swoon, is from the document quoted by Stoeber.

I left her in the care of Sébastien Scheidecker and ran up to the topmost floor of the house. There I threw myself on my knees and tried to pray that this unconsciousness would not continue long. I say *tried,* for, anxious as I was that my prayer should be heard, it seemed to be leaden and would not rise to heaven. It was my obligation to say, "Praise the Lord, all ye people, for His mercy watches over you for ever and ever." But all I *could* say was, "What have you done, oh my God? You have taken my wife from me! And yet I am supposed to praise You?" . . . I went down again. Sébastien was about to tell me of my loss, but I told him I had already been informed of it.

"Il se fâche" indeed! Yet, in the outpouring of grief that followed, Oberlin was purged of that momentary mood of angry rebellion. "That day I found sufficient strength to write the necessary letters and to take care of things that needed to be done; then I surrendered myself completely to my sorrow. It was so vivid that I kept pleading with God to let me die, too; it would be bliss for me to be buried along with that most precious half of myself; and the same God who had dealt me such a terrible blow, now treated me with the greatest kindness, as a sick man in a delirium whom one seeks gradually to bring back to his senses."

Madeleine-Salomé Oberlin, née Witter, was buried near the church at Waldersbach on January 21, 1783, aged thirty-six, in the fifteenth year of her marriage.

Several sentences (in chapter four) have already been devoted to Louise Scheppler as *conductrice*. It remains to record now her unique services to the Oberlin family and to tell of the wide range of her good works in the community. In July 1783, six months after Mme Oberlin's death, Oberlin was at Niederbronn to recover from fatigue and illness. Even at that early time, Louise seems to have seen herself as the responsible head of the family in his absence, for she wrote him at length, sending such news of the progress of the *ménage* as the birth of a calf; telling of the sadness of all the children, including herself, because of his absence; and expressing dismay at the news that the cure was to be longer than originally expected and the fear that this might be a portent that the children were also soon to lose their beloved *papa*.[19]

Louise, like the other girls who performed household services, was paid a small emolument in cash in addition to board, lodging, and free tuition as a trainee. When she assumed her new position in the family, she wished to be considered as one of Oberlin's own children and therefore asked Oberlin not to give her anything more than he gave to the others. Oberlin, wishing to satisfy that desire, yet feeling obliged to compensate her, arranged to have money sent to her by a friend in Strasbourg; but Louise discovered the ruse, returned the money, and wrote the following letter (without date, but possibly written during the same period of Oberlin's stay at Niederbronn): *"Cher Papa,* so you wish to deprive me completely of my hope of being allowed at last to offer you my feeble services without my receiving any pay except for my most necessary needs. Alas, I seem to be far from reaching that goal . . . Oh, how sad that makes me. . . . But it seems to me, my dear *Papa,* that you do not understand how I feel toward you . . . Oh, it is most difficult to love so tenderly without being allowed to show or to prove it. . . . I am, with a most heavy heart, your most affectionate Louise."

Ten years later, when Louise's father had died, leaving her with a small patrimony and with no further obligations to her own family, she asked Oberlin again to consider her "in every respect" his child and not pay her wages any more. "For my person I need only clothing, stockings, and wooden shoes, and when I need any of these, I will tell you, as a child tells her father." Thereafter the wish seems to have been granted. After Oberlin's death in 1826, his children urged Louise to accept a share of the inheritance, at least to the amount that each of them received. Again she demurred, requesting only that she be allowed to live on in the parsonage to the end of her days.

Some biographers have asserted that Louise at some time requested the privilege of changing her name from Louise Scheppler to Louise Scheppler-Oberlin. The assertion was first made by Baron Georges Cuviér in his citation at the bestowal upon her of the Monthyon prize "for her contribution to humanity" in 1829,[20] but members of the Oberlin family vigorously denied that any such request had ever been made, saying that it would have been uncharacteristic of Louise to have made it. No evidence supporting M. Cuviér's statement has ever been found.

To the casual reader it might seem that the first of the letters quoted above expresses an affection that is more than filial, that it is, in short, a love letter. In the circumstances, it would be no more than natural to assume that the young woman's emotions would at times be mixed. Indeed, slanderous voices were heard in the Ban de la Roche and in Strasbourg that spoke of scandal in the manse. But no one who has known Oberlin, either in person or from studying his life, could give credence to such hintings, for the probity of his private life is in every respect above suspicion, even if the phrasing of that letter from the twenty-year-old Louise might strike an uninformed reader as evidence of carnal affection. The fact is that Louise was literally Oberlin's collaborator; she carried on all of the functions that Mme Oberlin had performed except that she was neither his consort nor the biological mother of his children. Her own conception of the nature of her relation to him is indicated by the fact that she always addressed him exactly as his children did, with *papa,* or perhaps more often, *mon cher papa.*

The salient facts of Louise Scheppler's life are simple and therefore can be briefly told. One relatively short document covers them adequately, namely the *mémoire* nominating her for the Monthyon prize.[21] The opening sentence states that the nomination is not made because of particular traits or virtues possessed by the candidate, but because of an entire life consecrated to the exercise of all the Christian virtues. After that there are several paragraphs that review the nominee's early years, her training in the Oberlin household, and her new responsibilities after Mme Oberlin's death. ". . . For forty-seven years she shared all the cares and concerns of her distinguished master and was his chief support in all his noble enterprises. . . . It was, above all, through her that this man of God carried out the beautiful and sublime idea of training *conductrices* of schools for infants of preschool age, which have served as a model for entire nations."[22] Farther on there are comments on the nominee's concerns in the years after Oberlin's death, including her initiative work in establishing a training school for *conductrices;* her management of the communal loan fund; her making clothes for the poor; her charitable work in visiting the sick and bringing comfort to troubled hearts. "So that she is still the benefactress of a population of some 2,000 souls, all of whom honor her as a beloved mother."

Within the *mémoire* there is quoted in its entirety a letter written by Oberlin to his children shortly before his death, reviewing Louise's work, stressing the point that she was not *conductrice* in just one place, but that she went from village to village on a regular schedule. "The difficulties that she faced

would have discouraged a thousand other people . . .: the
unruly, rough manners of the children; the difficulty of
abolishing the patois . . . ; the bad condition of the roads and
footpaths . . . ; the necessity of coping with stones, water, heavy
rains, freezing winds, hail, deep snows on the ground and
avalanches from above. Nothing deterred her; and when she
had come home at night, breathless and wet, numbed by the
cold, . . . her knees bloody from rubbing against her frozen
garments . . . she addressed herself to the care of you, my
children, and of the household."

On July 20, 1837, Louise came home, "tired but content,
after working five hours in the afternoon in one of the *écoles à
tricoter.*" She had her supper, talked for a while with the
Rauschers, made two visits to neighbors, and retired. In the
night she was taken ill with pneumonia. She died on July 25,
aged seventy-four.

There is no doubt that Oberlin's extraordinary accomplishments were based in large part on the contributions of great
and good friends and helpers. These include Jean-Georges
Stuber, Sébastien Scheidecker, and Jean-Luc Legrand. But the
greatest helper of them all was Louise Scheppler.

9

Of Mysteries and Dark Enchantments

"Death is an open door,
We move from room to room.
There is one life, no more,
No dying and no tomb."
—Gordon Johnstone[23]

The greatest of the many triumphs of the nameless medieval artists who wrought the splendid sculptures of the gothic minster of Strasbourg is the Doomsday Pillar of about 1230. Around a free-standing column that supports the arched ceiling of the south transept there are clustered on three tiers three groups of four figures each. The lowest group shows the four apostles who recorded the history and the promises of man's salvation, each standing on a corbel rooted in the ground and adorned with his symbol: St. Matthew with the angel; St. Mark with the lion; St. Luke with the ox; St. John with the eagle. On the middle tier stand four angels holding their trumpets ready to sound the crack of doom. On high, Christ the Redeemer sits on the judgment seat, a throne supported by souls already redeemed from everlasting death. He is attended by three angels triumphantly displaying the symbols of the passion by which the promises are fulfilled.

High up in one of the galleries facing the Doomsday Pillar, some unknown artist has created, as a whimsical yet poignant commentary on the doomsday scene, a small figure of a man of uncertain identity: a portrait of the creator of the pillar himself, perhaps? Or of one of the nameless master builders of the cathedral? The little man, whoever he is, sits in a corner of the gallery, his arms resting on the balustrade, pensively gazing at the beautiful and awesome scene.

To an observer familiar with Strasbourg's intellectual history, this tableau might be seen as a symbol of a striking Alsatian trait: a propensity to ponder the ultimate destiny of the self, a proclivity to brood over last things. What it is that has generated this mood and sustained it through the ages is hard to say. Was it perhaps the collisions, sometimes of cosmic dimension, seeming to foreshadow Armageddon itself, that recurred ever and again in the purlieus of this European Megiddo, on this Plain of Esdraelon-on-the-Rhine? Whatever its causes may be, many Alsatians have possessed the trait, while others, coming from elsewhere, have acquired it here. The Strasbourgeois master builders of the minster and the creators of its singularly rich sculptures—who are mostly unknown but collectively honored under the name of the legendary Erwin von Steinbach—had it, and so did the Alsatian painters and engravers Hans Baldung Grien (c. 1476-1545) and Martin Schongauer of Colmar (d. 1491), from whom the journeyman artist from Nuremberg, Albrecht Dürer (1471-1528) acquired it. Matthias Grünewald (b. between 1460 and 1470, d. 1518) was infected with it as he worked on the great altar, his "mystical vision in colors," at Isenheim near Colmar. The writings of philosophers and theologians, too, are permeated by its spirit: Meister Eckhart, the father of German mysticism, was infused with it when he taught at Strasbourg from 1314 to 1322. Eckhart's pupil and disciple, the Strasbourgeois Johannes Tauler (c. 1300-1361), who founded the mystic Society of the Friends of God, had it and communicated it to the merchant Rulman Merswin (1307-1382), who was moved by it to sell his earthly goods and join Tauler's society and eventually to become its leader. It imbued John Calvin in the crucial years that he spent in Strasbourg (1538-1541). And finally, in our own time, it possessed the Alsatian Albert Schweitzer (1875-1965), the celebrated theologian, physician, philosopher, musician, and musicologist, who through his theological works, *The Quest of the Historical Jesus* (1906) and *The Mysticism of Paul the Apostle* (1930), led a generation of theologians of the twentieth century to an eschatological and mystical view of the life of Jesus that resembles some of Oberlin's ideas. It sent Schweitzer himself to Africa for works of charity in behalf of a primitive people in the

Gabonese bush that are sometimes reminiscent of Oberlin's projects for his disadvantaged people in the Vosges.

In all ages the Alsatians have indeed been "an earthy, sensuous people, endowed with rich inward gifts, troubled by visions and stimulated by prophecies."[24] For this observer it is not difficult, when standing in the presence of the Doomsday Pillar of Strasbourg, to see in the little man in the gallery an image of John Frederic Oberlin.

If Oberlin did absorb that mystical strain from the intellectual and spiritual ambience of the place where he was born and nurtured and educated, what form did its manifestations take? Here again we find that he was more a follower than a leader, an exploiter of the conceptions of others rather than a conceiver of new ideas, a willing (though perceptive) follower of trends rather than an innovator. Indeed, our interest in him stems from the very fact that he reflected and exemplified in a unique way and within the limited compass of a country parish the ideas and ideals of his time.

Among the more outré fashions of the day was one that appealed particularly to that special Strasbourgeois genius of mysticism. Mme Oberkirch, a perceptive observer living in Strasbourg and writing her memoirs at the very time that is under discussion here, describes the zeitgeist in Alsace as being marked by an incredible predilection for the miraculous.[25]

I would call it superstition, if I myself were not caught up, even against my better judgment, in what is more accurately designated as a symptom of the decline of a society. It is a fact that the Rosicrucians, the adepts, the prophets and everything connected with them have never, at any time, had such a numerous following as now. Even the imaginations of the most substantial, most sterling characters are preoccupied with them; they haunt the minds of the masses and conversations everywhere revolve around them. If my memoirs show signs of this preoccupation, it is only evidence that I have portrayed our time accurately. Later generations will hesitate to believe it; they will not be able to understand that even those who found it impossible to believe in God were capable of giving unconditional credence to such prophecies.

What was the cause of these excitements and delusions? Was it perhaps a generally felt *Unbehagen in der Kultur*—if Freud's expressive phrase may be borrowed and put to use here in a different context—a state of unease in the culture of the time, a condition of feeling not quite comfortable in one's own skin, occasioned by the onward march of the age of reason and its impending triumph over romantic idealism; a victory that was ultimately symbolized by the enthronement of reason in place of the crucifix and the Holy Virgin on the altar of Notre Dame de Paris?

The shock waves of change in that massive reevaluation of values once more were particularly jarring in the frontier province of Alsace, the buffer region between Gallic rationalism and Teutonic romanticism, between French Catholicism and German Lutheran Pietism. In Strasbourg, intellectual and religious leaders were under the influence of such visionaries as Lavater and Jung-Stilling; and even the most notable champion of revolutionary rationalism, Isaak Haffner, stood ready to defy the guillotine in defending his faith in the reality of a life after death. The collision of ideologies and the dislodgment of ancient verities now left many intellectuals reeling and sent them in search of new footings for their faith and new havens of security for their troubled minds.

Oberlin was, of course, keenly aware of the prevailing trends. He informed himself not only about the ideas of theologians and other thinkers, but also about such esoteric matters as Mesmer's theories of animal magnetism and Puységur's system of somnambulism. From reports in newspapers and journals and in letters from friends he knew about the prophecies of various putative seers and soothsayers, and at least once he consulted one himself. Evidence of such preoccupations exists in documents now in Strasbourg's Musée Alsacien. There is, for instance, an envelope marked in Oberlin's hand "Mlle Wipperman," which contains extensive notes on the visions and prophecies of that most celebrated clairvoyant of her time, who became the subject of two books by Justinus Kerner, *Documents from Prevorst* and *The Seeress of Prevorst*. Another envelope, marked "Revelations," contains miscellaneous notations on dreams, visitations, and apparitions. Furthermore, in the bibliothèque municipale there is a manuscript entitled "Spektra" which contains a discussion of the effects on their beholders of visions related in the Bible, as well as the list of more than thirty alleged happenings of an occult nature in the Ban de la Roche, which was referred to in chapter seven. Still another manuscript is (ambiguously) entitled, "Conditions of certain deceased persons, either presumed or made probable by dreams or visions of Ban de la Roche citizens." The number of cases described is fifty-two.[26]

Oberlin's own most intense and earnest studies on such mysterious subjects were applied to the apocalyptic prophecies of the Bible. Under the influence of his parents, of Lorenz, and of the Congregation of the Brethren he had entered his maturity as a believer in the resurrection of the body and in everlasting bliss for those who were worthy of redemption. His very first sermon had been a call to his auditors to prepare themselves for the life eternal. Always his utterances about death were full of happy promises for the righteous; his rhetoric was innocent of the funereal memento mori of the Trappists. He spoke of the promised glories of the life to come with the conviction of one who saw them as clearly as he saw the mundane realities that crowded—to borrow W. H. Auden's expressive phrase—the "prison of his days." And being the practical manipulator, the pragmatic manager that he was, he was not content with vague notions about a disembodied existence in some unimaginable, ethereal no-where, enjoying unnamed pleasures and unspecified rewards for a righteous earthly life. He wanted to know what forms those rewards would take, what shapes those many mansions in his Father's house would reveal. To that end, as to the end of all his learning, he began by searching the Scriptures, and then supplemented his own research there by reading the commentaries of his fellow seekers.

Among these were two Swabian theosophists, Johann Albrecht Bengel (1687-1752), who by his studies in biblical numerology calculated that the millennium would begin in 1836 (the date later adopted by Jung-Stilling), and Friedrich Christoph Oettinger (1702-1782), who fathomed the sacred mysteries by reviving the medieval system of the cabala. There was Johann Kaspar Lavater (1741-1801), "the Sage of Zurich," Swiss patriot and poet, physiognomist, and revealer of *Prospects of Eternity.* There were also three Englishmen: Thomas Bromley (1629-1691), disciple of the German mystic Jakob Boehme; and John Pordage (1607-1681), and Jane Leade (1623-1704) both Bromleyan Behmists. Finally, there was the Swedish seer Emanuel, Baron of Swedenborg

(1688-1772), mining engineer, public servant, and author of both philosophical scientific treatises and mystical visionary revelations.[27]

Oberlin became acquainted with Lavater's *Prospects of Eternity* in 1774, soon after the last of the three volumes had appeared, More than any other books on this subject, it appealed to Oberlin's more practical than philosophical mind, for these *Prospects* "are not philosophical thoughts concerning the immortality of the soul in the style of the Enlightenment; they are more in the nature of insights into the conditions and powers of human beings after death. Their purpose is to help the imagination to grasp the exalted dignity, the godlikeness of man's essence." On July 26, 1774, Oberlin wrote Lavater a letter of about a thousand words, from which the following is extracted:

> Permit me to express the liveliest gratitude for the edification, the encouragement, the eagerness to imitate Christ, which your *Aussichten in die Ewigkeit* have engendered among us. . . . Bless you for all the blessings this book has brought and doubtless will continue to bring to myself, to my wife, to my pupils, my *pensionnaires,* to my acquaintances and to my parishioners. . . . I had previously tried, with my small knowledge of nature, to make for myself some portrayal of heaven that was rather different from our ordinary ideas, so obscure and unworthy of our age, and this precious book has brought me the same conceptions, marvelously enlarged on new foundations, so much more numerous that it seemed to me really new and all the more precious. . . .

The correspondence between Oberlin and Lavater that began with this letter continued until Lavater's death in 1801. The ideas and outlooks of the *Prospects* remained as a very large ingredient in Oberlin's views concerning eternal life, while Lavater's most popular book, *Physiognomische Fragmente,* initiated and sustained his lifelong hobby of character analysis. The two men never saw each other face to face, although there were several occasions on which they might have met. The first of these was a journey not only planned but actually embarked upon, which was to take Oberlin ultimately to Zurich to visit Lavater, but the trip was aborted long before that destination was reached by an emergency in Waldersbach (described in chapter fourteen) that necessitated his early return. In view of Oberlin's disappointment and of Lavater's expressions of regret at that time, it seems odd that they did not manage to meet each other in Strasbourg, for Lavater was in that city on several later occasions, on at least one of which he was a guest in Stuber's house, where crowds of admirers came to honor him.

Oberlin's acquaintance with Swedenborg's writings began in the crucial year of Mme Oberlin's death, 1783, when a French translation of the *Marvels of Heaven and of Hell* (published in Berlin in 1782) came into his hands. Two of the three volumes from Oberlin's library are in the bibliothèque municipale in Strasbourg. They must have been much circulated and read in the Waldersbach parish, for they are worn and dog-eared, margins are shiny from much thumbing, some pages are torn and others are missing. Affixed inside the front of the first volume is a critique of about 1,200 words in Oberlin's hand, and scattered throughout the two volumes are marginal notes, mostly of a negatively critical nature and sometimes drastically phrased. (Example: "May God forgive Swedenborg for the temerity of his explications and reasonings.")

Both the critique and the marginal comments were apparently put there for the guidance of other readers, with the double purpose of justifying the circulation of the book while at the same time warning readers against undiscriminating acceptance of its revelations.[28] The first three sentences show the general purport of the whole essay: "I find in this extraordinary book such illumination, such instruction, and such wonderful reasoning that I do not know how to thank God for it. But, on the other hand, I find in it also some reasonings and some explications of the Holy Scriptures which are so bold and so rash, that I absolutely cannot admit them. This author wants to spiritualize all the meaning of the Holy Scriptures, but in a frightening way, so that there would be no certain meaning, and everyone could do with them as he wished."

Other strictures, expressed farther on, are epitomized in these propositions: "That Mr. Swedenborg errs in drawing from his visions fundamental principles and in taking up with too great a certainty all that is told him by spirits who are often very little advanced in their knowledge of the mysteries of God; that the resurrection of the body and the last judgment have not yet happened—one must take the Bible literally and cannot read it too assiduously; that Mr. Swedenborg is an important man, but in his ideas he has missed the true way, for—may the blessed have pity on him—he has separated the literal meaning of the Holy Scriptures from their metaphorical and mystical meaning. . . ."

In addition to the *Marvels of Heaven and of Hell,* Oberlin also purchased other books by Swedenborg as soon as they were published in French. Still to be seen in the Strasbourg bibliothèque municipale among the books from Oberlin's library are five books by Swedenborg.[29] In spite of all his negative remarks about their revelations, there is no doubt that he was captivated by their author: he is known to have used the works in connection with his own eschatological studies for many years.

Quite early in his speculations on the nature of the afterworld, Oberlin had looked into *The Way to Christ,* by Jakob Boehme (1575-1624), the German philosopher of mysticism. He had found it, "extraordinarily difficult," but had persisted in his effort to understand it because he sensed that "in truth, the spirit of God is here," and like the great Philipp Jakob Spener, the founder of Pietism, who had also acknowledged that he did not understand the greater part of it, he believed that "everyone should grasp something which bears in such a certain way the imprint of the Holy Spirit." It seems not unreasonable to suppose that Oberlin felt that he was getting the gist of Boehme from the more pragmatically inclined British Behmists, who were active in the organizing (about 1670) and management of the Philadelphian Society. The tenets and purposes of that organization resemble in many ways those of Oberlin's Christian Society, and in one of its organizational features resembles also the Moravian *ecclesiola in ecclesia,* as well as Swedenborg's New Church: for in the founding of each there was no intention to create a new sect that would draw members away from the established churches. Thus all of them together may have served, at least in this one respect, as models for Oberlin's Christian Society.

The names Bromley, Pordage, and Leade are found in many places in Oberlin's private papers in the bibliothèque munic-ipale.[30] Pordage appears typically at the head of notes on subjects such as "Divine Metaphysics," "Revelations of Paradise," "Eternal Nature," "The Seven Worlds of Pordage";

and among various charts and representations of the after-world, such as the "Pordagean Sphere of Eternity," and the "Eternal World and its Courts." One chart of "the moral and gracious order of the eternal world" bears Oberlin's marginal note: "After Dr. Pordage, J. Leade and several other English writers." The name of Jane (or Jeanne) Leade is most often associated with notations about the precious stones in the foundations of the New Jerusalem. Bromley's book *On Divine Revelation* is also in the collection. It has marginal notes in Oberlin's hand and underlinings.

Oberlin expended much time and loving labor in designing and executing graphic representations of the abodes of the dead; he charted and mapped them, sometimes in columnar arrangement, sometimes in spheres or hemispheres, sometimes in constructions combining concentric arcs and parallel lines. One chart, in which the correspondences between the heavenly mansions and the temple at Jerusalem are featured, was printed on Oberlin's little hand press in many copies, some of which are still to be seen in the Musée Alsacien. Although handbills such as these, which were made for local distribution, were all that ever appeared in print, the fact that Oberlin was interested in the subject became widely known, and several books falsely purporting to be of his authorship were published.[31]

The impact of these preoccupations was varied: on the one hand, they inspired the flattery of imitation; on the other, they brought down upon Oberlin another wave of hostility. They were probably among the evidences that Baron de Dietrich had in mind at a later time when he hurled at Oberlin the taunt "ridiculous mystic." Leenhardt reproduced a rough draft of a letter of May 17, 1785, to an unidentified friend in which Oberlin defended his devotion to these speculations, parts of which I paraphrase here.[32]

They say that I should not systematize the Bible. Is not all our faith systematized and arranged in tables? Our catechism, for instance, is a system that you will find nowhere in the Bible in that form. . . . And should I not assemble that which can give me an idea of those treasures for which I must sell all my goods and sacrifice everything? Can I not set them down and sum them up as I do my earthly credits and debits? . . . They say my representations are too fragile, too chancy. What do I care? None of our geographical maps is accurate and really true, yet I thank God that I have them. . . . They say that I should keep my representations to myself and not show them to my Ban de la Rochois. God forbid it! I live only for them; my energies, my knowledge, my talents; my fields, my livestock, my money, my garden, all must be shared with my congregation, *ma première femme*. . . . "They say that I will do harm to my parishioners. Really it hardly seems likely. Who could have shown me in 1767 another congregation of such poor devils that he who had enough potatoes to last the year and didn't have to boil up grass to eat in the spring was called rich; and who can now show me a community where so much good has been done to relieve misery; where each helps the other, where no one begs, where each brings aid and support to someone poorer than himself. . . . Let them compare this community with any other, German or French, and let them admit the difference."

After dwelling for a time with Oberlin in the thin air of those celestial regions, one is relieved suddenly to come upon evidence that he was at the same time as interested as ever in the news of the day. And yet, one is also amused to find that the news that seemed particularly significant to him also has something of an ethereal quality. He closes the letter quoted above with a "P.S.: Have you heard about the new way of flying? I was sent word of it from Strasbourg." It is characteristic of Oberlin that he wrote a memorandum about that event in his journal under the heading "A spiritual report on the machines for going in the air." In ten numbered paragraphs he alternates comments on the mechanics of aerostatic balloons with metaphorical homilies on spiritual matters.[33]

Oberlin's image of the afterlife is like an eclectic montage made up of many ideas gathered from the voluminous writings of the time on that subject. There is one element, however, that seems more than others to be peculiarly his own, namely, his conception of the immediacy of the righteous soul's passage from its corporeal earthly abode to its disembodied existence in the first stage of heaven. There is no doubt that he took literally the words of Jesus to the repentant criminal on the cross: "Today you shall be with me in paradise." As good an example as any to illustrate this is the following passage from the funeral sermon for elder Nicolas Banzét of Bellefosse.[34] Here again the childlike naiveté of the conception seems incredible to the modern mind.

Yesterday morning our dear departed rose as on every other day, took care of his livestock and did his accustomed work. . . . He did not know that the angel of death had already received the order to put an end to his earthly life and his sorrows. The angel, having received the commission . . . looked over to Bellefosse; his glance penetrated thousands and thousands of worlds; and his ears went along with his eyes; he heard Nicolas Banzét gasping in his struggle to breathe and moaning in his agony. Then the angel arose in rapid flight, and quicker than lightning he descended to Bellefosse. He walked into the poor, gloomy cottage, following the divine signal.

Now the hour strikes, it reverberates through the celestial worlds. The angel raises his arm for the death stroke. The fetters of the body fall away, the prison walls crumble and fall. And the soul, the weary frightened soul, sees and tastes the perfect, blissful freedom. . . . He . . . who, like a wretched worm, has been writhing under the burden of his sick earthly body, suddenly flies from the ground, free and light as a bird. He who had just been about to take earthly nourishment for his decrepit body, is now privileged to taste the joys of paradise. . . .

Let us go back once more to that crucial time in the Waldersbach parsonage. 1782 was the fifteenth year of Oberlin's pastorate. Although many of the projects, enterprises, organizations, and institutions that he had initiated in those years were well started and functioning, it was not a time to take one's ease, to indulge one's fancy in proud contemplation of one's accomplishments. Sorrows and cares were pressing in upon him: the youth of the parish were rebelling against the inflexible severity of the minister's moral code; the mood of the *pensionnaires* was refractory; the Christian Society was under attack from all sides; the lord of the manor was sending threatening messages from Strasbourg, where the "ridiculous mystic" of Waldersbach was the subject of general gossip; while in the loneliness of the primitive backwoods parsonage it seemed that the very elements were conspiring against the embattled pastor. It was in this winter that, one day, looking down from the Champ du Feu on the little huddles of cottages scattered across the snowbound valley, he dismounted from his horse, fell on his knees, and cried out: "Lord, have mercy on us; have mercy, for we perish."

Also for Madeleine-Salomé, perhaps even more than for John Frederic, it was a difficult time: only recently she had returned from her ninth accouchement with her child Frédérique-Bienvenue, now eight weeks old. Her life was filled with daily tasks, as mother and as the head of that large and complex household, suckling her newborn infant and mothering the six others, whose ages ranged from eleven years to twenty months; standing in loco parentis to the boarding pupils; directing, teaching, and counselling the housemaids who were in training as *conductrices;* and—perhaps most important and most trying of all—exercising her usual quieting influence on the vehement personality of her beleaguered husband. And amid all those fatiguing labors, agitations, and excitements, she was, unknown to him, panting under intimations of mortality whose singular explicitness would soon become manifest.

Such were the concomitant circumstances that formed the setting for that last conversation between husband and wife on Friday evening, January 17, 1783, that has already been described. So, consider now that Oberlin's mind at that time was much occupied with images of the unseen world and with the drawing of charts and sketches of his apocalyptic conceptions; keep in mind that he was in the midst of the series of sermons on the abodes of the blessed; and remember, finally, the valedictory mood of Madeleine-Salomé. Is it surprising that that intimate conversation turned on death and the new life that would follow after it? Recall also the solemn nuptial prayer that these two had written down at the time of their marriage, pleading that God, whenever one of them should die, would grant the other the boon of soon following after. Is it any wonder that the death wish that had often asserted itself in Oberlin's heart should return with perfervid intensity when, a scant twelve hours after their conversation, Madeleine-Salomé had died?

In the winter of 1782-1783, probably more than at any other time, Oberlin's mind and spirit were steeped in the bright enchantments of the invisible world. Near the end of 1782, a year in which he had devoted much of the quiet time left over from his many managerial activities to the studies that have been described in the preceding section, he launched a series of eight special sermons. On Sunday, December 15, he preached on the messianic prophecy of Isa. 9:1-6. Although the text was the traditional pericope for the last Sunday in Advent, the burden of the discourse is suggested by the title written on the manuscript: "Paradise and the Abodes of the Blessed." It was a German sermon for the congregation in Belmont; on Christmas day he preached the same sermon, but this time in French at Waldersbach.

A week later, on New Year's Day, he preached the second sermon of the series, and on Sunday, January 5, 1783, the third. Why the fourth sermon was not delivered on Sunday, January 12, is not clear from the record. Was it planned that the series would be interlarded with other sermons? Or was it perhaps a week of heavy snowfall that kept the people isolated in their houses? That it was again postponed on the next Sunday, January 19, is understandable: on the preceding day the pastor had been thrown into the deepest pit of despair by the unexpected death of his beloved Madeleine-Salomé.[35]

There is no available record of the Sunday service on the day after Mme Oberlin's death. Perhaps a colleague from Rothau or Barr or a friend from Strasbourg conducted the service. Nor do we have any details about the funeral on Tuesday, January 21, except that Madeleine-Salomé was interred near the church portal at Waldersbach. We do know, however, that on Sunday, January 26, Oberlin returned to the pulpit to preach the fourth sermon on the abodes of the blessed dead; and on that very day there occurred a mystic event that recurred intermittently during the next nine years.[36] The special, very private journal in which Oberlin recorded the experiences begins thus: "18 January 1783, Abigail's day, she died. ... On the 21st she was buried. On the 26th, in the night, she came and lay down beside me, in the guise of someone unknown; but her embraces, her kisses, the way her cheek pressed against mine, soon made me aware who she was, and the recognition poured a precious balm into my aching soul. ... 'You will be surprised,' she said, just before she vanished, 'how much I shall be with you.' "

"At first," the report continues, "the sorrow was nearly insufferable; I felt miserable, but without being ill, and my strength ebbed to such an extent that I could not walk without support. But then, gradually I felt the never failing comfort of God's presence, and my sorrow changed to a quiet, gentle, though melancholy devotion, mingled with praise and gratitude and the anticipation of our future eternal reunion."

Salomé made her presence known to her Fritz in many ways. Sometimes by day, when he chanced to extend a hand, he felt a gentle pressure on a finger, especially the little finger, and it reminded him how he and Salomé often, when passing each other in the hustle of their daily rounds, had been accustomed to exchange such brief private signals of affection. She came to him in various disguises. On February 20, 1783, for instance, she appeared "in the figure of my friend M. von Koch, Secretary of the Russian legation in Vienna. Our mutual joy was so great that we could not speak." Another time she appeared as his mother.

Soon she seemed to take over the functions of his personal guardian angel, in whose existence he had always believed and who had helped and sustained him in many a crisis. In that character she warned him of small mishaps, such as the leaking away of a precious wine from a defective cask in the cellar, and of larger calamities, like the impending collapse of a garden wall that might have caused mortal injuries. She counselled him, as she had always done, in the planning and execution of his work. Once, for instance, she warned him of the danger that a new project that he was about to start might not succeed if he should fail to bridle the tongue of the mercurial maid, Catherine Gagnière.

The journal entry for April 23, 1783, thirteen weeks after Mme Oberlin's death, is particularly notable because it is more specific than most.[37] It was Easter Sunday; the visitation is designated as the seventh, and as

the first in which she appeared in her own person: . . . For several days I had again suffered deeply in my spirits; my heart was torn and bleeding, my spirit was languishing. . . . The sources of my misery . . . were internal, for physically I was in good health. I had pleaded with God to grant me a true Easter festival, a resurrection from my sins, and had also prayed that I would be allowed to see and to speak with my beloved wife again. At the end of a refreshing night, she appeared as a vision in a dream. She was dressed as she usually was during her life. . . . She was as much taller than I was as I had been taller than she during her life, and when I walked with her I could not keep up . . . and I begged her to go more slowly, although I

understand that she wished to tell me by her rapid steps that
I ought to make greater haste in matters concerning my salvation.

She showed him paschal lambs that had been newly sacrificed
and told him that he, too, would be unable to withdraw himself
from such sacrifice. "For those who die before they have
allowed the effects of sacrifice to be fulfilled in them do not go
to their heavenly Master, but remain still in hands that are by
no means loving and gentle." He then led her through the midst
of the villagers into the church; but he was unable to determine
whether anyone either noticed this or saw his companion.
From then on, however, he felt that his wife could be, and
actually often was, with him, without, as she told him, being
seen by other living persons.

Rosenberg cites twenty-two specific visitations. There is no
point in repeating them all here; those that I have cited are
typical. Oberlin himself made a brief statement about them
which, together with the comments and examples given above,
afford a sufficient conception of what the visions were like. In
1824, long after the visitations had ceased, Dr. Gottlieb
Christian Barth, clergyman and physician of Möttlingen in
Württemberg, visited Oberlin and talked to him, among other
things, about his visions. Barth described the visit in a letter to
his friend and successor, Johann Christoph Blumhardt,
theosophist and millenarian, and also a friend of Oberlin's.
"When I saw Oberlin," Barth wrote, "he was eighty-four years
old. But that clear minded, sharp witted, classically educated
man, who treasured the Bible above all else, talked about the
invisible world as if he were at home there."[38] Oberlin told
Barth,

> After the death of my wife, I saw her almost daily, for nine
> years, both in dreams and awake, sometimes here where I was,
> sometimes in the place of her abode in the world beyond, and
> I learned from her remarkable things, including political
> events, long before they happened. But she did not appear only
> to me; she came also to other members of my household and
> many people of the Steintal, often warning them of impending
> misfortunes, foretelling things that were to come, and giving
> information about things that are beyond the grave. Then, in
> 1792, a farmer, Josef Müller of Belmont, was seeking contact

in the other world with his uncle, a man named Morel, who, together with his family, had often had visions. It happened that my deceased eldest son, Frédéric-Jérémie, escorted Müller to the place [in the afterworld] where his uncle was, and Frédéric told Müller that his (Frédéric's) mother had now been elevated to a higher abode of the blessed. He had instructed Müller to tell me that from now on she would not be able to appear on the earth.

Oberlin often used the word "dream" when speaking of these experiences, no matter whether they occurred during sleep by night or waking by day, but he testified that he could readily distinguish between them and all ordinary dreams "as one distinguishes one color from another." He never thought of them as being occult, or spiritualistic, or supernatural in character; there was nothing spectral, nothing eerie, nothing scary about them; he simply was aware of his wife's presence with all of his senses, as he would have been aware of her physical, living presence. At the same time, however, as he specifically stated, there was nothing carnal, nothing voluptuous about these encounters nor about his recurring desires to be in her company. He expressed no surprise that such visitations could happen; he was too familiar with the many theophanies reported in the Bible to have any doubts about their possibility. Such things as Jacob's vision of the ladder reaching into heaven with angels ascending and descending, or the apocalyptic revelations seen and described by St. John, or the countless repetitions in the biblical narrative of such phrases as, "an angel of the Lord appeared to him in a dream and said . . . "; all these were, in his strictly literal conception of the Scriptures, "gospel truth"; he believed in them just as he believed in such things as the virgin birth, the feeding of the 5,000, the changing of water to wine at Cana, and all the host of miracles recorded both in the Old and the New Testament.

The barrier, called death, between God's elect living in this world and the souls of the redeemed living in the next had never seemed to him great enough to make the breaching of it seem supernatural. In his adolescence he had written in his journal, on the subject of parting at death from his parents and others whom he loved: "It seems to me that, in dying, I will in no sense be separated from them; I see in it nothing but that the master of the house will show me another lodging, a little farther from that of my parents, which will bring it about that our visible discourse will be interrupted for a time. Meanwhile, we shall always be in the same house; I will be lodged nearer to the Lord, whose presence will be diffused throughout the house."[39] Furthermore, an English friend of the Oberlin family, recollecting a visit that he had made to the parsonage soon after the death of Frédéric-Jérémie, wrote: "[The family] spoke of their beloved Fritz not as someone deceased, whose loss one mourns, but as a friend who has passed from this life to the other, a friend whom one saw and heard and whom one would find again, sooner or later without fail. They felt the pain of the loss keenly, but consoled themselves with the thought of their reunion."

One's puzzlement about Oberlin's "visions" is compounded by the fact that he was not the only one who experienced them: on January 28, two days after Oberlin's first "dream," Madeleine-Salomé appeared to Sara Caquelin, "and soon," as Leenhardt puts it, "it was a real epidemic, and Oberlin, who wrote them all down, received accounts of these apparitions from all quarters. . . . People told how Madame had shown them their faults and had told them something of heaven, and there was produced a veritable flood of fantastic stories of which Oberlin does not always seem to have grasped the unhealthy and absurd nature and which for a long time left unhappy traces in their minds."[40] Leenhardt hints that Oberlin's own son, Charles-Conservé, "was in large measure a victim of these aberrations."[41]

It is, indeed, even more difficult to explain the apparitions seen by the people than it is to rationalize those of Oberlin himself. The only contribution that I, for my part, feel capable of making is to point out that in that closed, remote, and isolated subculture, Oberlin lived with these people almost as intimately as with his own children. The sobriquet *papa* that they bestowed upon him was not just a vacuous cliché; he was in all things their preceptor, their mentor, and their model, and he exercised profound influence over the actions and the thoughts of many, and even over the dreams and fantasies of some.

Furthermore, Oberlin was singularly exposed to a peril that has at all times and in all places threatened the intellectual and spiritual integrity of many a country parson, namely, the danger of rustication, of being absorbed in the primitive culture and patterns of thought of the environment. Superstitious tales of spectral apparitions and bizarre occurrences circulated in the Ban de la Roche as they have at all times in many similar communities. The young, city-educated pastor collected them, at first perhaps as a kind of folkloristic exercise, perhaps partly because he wanted to know the enemy superstition thoroughly, in order to combat it more effectively. Then gradually the stories began to beguile his own mind and to affect his own psyche. This process of absorption into the local folkways and mores is shown, perhaps, by his failure to see that while he was extracting many gross superstitions from the souls of his simple folk, he was implanting other errors of his own kind in their place. One fancies that one sees corroboration for this reading of the matter in the fact that the visions began to fade just when the great events of the revolutionary year 1789 captivated Oberlin's mind and broadened the horizon of his interests beyond the narrow intellectual confines of the little enclave that was his parish. Thereafter the visitations became less and less frequent until, in 1792, they came to an end with that message quoted above, to the effect that Madeleine-Salomé had been translated to a higher stage of existence that was allegedly inaccessible to earthly communication.

In attempting a summary evaluation of the causes and effects of these experiences, one cannot say that they are entirely negative. Indispensable to their existence were certain qualities of Oberlin's personality and character: particularly his extraordinarily deep spirituality, and his unshakeable faith in the Bible, literally interpreted, as an inerrant guide to wisdom about the nature of the universe and to his conduct of life at all "levels of existence." And it was exactly these same qualities that underlay the ultimate success of all the practical measures that he took to improve the conditions of life for his people. If those strange, mystical phenomena could be expunged from his life, his personality would seem less enigmatic to us, two centuries later; but without the character traits that sparked them and fueled them, his name and his deeds would probably have been erased from human memory long ago. His practical accomplishments stemmed from the same roots that nourished his apocalyptic imaginings.

It is also important to remember that those mystical experiences gave Oberlin the strength not only to endure a

great trial, but also to emerge from it with his character un-
scathed and his capabilities still equal to the great tasks that he
prosecuted and completed in the forty-four years of his
ministry after his wife's death.

In his summation of that phase of his life, Oberlin himself
did not suppress its negative aspects. In a sermon of 1787 he
declared: "One pays for visions by thorns in one's flesh and by
great suffering." And in another place he says, *"Avec des
visions on peut être damné"*—with visions one can be damned.
And if, in the end, we shake our heads and say, "I cannot
understand this," perhaps we can find some comfort in the
thought that Oberlin himself would not have expected us to
understand it: on the first page of the notebooks in which he
had recorded the visions, he wrote, "The friends who might by
chance see these leaves, which I write strictly for myself, are
asked to think of Christ's warning: 'Do not throw your pearls
to the pigs: they will only trample on them, and turn and tear
you to pieces.' "[42]

Our preoccupation in this chapter with mysteries and dark
enchantments may leave in some minds the impression that
Oberlin during the years after his wife's death must have taken
a kind of spiritual leave of absence from his terrestrial life and
his mundane concerns. That would be a serious misapprehension. It may well be that his quiet evening hours were often
occupied with reveries, his hours of sleep thronged with
phantoms and visions; and that sometimes interludes of
mental inactivity, as when riding or walking from village to
village or riding by night to Strasbourg and back, invited
strange meditations and idle fancies. Yet the world, take it all
in all, was still very much with him. The multitude of his social,
religious, and pedagogical projects continued to command,
and to receive, his alert and active participation. The cares of
his complex household were greater because of the absence of
his wife; for this he had to compensate by giving more time and
attention to the four little girls and three boys whom her death
had left motherless, as well as to the young women who lived at
the parsonage as teacher trainees, and to the boarding pupils,
who were also, in a sense, orphaned by the death of Mother
Oberlin.

There is no evidence that Oberlin experienced any mystical
visions after 1792. We know, however, that his interest in the
ways and scenes of the life after death continued, and surmise

that in times of quiet solitude he often longed for release from the world and its cares, as he had at many other times, beginning in his youth. In his sixties and early seventies, however, it became a less fervent longing than in those sorrowful nine years; but it returned again as an implacable yearning in the last decade of his life.

Part 4

Revolution and Liberation: 1789-1804

10

"Christian Patriotism"

In situations where questions arose concerning the relationships between individual citizens and established authority, Oberlin had one fixed rule of conduct, namely, the imperative set down by St. Paul and abundantly stressed by Luther: "Let every soul be subject to the higher powers. For there is no power but of God: the powers that be are ordained of God." (Rom. 13:1) As examples of the practical application of this precept, consider once more Oberlin's relations with that personage who, in the experience of his people, most immediately and most palpably represented the concept of political power, namely, the grand seigneur of the Ban de la Roche, Baron Jean de Dietrich.

It will be remembered that in 1772 there had been an ill-tempered correspondence between Oberlin and Dietrich. Now, in 1788, there was another exchange of unpleasant letters even more acrimonious in tone than the first. Relations between the two men in the intervening sixteen years had been tranquil enough, and as late as 1786-1787, Dietrich had made good his long-standing offer to build a new parsonage in Waldersbach at his expense.[1] (Oberlin himself had caused the building to be postponed by insisting that no new residence should be built for him until all the schools were decently housed.) In view of that generous act of good will, one is surprised at the haughty and sometimes insulting style in which the seigneur addressed his pastor in the very next year. Neither the magnitude of the new request that Oberlin was now making, nor the alleged delinquencies and derelictions that Dietrich threw up to him in his response, seem serious enough to justify the contumely and insolence of office that the baron's letters display.

The letter from Oberlin that opened the exchange is lost; it is therefore impossible to judge the style or tone in which it was written.[2] From Dietrich's reply it seems that Oberlin had informed him that a larger seating capacity was needed in the church at Belmont and had asked him to furnish from his forests, either gratis or at greatly reduced cost, the timbers needed to build a new gallery. Requests of this kind were an old story. The people of the Ban de la Roche believed that their proper share of the products of the forests had been illegally reduced through the years by the successive proprietors of the fief; the matter had been in litigation for almost a century. Dietrich, who was by far the most generous of all the lords that the little fiefdom had known, had in the past more often than not acceded to similar requests with good grace.

This time, however, he opens his testy reply with a sarcastic taunt in which he seems to impute to the suppliant something like sentiments of rebellion coupled with ecclesiastical delusions of grandeur. "It is too bad," he writes, "that you, *Monsieur le Ministre,* passed up the opportunity [some fourteen years earlier] to emigrate to the American colonies: you would surely have played an important role in the American insurrection and might actually have been crosiered and mitred there." Thereafter he lists eight major benefactions that he has bestowed on the Waldersbach parish during his tenure as proprietor, the cost of which amounted to 96,200 livres. He accuses Oberlin of ingratitude, "the most odious of all vices," of haughtiness bred by the exercise of authority that his clerical office allows him, and of inciting the people to disrespect for their seigneur. He objects to Oberlin's having reminded him of the sacredness of Holy Scripture. "Who questions that? If your intention is to attack my religion and morals, I would suggest to you that they are purer than yours. I don't believe that anyone would designate me as *a fanatic and a ridiculous visionary,* like you, nor have I ever scandalized people by making *equivocal and lubricious remarks, as you have done more than once at my table. I call upon other guests, notably the Catholic curé of Rothau,* and M. *Jaeger, as witnesses. More than once I was inclined to reproach you for this indecency.* . . . Your duty is to practice what you preach."

The italicized passages were underlined by Oberlin; and in the margin of the baron's letter he wrote, with a fat exclamation point: "Oh impudence inconceivable!"

The baron then emphatically turns down the "insistent demand" for building material: he will give it neither gratuitously, nor for any sum of money that Oberlin could collect from the people. Continuing in his sarcastic tone, he remarks that apparently the church has become too small "only since last spring," for he had heard nothing about it before that. In the end, however, he relents somewhat and says that, in order to "make an end to these stupid proposals and so that the people should no longer be deceived in their great delusion" concerning their rights to the forests, he will ask the sovereign Conseil d'Alsace to survey the forests of the Ban de la Roche and to release to the villages any forest lands in excess of 9,000 or 10,000 acres. "Here you have, *M. le Ministre*," he concludes, "the answer that your indecent letter deserves. I have written it in French so that you can easily communicate it to your parishioners. You may be assured that I accord justice to all your good qualities, and that I am very sincerely your humble and very obedient servant."

To this letter Oberlin replies with reasonable dignity and restraint, yet with firmness. Is it true, he asks, that he has incited the people to disrespect for the seigneur? No; precisely the opposite is the case. It is easy to calumniate a man: where and who are the calumniators in this case? Has the authority that he exercises in the community turned his head? Not at all: his enemies can say this only to people who do not live in the community; the villagers "do as they please and I am not consulted by them except in indifferent matters." (This, of course, is a crassly inaccurate estimation of his own authoritarian conduct.) He is "charmed" by the recital of the seigneur's past benefactions and again expresses gratitude for them. The baron, he grants, is indeed "not a ridiculous visionary"; the minister, for his part, believes in visions because he believes in the Holy Bible. "Where there are no visions, the people are lost." He closes his letter with a reiteration of his request regarding "the known subject, which is indeed within my province and my commission," and with assurances of his "most profound veneration" for the baron "as long as I shall breathe."

This letter elicited from Dietrich the reply that, much as he wished to be convinced that Oberlin's assurances of innocence were well founded and therefore did not justify his seigneur's reproaches, he could not do so. "In all the earldom public opinion is against you; you are considered generally as the dictator of your communities and they do not act according to your counsels." Meanwhile he has heard of

> the petition insolently addressed against me by trustee Bohy, your schoolmaster of Solbach, who never has acted but as your agent.[3] All the world was scandalized by it and has told me so, except you, who should have been the first to turn to me. If you should say that you knew nothing about it, you would offend the truth. . . . That action has aroused the ill will of my vassals, and they deserve it that I will henceforth be more economical with my benefactions and my bounty for them. The fief belongs to the king: I am obliged to maintain it in its entirety. It is not my fault if the residents possess nothing. . . . Their behavior now forces me to suspend the surveying of the forests. All your citations of Holy Scripture and all your invocations of God will be useless. . . . I consider myself, thanks to the efforts of your father,[4] well enough educated and sufficiently Christian to be able to do more for others than any theologian has yet accomplished.

He reiterated his declaration that, in view of all that he had done for the communities up to now, he would surely not help to build the new gallery in Belmont. He closed the letter, however, with a statement that he was willing "to forget all that has happened" and with new asseverations of his "old sentiments of amity and esteem." In the margin of this letter Oberlin wrote: "How shall one respond to this letter?!"

The rapid change in the mood of the feudal seigneur from generosity to obduracy, from benignity to truculence, can best be explained as a reflex of the times. Serfdom had virtually disappeared in France as a dominant economic and social mode of life except in a few remote enclaves such as the Ban de la Roche. In many areas, however, some feudal or manorial obligations remained to plague the peasants in the form of various fees and imposts collected by the landlord, and of tithes imposed by the church. With Baron de Dietrich's accession as seigneur of the Steintal in 1772, those fees and imposts had been lightened, so that, by contrast with their former condition, the peasants there had felt relieved and reaccommodated themselves, for the time being, to the feudal condition. The ancient conflict over forest and grazing rights, however, had remained, for both here and elsewhere in France landlords were inclined to recoup the losses they had incurred through the abolition of vassalage by new encroachments on various kinds of "common lands," where the peasants had traditionally grazed livestock, gathered firewood, and cut trees.

Dietrich's chief profits from his holdings in the Ban de la Roche came from the iron works in Rothau, and they depended on the availability of a steady supply of fuel, most of which came from the forests of the Steintal. The increase in productivity of the foundries under Dietrich's capable management called for an ever-increasing supply of wood, while at the same time the gradual growth of the peasant population also increased the demand for wood, both for construction of houses and for fuel to heat them in the long cold winters.

Pressures similar to these were being felt more or less all over France and were increasing rapidly as economic conditions steadily worsened in the last years of the decade. Thus even Baron de Dietrich, whose relatively benevolent and paternalistic policy probably had made him as secure in his position as any grand seigneur or landlord in France, must have read the signs and portents and shared the presentiments of disaster for the old system which had been, in varying degrees, the source and guarantee of the aristocracy's wealth since medieval times. It seems reasonable to suppose, therefore, that in 1788 the baron's actions and utterances were those of a man who sensed that the foundations of his great fortune and influence were cracking. It does not seem likely, however, that he had any presentiment of the swiftness with which disaster would overtake him and his family.

There is evidence of only one instance before the Revolution of 1789 when Oberlin fell into conflict with a superior authority other than his seigneur. The Conseil souverain d'Alsace, in response to defamatory reports received from unnamed persons, charged Oberlin with having encouraged French citizens to emigrate to Poland and called him to account for that misdemeanor. Oberlin responded to the summons, of course, and appeared before the court at

Colmar.[5] There he testified that two citizens of a neighboring community had come to him with a placard, printed in German, that had recently been posted in their town, and had asked him to translate it for them. He refused *"absolument"* and remonstrated with them, as he had "a thousand times" with his own parishioners, that: "Anyone who is willing to work will be better supplied with his daily bread in his own country than elsewhere." The visitors, however, persisted in their request, saying that they themselves were not actually thinking of emigrating, but the placard had attracted so much attention that they were curious to know exactly what it said. Oberlin then scanned it and saw that it was addressed only to subjects of the German Reich and that it specifically stated that any prospective emigrants would be required to show certifications of German citizenship from both their seigneurs and their *magistrats supérieurs.* Thereupon he gladly translated the document, for he considered it his duty "to prevent any poor deluded person from getting into trouble out of ignorance of what was required." He had one of his pupils make a copy of the original German placard, gave that to the visitors with his translation, circulated the original among the *régents d'écoles* for their information—calling particular attention to the legal conditions—and thereafter destroyed it.

In his concluding statement to the court Oberlin testified: "The surest way to protect the people from being led into temptation is to conceal nothing, to avoid the appearance of being either despotic or secretive, and to disseminate clarifying commentaries about such seductive invitations." The incident ended with the *conseil* expressing to Oberlin its apologies for having discommoded him and with compliments of respect on account of his conduct in the affair.

As the great events of 1789 began to unfold, Oberlin found more and more occasion to exercise his habit of making discussions of public affairs a part of the weekly prayer meetings and church services. After the historic meeting of the States-General the reapportionment of power among the social classes became the subject of general conversation, and rumors passed through the land that there were to be no more bishops, nor seigneurs, nor tithes, nor dues, no more titles nor distinctions. And so, eventually, Oberlin also felt impelled to declare his position on that subject. As a loyal Lutheran minister, he preserved his deep respect for personal liberty, and, at the same time, his commitment to good order. The following paragraphs from a sermon give an example of his wrestlings with that ubiquitous and eternal dilemma.

The differences in the estates of man are indispensable in a thousand ways to good order and to the prosperity of life. Differences must exist between masters and manservants, mistresses and maidservants, between superiors and inferiors, between kings and subjects. These differences are subject to the same law as differences in appearance, in body, in character, talent, and ability. One person, for instance, will have more intellect [*esprit*] than another and will be more capable of comprehending things and their combinations in their entirety and to formulate plans for the prosperity of all and will therefore have greater ability to command. Another will be physically stronger and will therefore be more capable of performing those labors for the common good that require strong bodies and sinewy limbs. Thus each has powers and capabilities for the common good that another lacks, and it is proper and right that each is entitled to the respect and esteem of the other. *Voilà,* nature itself is based on that law. So, the more closely differences of character and condition conform to that law, the more productive they will be of good order, of harmony, and of prosperity for the public.

All this is incontestable, and whoever presumes to abolish that difference and to introduce equality in places where nature itself has established variety, does not know what he wills: he wills something that is not good, something that is not possible.

If the sermon had ended here, one would have the impression that Oberlin must surely have been an unconditional defender of the old regime, an apologist for the privileged aristocracy with all its wanton abuses of power. The next paragraph, however, establishes the ground on which he could support the nascent new order; could support it not only nominally, but with an enthusiasm little diminished by this and other strictures which his interpretation of God's will imposed upon him.

But also incontestable is the fact that the father of lies, the prince of this age, who from the beginning of the world to this day has sought to throw everything into confusion, always under the appearance of a splendid order, has desecrated these necessary and useful distinctions of class and in a thousand ways has brought society to a state of confusion and misery by misusing that which ought to create tranquility, peace, and prosperity.[6]

Oberlin goes on to describe the countless "maneuvers and manipulations that human beings have used to enslave each other, and to consolidate the differences that exist between them by prejudicial laws and by exaggerated judgments that are contrary to and abusive of all good order." He contrasts this state of affairs with the kingdom of Jesus Christ which will prevail in eternity and which all men should seek to establish also on earth, a kingdom "which is based on devotion, on sacrifice of one's self, and in which he is always the greatest who is the servant of all."[7]

Oberlin accepted the slogans of the Revolution and used them often in his public addresses, but to him "Liberté, égalité, fraternité" meant neither the forcible removal of superior authority, nor the abolition of private property; the ideal on which his eyes were fixed was even loftier—and thus even more unattainable—than that of the revolutionary activists who were eventually to accuse him of opposition to their aims. To him revolution connoted a transformation not only in the social order, but in the heart of every citizen of whatever degree and station. His ideal society was not necessarily a classless state, but one in which the concept of special privilege, irrespective of class, was displaced by the ideal of universal love, humility, and mutual devotion. While he surely conceived of democracy as being closer to his ideal than feudalism, he did not consider dispossession as essential to the establishment of the kingdom of God on earth.

Although he customarily ascribed to the watchwords of the Revolution his own deviant interpretation, thus using them in a special, one might even say Pickwickian, sense, it would not be fair to accuse him of either obscurantism or hypocracy, for he repeatedly and abundantly explained his meaning. Consider, as one example among many, a communication of 1794 addressed to the young adults of all the congregations in his parish.[8]

> I desire that the numerous members of the French Republic
> should be animated by truly republican sentiments; I wish them
> to understand that public happiness constitutes private happi-
> ness, and that every individual ought therefore to endeavor to
> live for the public good; and to remember that their actions
> will only secure the favor and love of God, *according to the
> motives with which they are performed* [emphasis added].

From there he went on to say explicitly what he meant by the
word "republican."

> We are Republicans when we neither live, nor act, nor under-
> take anything, nor choose a profession or situation, nor settle
> in life, except for the common good. . . . We are Republicans
> when out of love for the public, we endeavor, by precept and
> example, to stimulate our children to active beneficence and
> seek to render them useful to others. . . . We are Republicans
> when we . . . imbue our children's minds with the love of science
> and any knowledge that will make them more useful in the
> stations which they will occupy and when we teach them to love
> their neighbors as themselves. We are Republicans when we
> preserve our children from that self-indulgent spirit that seems
> once more to have gained ascendancy over the nation. . . . God
> grant that the Republic and all true Republicans may prosper.

The chief change in his rhetoric was that now he used the
term "good republicans" where formerly he had spoken of
"good Christians"; his definitions of the new term, however,
were the same as those for the old; a community of "true
republicans" (in his own meaning of the phrase) was now
equated with his persisting ideal of *ein Gottesvolk*. It is
utterances such as those cited here that have led Heinsius to
remark that "the great and often abused words: liberty,
equality, and fraternity, had, when they came from his lips, a
more genuine sound and a deeper meaning."[9]
The singularity of Oberlin's interpretations of the revolutionary slogans had but little effect on the intensity of the
fervor of his patriotism. Distracted now by the events of 1789,
he tore his eyes away from those mystical visions of paradise
that had so long beguiled him and turned both his dreamings
and his energies again, and with renewed vigor, to the affairs of
this world and to the realization of his daily prayer: "Thy

kingdom come; Thy will be done *on earth* as it is in heaven."
One of his immediate objectives now was to arouse among the
people an enthusiasm for the new order equal to his own—and
incidentally, perhaps, to create opportunities to direct the
general enthusiasm into what he considered to be the proper
channels, namely, those that would lead to the realization of
his persisting aim to establish God's kingdom on earth. Among
the means that he used to attain that end were patriotic
festivals, for which he had a great fondness and in the design
and execution of which he showed considerable skill. One
occasion for such a fete was the first anniversary of Bastille
Day, July 14, 1790. For it he built an "altar of the fatherland"
on the plateau of the Perheu, to which the whole community
repaired in a festive procession for the swearing in of the newly
elected communal officials and a service of thanksgiving.

The greatest festival of all, however, fell on November 13,
1791, when the adoption of the constitution, limiting the power
of the king and establishing a legislative body, was celebrated.
At that time there was no objection in Alsace to the participation of the clergy in political celebrations. The Catholic
priests, to be sure, had been compromised and placed in a
difficult position by the flight of their bishop, Cardinal de
Rohan, but nearly all the Protestant ministers took the oath of
allegiance. (In Strasbourg, Stuber was even placed in a
position of political responsibility by being elected to the first
constitutional council of that city.) So it seemed only natural in
the Ban de la Roche that Oberlin should lead the people in this
celebration, as he led them in all things else. The festival is
described in detail by Stoeber, who had himself been an active
participant in it.[10] Its site was the church at Fouday and the
program included the investiture of the new constitutional
maires and elders. The whole community gathered in the
church and on the hillock around it. The act of investiture was
performed at the altar with Oberlin decorating each initiate
with the tricolored sash as the symbol of his office. After words
of admonition and prayer he sent the company of the fifteen
officials thus decorated to fetch the constitutional documents
and emblems from the chief elder's house. The church bell
began to ring and the drums to beat as the fifteen marched out
of the church; and those rhythmic accompaniments continued
until they came marching back to the altar with banners
unfurled and the chief elder, now walking in the midst of the

company, carrying the documents. These were ceremoniously laid on the altar and the congregation knelt in a prayer of thanksgiving for the gift of liberty and in petitions for protection and guidance of the new government by the Lord of nations, who had "miraculously brought down the greatest by the strength of the least and disarmed the mighty by the power of the weak." Thereafter Oberlin delivered an address in which he compared the revolutionary movement with his own paraphrase of the prophet's vision of a stone that had not been loosed by hands of man, but in falling had shattered to dust the monstrous colossus of the aristocracy and the Antichrist, so that they would be "swept away like chaff before the wind from a threshing floor in summer until no trace of them remained," that "the stone would grow into a great mountain filling the whole earth," and that "the God of heaven will establish a kingdom which shall never be destroyed." At the end of his discourse he pronounced the benediction thus:

> The Lord bless all those who are devoted to the founding of His kingdom and watch over them;
> The Lord make His face to shine upon the friends of the constitution and of the public welfare and humble and convert all those who love only themselves and their own families;
> The Lord lift up the light of His countenance upon France and upon the whole earth and establish His peace upon it and unite all peoples under the scepter of Jesus Christ, the exalted Lord of the whole universe. Amen!

Was ever the priestly blessing paraphrased in more patriotic terms? And was there anywhere on that great festival day in all of France another orator who took his theme from the second chapter of Daniel? At this stage Oberlin saw the Revolution as nothing less than the veritable coming of God's kingdom on earth.

Less than a year later, when the newly won freedom of the nation seemed to be threatened, when Austria and Prussia had declared war on France, and the young hotspurs of his parish were joining their compatriots in the general rush to the colors, Oberlin could not let the recruits go without a send-off in the form of a special religious service. In his sermon on that occasion he reviewed with the young men, all of whom he knew as well as he knew his own children, the precepts of patriotic

Christian conduct that he had instilled in them. He admonished them to be models for other soldiers:

> You have had a general education and religious instruction such as most of your future comrades in arms have not had. Therefore you shall be a lamp to their feet, an example, a model of conduct. Let all the people whom you meet know by your behavior that there are no more excellent people than those who live by the gospel. . . . Remember that God, our God, the God of the French constitution, the God of arms and of victories, is a God of love. . . . When you enter a strange land, remember that we are not enemies of the people there. . . . The French princes, the deserters, the emigrés, and the King of Prussia and the German Emperor are our enemies, but their subjects are not. . . . Be compassionate toward them, be fair and just to everyone. . . . And if any one of you should find his grave far away from here, he will know that the lands to which our God and our duties have led us are always those that are nearest to heaven.[11]

These, one remembers, are the words of a man who had himself once made up his mind to go to a land across the sea because his duty seemed to call him there. And they acquire a greater poignancy when one remembers that almost exactly a year later, Oberlin's own eldest son, Frédéric-Jérémie, died as a soldier in the first battle in which he was engaged.

But his patriotism did not by any means exhaust itself only in ceremonials and oratory. Consider, for example, the affair of the assignats.[12] The new revolutionary government found that many essential things were in short supply. The most embarrassing shortage of all was cash. To redeem the huge public debt and to reduce the growing deficit, the National Assembly issued, on December 9, 1789, treasury notes at 5 percent, called assignats, in the amount of 400 million livres. These were intended as short-term obligations pending the sale of confiscated crown and church lands. They were made legal tender in April 1790, and thereafter bore no interest. Inflation followed; by 1796 there were 39 billion livres in circulation with an actual value of less than the cost of printing them.

Oberlin anticipated that development early, and his quick and energetic reaction is strikingly symptomatic of some of his chief characteristics: his loyalty to the revolutionary government, his lofty sense of national honor, his literal adherence to the Christian ethic, and his naiveté in matters pertaining to political economy. As early as February 15, 1792, he preached a sermon in which he admonished the people to keep the assignats in circulation, and to deal in them only at their face value. He described them as IOUs of the nation for which the whole population, through its deputies, had in good faith pledged not only its property, but also its faith and honor. Anyone who would acquire assignats at a reduced price, seeking to gain a selfish profit thereby, he said, was not only unfaithful to his mandate that Christians should act only in accordance with the public good, but was also an enemy of the kingdom of Christ, which was in constant conflict with the powers of darkness; while anyone who kept faith with the assignats was a patriot, and "every true Christian is a patriot."

Oberlin probably never labored under any delusion that the idealistic measures he urged on his little flock would ever be emulated on a scale sufficient to have a palpable effect on the nation's fiscal condition; yet his conviction of the rightness of his view of the matter was so great that, as the rate of inflation accelerated, he sought some effective means by which he could keep the conscience of his people clean in the midst of general debasement. On May 30 he initiated a procedure which, in its simplicity, has the stamp of genius. All citizens, both male and female, he said, should make up their minds that every time they use a five-livre assignat to pay an obligation or to make a purchase they will voluntarily make a small contribution toward maintaining the honor of France by taking a voluntary loss of two sous in the transaction. Thus, when an assignat has changed hands fifty times (one livre equalling 20 sous; 5 livres, therefore, equalling 100 sous), its value will have been reduced to zero and it will therefore be equivalent to a note of hand given by the nation that is now extinguished, that is to say, paid in full; yet no one will have suffered a calamitous personal loss along the way. Thus, he said, it would be possible for all the citizens to contribute to the gradual retirement of the assignats and therewith to the "liberation of all righteous persons from the rapacious claws of blackhearted speculators." He therefore called on all patriotic and honorable citizens to bring to him all assignats in their possession. Learning from them at what price each one had been acquired, he would write that figure on the reverse side of each, so that no one to whose hand it might thereafter come could cheat by demanding a higher price for it. From then on its value would be reduced by two sous with each transaction and its new, lower value written on the reverse side "in small but legible figures." For anyone who might find that a too difficult task, Oberlin offered "the services of my pen."

"By this means," he wrote, "every poor but honorable citizen will be able each time to make a contribution of two sous to the nation and the constitution because he expends the assignat for two sous less than he paid for it. And since the constitution obviously is of God himself, the citizen thus makes the meritorious sacrifice also to Him. Furthermore, he performs an act of charity to all the poor of the nation and, at the same time, strikes a blow against the devil and his cohorts, the dastardly and execrable speculators who practice their usury with the sweat of the poor and the blood of widows and orphans."

In order to promote this, his own kind of dealing in assignats, Oberlin laid in a store of goods—agricultural implements, clothing, wooden shoes, prayer books and hymnals, schoolbooks and supplies, and the like—for the people to buy using as currency the discounted assignats. Once he had got his system established in his parish, and apparently unaware that it could work there only because of the singular isolation of the community, he optimistically brought it to the attention of the National Convention. "The people in these hills," he wrote, "can now buy neither eggs nor butter unless they have silver coins, not because of disdain for the assignats (for we have here many enlightened and eager patriots), but because we cannot buy with them the grain and fodder that we lack." One is not surprised that that body did not forthwith decree the national adoption of the Oberlin system for retiring the assignats; but it did enter in its protocol of 19 Frimaire, year III (December 9, 1795), a resolution to "make honorary mention of the civic sacrifice made by the citizens of the Ban de la Roche by printing the description of the plan in the daily Report of Correspondence, and by reporting the ingenious invention to the committee on finance, in order to make known to them this freewill offering of poor men's mites to the sum of moneys that have been set aside for retiring the assignats that are still in circulation. Resolution adopted."

The government finally found its way out of the imbroglio by demonetizing all paper currency and redeeming the assignats at 3,000 livres to one franc in gold. All unredeemed assignats were then declared void on May 21, 1797. Oberlin, however, in order to give his honest folk something of value in return for their dwindling assignats, using funds from his tithe box to continue purchasing goods to be resold to them, steadfastly continued on the course that he had conceived to be right long after the Republic itself had repudiated the assignats as legal tender. As the soiled and ragged old chits one by one came down to zero, he wrote across the face of each: "Praise be to God; another debt of honor of the nation has been paid!" The last of the assignats was thus honorably retired in 1818, twenty-one years after the state had summarily repudiated its legal responsibility for them.

As a way of coping with the problems of the national economy, Oberlin's action seems surely a futile exercise, a quixotic venture in naive idealism. Yet for themselves, both Oberlin and those who faithfully went with him to the end must just as surely have found personal satisfaction in the thought that "he that is faithful in that which is least is faithful also in much." To appreciate the full scope of Oberlin's own sacrifice in this business, one must recall that during the years of revolution his salary was virtually zero; he and his family lived on the tuition fees of his boarding pupils.

Of the beginning of the general traffic in assignats Carlyle wrote:

> So now, while old rags last, there shall be no lack of circulating medium: whether of commodities to circulate thereon, is another question. But after all, does not this Assignat business speak volumes for modern science? Bankruptcy, we may say, was come, as the *end* of all Delusions needs must come: yet come gently, in softening diffusion, in mild succession, was it hereby made to fall;—like no all-destroying avalanche; like gentle showers of a powdery impalpable snow, shower after shower, till all was indeed buried, and yet little was destroyed that could not be replaced, be dispensed with! To such length has modern machinery reached. Bankruptcy, we said, was great; but indeed Money itself is a standing miracle.[13]

What terms, one wonders—of irony? of admiration?— would Carlyle have found, if he had known of it, to describe the wondrous invention of the visionary vicar of Waldersbach in the wilderness of the Ban de la Roche?

11

Citizen Oberlin

The anticlericalism of the revolutionary regime created new problems for the churches in the Ban de la Roche, as it did in all of France. Yet, even after the defamation of Christianity and the desecration of the churches had begun, Oberlin persisted in his support of the government. There can be no doubt that it was a time of great tribulation and trial for him, but he found comfort and strength for the ordeal both in the Bible and in the history of the early church as it is recorded by St. Paul. In his sermons and other discourses he often dwelt, during this time, on the primitive Christians as a model of conduct for believers in all times of persecution. On one occasion he said: "Those who refuse spiritual aid have never known its value and therefore have nothing to lose; but those who have inner resources will now discover them." Thus, in respect to the persecutors of the church, he could speak in the words of Jesus on the cross: "Forgive them, for they know not what they do." Another source of strength was his basically optimistic spirit, which would have enabled him to speak, if he had known of them, in the words of his contemporary Warren Hastings: "This, too, shall pass." For he believed that excessive passions would be moderated, and in the end the cause of religion would emerge purified and strengthened. On one occasion he was even able to express this sentiment in jocular terms. When he was asked, by someone whom Mlle de Berckheim identifies only as *Citoyenne* D., what he thought of the state's subversion of religion, he answered:

What we are going through is like a great Saturday house-cleaning. Everything is to be made beautiful for the coming Sunday: the furniture is removed from the rooms, a great dust is stirred up, everything is set topsy-turvey, there is much beating and brushing; the disorder is terrible; one breathes in a cloud of dust; one feels as if he were living in a hovel. . . . But everything is put to rights again; the salon is restored; the furnishings are replaced one by one; order and propriety emerge from disorder as a fruit of the great upheaval that at first seemed so terrible. Sunday comes, and all is lovely and shining. The master of the house, who had moved out on Saturday, returns, and I do believe he thinks, even if he doesn't say so, that everything is lovelier than it had been on the preceding Friday.[14]

Oberlin kept abreast of political events by diligently reading the newspapers, which, as always, he shared and discussed with the people. Another source of information was his correspondence with the Abbé Grégoire, which continued despite the fact that Grégoire was now one of the leading members of the National Convention and the most important clerical personage in France. At about the time that the abbé was leading the convention to its adoption of his resolution to abolish the monarchy, he wrote a warm, fraternal letter, in which he thanked Oberlin for having written him "the latest news from the Ban de la Roche," and asked him to join with him "in hating the race of kings, for they have done only evil in the world, still do only evil, and will continue to do nothing but evil" until they are utterly destroyed. "I say to you, I would prefer the ten plagues of Egypt to one king; my heart shudders when I think of that horde of royal evildoers."[15] The abbé also expressed his nostalgic desire to lay down the burdens of office and refresh his soul for a brief season in the quietness of the parson's study in Waldersbach. Seeing no prospect of such fulfillment, however, he closes his letter with: "Hail to all the Steintal! Keep writing to me about the progress of morals, of knowledge, and of industry in your parish, and be assured that my love for you is as great as is my hatred of kings."

As ardently as Oberlin supported the Republic and prayed for the confounding of its enemies, his rhetoric never rose to so high a pitch of emotion as that displayed by the good abbé. Compared with it, Oberlin's homely image of "the torment" as a rousing good housecleaning creates an impression of naive innocence. There was, of course, a difference in the circumstances in which the two vicars of Christ were living and in the immensity of the provocations to which each was exposed. Unfortunately, we have none of the letters that went from the parsonage of Waldersbach to the legislative halls of Paris, but the tone and content of the abbé's letters show that he found strength and comfort in the messages that came to him from that tranquil source.

But in 1793, the hot breath of the Reign of Terror began to be felt in the Steintal, too. In December of that year Oberlin was enjoined by officers of the district *directoire* at Barr to appear before the *Comité de sûreté générale* in Strasbourg for the purpose of making his profession of political faith. He rose to the challenge without hesitation or fear. Following is the statement that he wrote out for oral delivery on that occasion.

> I scarcely know on which articles of the Constitution my explications are desired.
>
> I approve absolutely of the rigorous way in which the infamous speculations in assignats has been stopped. These assignats; I respected and cherished them from the beginning as a happy means of saving the fatherland.
>
> I approve absolutely of the abolition of empty ceremonies, and of the banishment of all dogmas of religion that are sterile, unfruitful, and serve only to create strife.
>
> I have always restricted myself in my teaching to that which enlightens my brethren and makes them more virtuous, more diligent, good patriots, good parents, good soldiers, zealous republicans, yet faithful and commendable in all situations.
>
> The *rabbat* and robe that I formerly wore I took off some time ago at a public service; I have always felt repugnance against wearing those vain distinctions.
>
> As regards the question of royalty, I am firmly of the opinion that it should be absolutely abolished. It was several years ago that I began to instill republican sentiments in my auditors.[16]

It is impossible to know whether Oberlin added anything to these remarks when he stood before the *comité,* but it does not seem likely that he did. One has the impression that he wrote down his thoughts in such explicit terms, rather than as disjointed notes such as he used when preaching, exactly because he wanted to avoid the danger of making an indiscreet utterance extempore.

Whatever else may have been said in the course of the hearing, the decision was probably strongly influenced by the testimonial that the *Comité de surveillance* of Waldersbach had sent to its parent body. It certified that citizen Oberlin during the twenty-six years of his ministry had shown himself to be "a rare human being." "He has devoted himself with all that he is and all that he has to the relief of the indigent; he has preached not only in his sermons, but also by his example the true maxims of the Supreme Being; ever since we have been fortunate enough to have a Constitution, he has accepted it with a joyful heart; he has done everything possible to encourage our young men to go to its defense, has explained it to us and taught us to accept it and to love it. He has always expressed the sentiments of a true republican."

This document, signed by the five members of the committee, was dated December 18, 1793. Three days later the incident was closed with the laconic response from Barr: "Seen, verified, and approved," and signed by the four members of the *Comité de sûreté générale*.

By the end of 1793 anticlerical activities in France had reached their highest intensity. Churches across the land were plundered, many were destroyed, and others were put to use as powder magazines and cavalry stables. After the execution of Louis XVI, royalist insurrections broke out in the Vendée and spread to other *départements* of the west central region. Civil strife descended to depths of savage slaughter such as only religious causes seem capable of evoking in internecine wars. Everywhere the communions of the faithful lived in apprehension and fear. The Ban de la Roche was still relatively quiet, but a shudder of anxiety seized many hearts there when the community was suddenly deprived of the comfort and strength that it was accustomed to receive from its pastor: on January 20, Oberlin fell seriously ill of what he later referred to as *ein Faulfieber, une fièvre putride.* That designation is, of course, too vague to give any idea of the nature of the disease; one thinks of typhoid, but it is impossible to know in the absence of any further information. The illness lasted about ten weeks, from January 20 to March 30. For many days the patient lay in imminent danger of death. On the day that he resumed his duties, he walked to the altar supported by two of the elders.

Meanwhile the opposition to the churches and the clergy had grown ever more virulent. In Strasbourg the most rabid Jacobins had mounted their campaign against the mayor, Jean de Dietrich's son Frédéric, which ended in his decapitation. The office of chief prosecutor of the revolutionary courts had been captured by the notoriously bloodthirsty Eulogius Schneider, formerly vicar of the constitutional bishop Brendel; and the guillotine, erected in front of the hotel Maison Rouge on the present Place Kléber, had begun to perform its gory function. Most of the Strasbourg churches were requisitioned as warehouses for the military quartermaster corps. On November 17, 1793, all public services of worship in Strasbourg were interdicted; soon thereafter the minster became the Temple of Reason; the episcopal seminary was used as a prison in which both Catholic and Protestant clergymen were incarcerated. Professor Jérémie-Jacques Oberlin was arrested on the instigation of Louis de Saint-Just, and along with the other members of the city council was transported in chains to Metz, where all were imprisoned as "traitors to the Constitution." In the outlying towns and villages of Alsace, the churches had either been closed or converted into clubhouses in which every ten days "educators of the people" lectured on the principles of "natural morality." Some ministers and priests resigned their office and took up secular vocations, some even renounced their faith, while others stood firm and went secretly to private homes to baptize children and administer communion to the faithful or extreme unction to the dying.

Amid all this turmoil and persecution, Oberlin seemed, for a time at least, to enjoy a kind of immunity. The two things that had made this possible were the isolation of his little community, and the loyalty to him of both the majority of the people and of the newly elected civil authorities. But these could not protect him throughout the time of ever-increasing terror.

When, in April 1794, all churches were finally closed, Oberlin did not choose to "enter the melee of political demonstrations" against that edict; nor did he subside into a dishonorable indifference that would have resulted in meek submission to the fait accompli. In 1792 he had applied for, and had been granted, a license that allowed him to practice any vocation that he wished. It is presumed that his chief reason for seeking the license had been that his having it would prevent any injunctive action against him for engaging without authorization in the kind of trade within the community that made the business of retiring the assignats possible, namely, the buying and selling of merchandise. His possessing the license now might incidentally have made it easier for him to take up vocationally one or another of the trades that he had learned to practice as an amateur for the benefit of the community, and thus a change of vocation might have been less difficult for him than it proved to be for many ecclesiastics who took that course. It was, however, a road that Oberlin could not possibly have travelled; both his dedication to the ministry and his loyalty to the community made it unthinkable. The decision that he did make was to remain at his post and serve his people and his God as best he could, compromising where necessary on nonessential points, yet never denying the fundamental rightness of his faith, regardless of the consequences. That decision he carried through with such success that many people marvelled at the adroitness with which he managed to follow the advice of Jesus to the apostles, as he sent them forth as sheep in the midst of wolves: "Be ye wise as serpents, and harmless as doves."

In his journal he wrote on this subject: "I was forbidden by the revolutionary government of Robespierre and the Jacobins to perform any ministerial functions whatsoever. I therefore established a club in place of the divine services in order, under that name, to continue our assemblies."[17] He called the new organization the *Club populaire*. The government had decreed that meetings should be held in each community, at which an elected orator should speak on subjects such as the Declaration of the Rights of Man and of the Citizen, the new constitution, and the rational doctrine of a Supreme Being. The club was to be the instrument for compliance with the decree.

The first meeting, called by Oberlin for the purpose of organizing the club, was held in the Waldersbach schoolhouse. Since the room was too small to seat those who had responded to the call, Oberlin had no difficulty in making the point that a better hall for the meetings hereafter would be the Temple of Reason and the Eternal, as the churches were now officially called. Agreed: the churches would now be the clubhouses.

Now, he said, we must have a president and a secretary, and we should select men who have held office in other clubs and therefore know how to function. The schoolmasters Sébastien Scheidecker and David Bohy, who held offices also in the Agricultural Society, were proposed as copresidents, and Jean Claude as secretary. They were elected.

The secretary was then asked to read the resolutions of the district of Benfeld, which, according to the decree of 8 Nivose, were to be the general mode for organizing people's clubs. They were adopted as bylaws. The next item on the agenda was election of the principal orator. No one in the community was as well qualified for that office as citizen Oberlin. He was elected.

The schedule of meetings was discussed next. The new revolutionary calendar divided each thirty-day month into three *décades,* and a decree of the National Convention gave the last day of each *décade* the name *décadi* and proclaimed it as a day of rest. The bylaws called for a meeting on each *décadi.* Some *clubistes,* however, objected that such an arrangement would be contrary to the laws of God ("six days shalt thou labor"). Citizen orator Oberlin took the floor. He quoted from the second chapter of Paul's letter to the Colossians: "Let no man therefore judge you in meat, or in drink, or in respect of any holy day, or of the new moon, or of the sabbath days." Then, launching into his first discourse as principal orator in the Temple of Reason, he proved to the satisfaction of all that resting and going to meeting is as pleasing to the Eternal on *décadi* or tennight as it is on sabbath or sennight. *Décadi* was adopted by a majority vote as the meeting day and a day of rest.

Continuing his discourse, citizen Oberlin said that he saw a possibility of interpreting the bylaws in such a way that they would not seem to prohibit the celebration of communion. What did the citizens think about that? After considerable general discussion it was decided that it would not be wise at this stage to do anything other than conform literally to the regulations. Oberlin was in full agreement with that decision. "But you must not think," he said, "that just because we cannot celebrate communion together publicly here in the Temple of the Eternal, we can simply dispense with that most important sacrament." He then gave an oration in which he told how the apostles and their converts celebrated the rite of the last supper secretly in their own homes and suggested to the *clubistes* that they go and do likewise. If a family had not enough confirmed adults to make a proper celebration and wished to invite guests, it was meet and right so to do; for the pleasure of doing whatever he desired to do in his home was one of the celebrated rights of man. Take the bread that the Eternal has given you, he advised, cut it in small pieces on a plate and pour a cup or a glass of wine; read the words of institution from the book of Matthew; then let the householder offer the bread and let the cup go around; read the communion prayer from the prayer book and, if it can be done, sing a hymn. Thus did our forefathers celebrate their communion in the first Christian congregations.

At the conclusion of the oration, citizen Oberlin announced that a fellow citizen had died, leaving unpaid debts. If the friends and neighbors of the deceased would together assume the burden of paying those debts, they would not only be acting according to the will of the Supreme Being, but would also promote the republican ideals of *égalité* and *fraternité*.

If one remembers that in his own mind and heart—and with his own peculiar interpretations—Oberlin virtually equated the Rights of Man and the constitution with the kingdom of God on earth, it is not difficult to imagine the many ways in which he used the *Club populaire* as an instrument to serve the purposes of both divine and secular authority. A single example of a combined church service and club meeting will suffice. Fortunately, we have a detailed description of such a meeting from the journal of Mlle de Berckheim, who was living at that time at Rothau as a refugee from the Terror.

"We had come just in time to hear the catechizing of the young folk; the girls, standing in one line, and the boys in another, were being interrogated in the presence of the whole community by one of the *clubistes*. The subject was the Rights of Man, which all the young folk knew by heart."

The president then read the minutes of the meeting on the previous *décadi,* which mentioned a discourse by one of the members. The same member was then called upon to continue with that which he had not had time to say at the preceding meeting. Oberlin, who was sitting in one corner of the *clubistes'* pews, took off his greatcoat and mounted the "tribune," which was the pulpit. He began with a prayer, as he had always done at the beginning of a divine service. Mlle de Berckheim "admired him because his discourse was so well suited to his people in their present situation; also because it took courage to speak, in these times, as he did. . . . I saw in him again the same man whom I had known before, with the same holy enthusiasm, the same frank and original mode of expression that finds its way to every heart. After the sermon there was again a prayer; the whole congregation kneeling, most of the women with their faces buried in their hands."

Thereafter a citizen took the floor. He uttered some reflections on the abuse of liberty and commented on new developments to which the new freedom had given birth. These included a report on a new method of tanning hides that offered great time-saving advantages. He also mentioned the telegraph.

"After that there was the reading of the village news, and at the end the *Klingelbeutel* was passed for the benefit of the poor. The *clubistes* then stayed for a continuation of the meeting, but the women and the young people streamed out in a great crowd."[18]

The differences between the Sunday services that had become traditional in the Ban de la Roche and the meetings of the *Club populaire* were neither numerous nor substantive. There had always been services of worship that included catechization of the young and in which the questioning had by no means been limited to subjects that were strictly religious, except in the sense that Oberlin, with his views on the unity of all life, ascribed religious significance to all things and all actions. Thus the public examinations of the young confirmands had included all the subjects taught in school, while in his sermons the minister had never hesitated to weave into his discourse whatever subject seemed to him to be in need of airing for the good of the people or for the prospering of their earthly labors. Also the reading, and sometimes the discussion, of the news of the day had been part of the weekly order of service. Although Oberlin did conform to official edicts to the extent of suspending the public celebration of the Christian sacraments, he promoted and participated in their observance in private homes, and the prayers that he spoke at the *décadi* club meetings were unmistakably Christian in form and content.

Once the *Club populaire* was organized and functioning as a cryptoecclesiastical instrument, Oberlin probably felt less inhibited and frustrated by the interdiction of religious observances than by that of his pedagogical activities. His complaints about this were frequent and vigorous, until finally, through the good offices of the district *agent nationale,* M. Stamm, he managed to bring the matter to the attention of highly placed personages in Paris and ultimately to the National Convention itself.[19]

In his petition he wrote that he understood and acknowledged that it had been necessary to adopt general measures to prevent the propagation of "evil principles," including those disseminated by some of his ecclesiastical colleagues. He had obeyed and submitted to those stern measures, though with an aching heart, for *his* instruction had *always* honored the Revolution. Coming back after a severe illness, he said, he was eager to make up for lost time. There remained so much for him to say in order to dispose the young people to give up the old system of Sundays and holy days and to adopt the new republican calendar. But he found that he was forbidden to teach, and he had submitted, if for no other reason than to set a good example of civil obedience. He hoped that the authorities would themselves soon be convinced of his decided patriotism and devotion to the public good and would therefore see fit to restore to him the privilege of teaching; or at the very least of showing the young people his natural history collection and explaining it to them, for many of his pupils of both sexes were daily pressing him to do so. "Knowing then that the *Convention nationale* and all other judicious officials would not be opposed to having all the people conscious of the marvels of nature, I do not believe that I ought to refuse them. Yet I also believe that it is my duty to inform you of this and to consult you about it. If it displeases you and you still cannot allow it, for reasons best known to you, I will submit willingly [*de grand coeur*]. I await your decision and beg you to inform me of it."

In view of the fact that Oberlin was already actually doing what he here was asking permission to do, namely, giving object lesson instruction in natural history, this document is not entirely innocent of cunning in its phrasing. Furthermore, for the delectation of the *citoyens administrateurs* at Sélestat, he sent along with the petition a packet of indigenous dried herbs to be used in brewing a "delicious and therapeutic" potion that he called *"une thé nationale."*

The reply from Stamm came promptly in the form of a warmly fraternal letter, in which he fulsomely praised his good *citoyen* correspondent both for his exemplary submission to the edict and his equally laudable desire to resume his teaching, for "it would be a shame to lose such a teacher as you are." Nevertheless he could only advise him to contain himself in patience until a resolution should come of certain points of law about which he, Stamm, had made inquiries in Paris.

The period of waiting, alas, extended through the entire summer of 1794. But when the response finally came, it contained the surprising news that the National Convention had not only granted citizen Oberlin permission to resume the teaching of any subject that he pleased, but had also adopted and recorded in its protocol the resolution already cited in chapter five above, praising Stuber and Oberlin for the excellent contributions that they had made in four decades of labor to the education of youth and the "universalization" of the French language and culture.

Recognizing in this handsome accolade the fine hand of Abbé Grégoire, Oberlin wrote to him (in September 1794), along with a letter to the president of the convention, a warm personal note of thanks. The praise, he said, had seemed all too fulsome to him, yet he could not deny that it had given him new and welcome encouragement, because "there are certain persons, some of them acting like mad men, who take pleasure in . . . proclaiming that certain of the most essential fields of knowledge, morals, and virtues are not valid in these times." He reported that the *citoyen president* of his *Club populaire* had read the commendation aloud to all the people in the Temple of the Eternal. "Ah, *citoyen*," Oberlin continued, "what satisfaction you, too, would have taken to see the tears of joy and gratitude in the eyes of all these good people, who are, in truth, the only true republicans, when, it being the end of the meeting, a special benediction was spoken for the *Convention nationale* and for those who had been the authors of that document."

Five months later, on March 22, 1795, there was a great service of thanksgiving in the Ban de la Roche: the interdiction had been lifted and the public worship of God could be resumed in its traditional forms.

Thus Oberlin had brought his parish through the years of persecution with its three churches intact. To leave the impression, however, that this had been accomplished with the full and undivided approval of *all* citizens of the parish would not be completely accurate. Even after the interdiction had been lifted in February 1795, there remained widespread confusion about the status of church properties.[20] Thus it was possible for a small group of disaffected members of the Waldersbach *Club populaire* to propose that the old parsonage be sold and the proceeds of the sale be given over to the civil authorities. Oberlin wrote a reply to that proposal, to be read by the secretary at the meeting of the club on July 2, 1795. He called attention to the fact that the confiscation of Protestant church properties in Alsace had not been authorized, but on the contrary, such properties had been (through the exertions of M. Koch, an adroit jurist of Strasbourg) specifically placed under the protection of the law. He spoke at length about the folly of any proposal that his parish, one of the poorest in Alsace, should voluntarily take an action that would increase its poverty still more. He reminded the citizens of the general discredit in which the parish had languished before Stuber and he had restored it to an honorable state. He concluded the memoir with the following words:

> People prattle about the Republic, but remain egoists. I have given you a better example. Whatever money I have had, I have used . . . for betterment of the parish: for building schools and community centers; for buying medicines and agricultural implements; for the renovation and maintenance of the churches; for roads in all parts of the parish and for a highway leading into this previously inaccessible valley; for prizes to encourage the schoolchildren; for installing and remunerating deaconesses; for a circulating free library for schoolchildren and families; for the elimination of beggary; for the support of the poor; for reestablishing the credit of the community; for the payment of private debts, etc. . . . Ah well! Spare your feelings of remorse! No man can exonerate you from the duty of gratitude and decency [*honnêteté*].

No proposal of that kind was ever made again thereafter.

Having virtually identified the proclamation of the Rights of Man with the beginning of the millenium, Oberlin looked about him to see where, in the spirit of the Revolution, he could make improvements in the life of the people within that small sector of the nation for whose welfare he had long ago assumed nearly complete responsibility. The accession of the people to national legislative power intensified his consciousness of the importance of education and enlightenment of all citizens. During the first two decades of his ministry, while he had concentrated on the improvement of the schools and the initiation of infant education, he had not neglected continuation of Stuber's projects in adult education. To approximate more clearly the ideal of an informed and intelligent citizenry, which he recognized as essential to democracy, he now redoubled his efforts to create still better learning facilities for adults.

The circulating library for which he had gradually and laboriously collected a considerable stock of books—most of them personally searched out by him in the bookstores of Strasbourg and paid for out of his own purse—was increased in 1792 by the acquisition of new periodicals and books, including such works as Fénelon's *Télémaque;* the *Fables of Aesop*; an anthology of the writings of Alexander Pope entitled *Principes de morale;* manuals on good farming and on beekeeping; works on education by Berquin, Campé, and Basedow; *L'Imitation de Jesus Christ* by Thomas à Kempis.[21]

A significant new project in the cause of public enlightenment was the free distribution to all householders of a new almanac, compiled and published by Oberlin. Using this as a means of circulating authentic information about the calendar and about meteorological and astronomical phenomena, he hoped to displace the astrological charts, the horoscopes, and the compendia of superstitious precepts that he saw in all too many of the houses that he visited. The book also contained a calendar of the church year with appropriate biblical texts for the holy days; special notations on national anniversaries, patriotic holidays, and community celebrations; practical hints and useful tricks of their trade for housewives, farmers, and husbandmen; advice on hygiene and health and the care of the sick. Believing that "nomen est omen," and noting that in 1791 and 1792 many French babies received the baptismal name Mirabeau, and that from 1792 to 1794 many were christened Robespierre, he tried to combat the practice of giving faddish or meaningless names by including a catalogue of recommended names in his almanac. The list runs to about 350 names and is particularly notable in that it greatly enlarges the usual repertory of names denoting Christian virtues and graces. Examples: Deliverance, Repentance, Sagesse;

Tranquille, Bénigne, Généreuse; Tempérant, Tolérant, Immortel; Obeissant, Paisible, Simple.[22]

Oberlin had long ago established the practice of holding weekly meetings with groups of his parishioners. The programs were of two kinds. Some, called *catéchismes,* consisted of prayers, devotions, and Bible studies; they were held every Thursday, with meetings for women alternating with those for men. On Sunday afternoons there were meetings of the Agricultural Society, which were, as we have seen, largely devoted to readings from secular books and periodicals on subjects of general interest and to discussions of current happenings in the community, the nation, and the world. To these only men were invited. At the meeting of that group on May 8, 1791, Oberlin spoke on the role of women in the social order.

"Since God directs all events on earth," he said in his opening remarks,

> reading the magazines, the newspapers, the village bulletins and other papers of the day—especially in these times so rich in great events—is to read, as it were, the history of the works of God. Every friend of God desires to know His works, and every citizen is interested in that which is of interest to his country. Exceptions to this rule are to be laid chiefly to failures in education. Therefore: since it is the feminine sex that chiefly influences our education; since it is the women who almost exclusively fashion the earliest years of our lives and give the first direction to our tastes, our passions, and our inclinations, it is meet and just and proper that women, too, should instruct themselves about the rules and vicissitudes of our new constitution. For that reason, all doors, even those of the august halls of our esteemed National Constituent Assembly are thrown open to women.[23]

He then proposed that the Agricultural Society's place of meeting be shifted from the schoolhouse to the more spacious church and that "all persons of the female sex be invited to attend." Anticipating the likely objections of male chauvinists lurking in his flock, he threw in the remark that the "females can occupy the back benches, near the wall, and thus will not embarrass us at all." The club meeting described above by Mlle de Berckheim must have been one of the last in the Ban de la

Roche at which the presence of women was not tolerated. Coming from the man who had been the first person anywhere to employ women as teachers in public schools, this action may seem overcautiously modest, yet it is not without significance, for it extended the practice of coeducation of the sexes that already existed in the schools to the instruction of adults.

At the same time Oberlin was devising other plans to involve women more actively in the affairs of the community. It is known that in the last weeks of 1790 his reading included a book of A.G. Spanenberg, Zinzendorf's successor at Herrnhut, on the foreign missions of the Moravian Brethren, and that he was particularly interested in what he read there about women participating in missionary work. Early in 1791 he devoted a series of the regular Thursday evening Bible study meetings to the Epistle of Paul to the Romans. On Thursday, May 12, four days after the Sunday meeting described above, the subject of discussion was the last chapter of the Epistle, which begins with an extolment of the role played by women in the primitive church at Cenchreae.[24]

Oberlin was also aware that there were certain male lay members of the primitive churches who assisted the bishops in various functions, and who were called deacons by the Apostle Paul. He had, indeed, shaped the functions of his own church officials on that model, though he continued to call them *anciens* (elders), according to local usage, since in Alsace the term *diacre* designated an assistant minister, that is to say, an ordained clergyman. Now, encouraged by the example of the Moravian Brethren, Oberlin interpreted St. Paul's words about the women at Cenchreae as evidence that their functions were similar to those of deacons and made bold to designate them as deaconesses.

So now, with the sanction of St. Paul, the example of the Brethren in his mind, and the democratic ideal of *fraternité* in his heart, Oberlin took a first step toward creating a cadre of the elect among the women of the parish, referring to them as deaconesses, and expressing his confident hope that they would lead all the people to a better earthly existence through the intensive practice of Christian charity. This happened nine years and a day after the dissolution of the ill-starred Christian Society. As he improvised the apparatus of organization, he honored the laborious canons of democratic process. "What was this office of deaconesses ordered by the Apostles? Have you ever thought about it? Does the office exist among us? Is it to our advantage or to our disadvantage that it does not exist? How could we make up for this failure and thus approach the example that God has given to all Christians through the primitive congregations?" He closed the discussion with this admonition: "So now, my dear sisters, the women of this parish can look about them and see whether there are deaconesses among us, and if they find that we have none, they should consider: first, whether they wish to have them; and second, how one should go about it to get them."[25]

At the very next women's *catéchisme* on May 26, Oberlin developed further his conception of the character of a deaconess. She should love Jesus, so that she will not forget to remind others to study and to keep His commandments; be humble, so that she will not domineer or bully her charges; know sorrow and pain, so that she will also know compassion and will not judge, but console and support and encourage. If she has both love and humility, she will be faithful to her husband, will be concerned about the souls of her own children, and, like Jesus himself, will feel drawn to all children in love and devotion.

To bring the new organization into being, he gives, in the same document, the following advice: "Wherever five, six, or seven women are known to each other as being equally concerned about their salvation, let them . . . converse about their desire to elect a deaconess and set a time for the election, preferably allowing an interval of about a week for prayerful meditation."

Oberlin's advice concerning the act of installation constitutes an expression not only of his democratic view of the new office, but also of his ideas on the proper mutual relations between citizens and their elected representatives. "Let the electors ask the electee if she will have the goodness to watch over them; to reprove them when they err; to admonish them; to commend them to God's mercy; and in all possible ways to help them on their way in the great work of sanctification. If the elected person assents, then let the others each lay a hand on her head and bestow on her the office of deaconess. Thereupon all the women will promise their new deaconess that they, as her sisters, will render to her the same services that they have commissioned her to bestow on them, namely to reprove her if she errs, caution and admonish her, and commend her also to God's mercy." Thus the deaconess is to have no authority to which she will not herself be subject and will bestow no privileges that she may not expect for herself. She will be *prima inter pares,* nothing more and nothing less. "For are not all men and all women equal in the eyes of our sacred constitution?"

There is no record of any further activity in this connection for several months. This may seem surprising, for it was Oberlin's usual way, once he had launched a new project, to execute it promptly, steadily, and vigorously. In that particular summer, however, there were many happenings to distract the minds of the citizenry. In October 1790 there had been formed, with Oberlin's blessing, units of the national guard that held regular military exercises on the Perheu.[26] Believing that the *départements* of the Rhine were particularly threatened by enemies of France and of the constitution, the leaders of the guard sent to the *directoire* of the *département* Bas-Rhin a petition (replete with the high-sounding patriotic phrases of the Revolution and signed by thirty-two citizens) requesting the issue of arms. The petition was granted, and on July 12, 1791, each volunteer received a musket with bayonet. Amid such excitements as these it would seem only natural if the gentle cause of deaconry were relegated to secondary importance, though Oberlin, for his part, considered it no less responsive to the imperatives of the constitution than national defense.

On Sunday, August 14, 1791, he approached the matter again, de novo, but this time before all the people in the church at Waldersbach, and again a week later in the service at Fouday.[27] He now significantly broadened the base of the electorate, making all women in the parish eligible both as electors and as candidates for election. He proposed that a total of thirteen to sixteen women be elected: two or three each for Waldersbach, Belmont, and Bellefosse; two each for Fouday and Solbach; and one each for Trouchy, La Hutte, and Pendbois. He suggested that the term of office be one or two years with no limit in the number of times the same person could be reelected. One cautionary remark is interesting because it signalizes the democratic organization's respect for the individual personality, its totally voluntary nature, and also the obligation of a dissenting individual to be tolerant of the order established by the majority—and especially when that order is sanctioned by holy writ. "If any person feels aversion or hostility, believing that she can work out her own salvation without help from the deaconesses and therefore chooses neither to participate in the election nor to be molested by any kind of elder or supervisor, she should be granted complete freedom and should not be in any way embarrassed or constrained, so long as she does not arrogate to herself the right, for her part, to embarrass or to manage the others. . . . For her to try to hinder them in establishing an institution created by the disciples and apostles of Jesus Christ would be to proclaim herself as wiser than they and thus to reveal herself as anti-Christian."

Although it is possible to view this action of Oberlin's as a step forward in the history of women's rights, it is doubtful whether women's liberationists of our time will find comfort in the style of communication between men and women that Oberlin felt constrained to impose. "If one of the deaconesses in the course of her work should find it necessary to have recourse to the parish alms box to aid an indigent person or family, she should speak about it to the chief elder, but only in the presence of his wife"; and if she should have occasion to consult with the minister, she should remember that "no woman should ever go unaccompanied to any man, no matter who he is, save to her own husband." Also one of the prime requirements that he sets down for a woman who desires to be a deaconess is that she must be submissive to her husband. These strictures, of course, should be judged not by standards of today, but by those of that time and place. They were doubtless motivated by Oberlin's awareness that delicate situations could develop for women charged with social duties and endowed with vocational prerogatives that were totally unprecedented in the Lutheran church discipline of Alsace. (One wonders what Oberlin's reaction would have been if he could have known that in 1973 a woman, Marie-Louise Carron, would be installed as minister of the Waldersbach parish.)

So the office of deaconess was successfully established in the twenty-fifth year of Oberlin's ministry. In the remaining thirty-five years of his life, and long after that, it was well served by a large number of women of that remarkable community. The work that they did encompassed services that we think of today under titles such as family and child welfare, visiting nurse services, and the like.

There is an interesting parallel between the founding of the office of deaconess and the beginnings of infant education. Just as Sara Banzét had started a program of bringing small girls together for instruction in knitting and in Bible studies before Oberlin founded the first *écoles à tricoter,* a young unmarried woman, Sophie Bernard, had on her own initiative begun, at some unrecorded time but surely well before 1791, to take neglected and helpless children into her care and to make a home for them. Her name and work first became known to the outside world through Sarah Atkins's Oberlin biography. Even after she had married and acquired a family of her own, she and her husband continued in their work of charity for many years, taking in orphaned, neglected, abandoned, and otherwise disadvantaged children, and rearing them in the dilapidated old house in which the Oberlins had raised their family. Her example had a wide and lasting influence in the community. "When a poor father or mother dies, leaving a numerous family, it is a thing of course for some poor person to take upon himself the charge and care of the orphans; so that many of the households contain one or two of these adopted children, and they seldom think of mentioning that they are not their own."[28] Sophie Bernard was one of the women elected to be the first deaconesses. Two others were Catherine Scheidecker of Fouday, and Maria Scheppler of La Hutte.

12

Refuge and Liberation

Jean de Dietrich's son Frédéric, born in 1748, was probably the brightest and best among the several generations of Dietrichs, who had been notable for their intelligence and their managerial competence, both in their private business affairs and in many positions of political and commercial leadership in Alsace. He had been the royal commissioner for mines, foundries, factories, and forests for all of France. He was a friend of Turgot and of Lafayette.[29] When the first constitutional mayor of Strasbourg was to be elected, the overwhelming choice of the people was Frédéric de Dietrich. Wherever he appeared in public he was greeted with enthusiasm. He organized and presided over a society called the Friends of the Constitution. His salon was the gathering place of the social, political, and military elite of Strasbourg. At one of his soirees, the "Marseillaise" was heard for the first time, in the presence of its author and composer, Claude-Joseph Rouget de Lisle, captain of engineers, who was stationed in Strasbourg.

However, the most radical group in the Strasbourg Jacobin Club, led by Eulogius Schneider, turned against Dietrich and eventually sought to depose him, not only from the presidency of the patriotic club, but also as mayor. They accused him of treason and of "favoring Germanic elements." In June 1792, Dietrich received a letter from the highest representative of the national government in Strasbourg, accusing him of plotting to deliver the city to the enemies of France. As an answer to

239

that indictment of treason, the Municipal Council of Strasbourg sent a protest and a declaration of loyalty to Dietrich signed not only by its members, but also by thousands of plain private citizens. It was unavailing: the Terror was irresistibly on the march.

After the proclamation of the Republic and the seating of the National Convention, the Strasbourg Municipal Council was dissolved, and therewith the political influence of the Dietrich family ended. Frédéric was summoned to Paris to answer the charges against him. On his way there, however, he learned that on his arrival he would be placed under arrest. He therefore changed his destination to Basel, where he took refuge in the home of his wife's parents. For that apparent defection the authorities in Paris placed his name on the list of *emigrés*. Six weeks later, when it seemed that his classification as an *emigré* might seriously endanger the lives and property of his family, he voluntarily returned to France. He petitioned for a hearing of his case before the National Convention, but the request was refused; he was to be tried by the revolutionary tribunal at Strasbourg. When he returned there in November 1792, there were so many large and noisy demonstrations in his favor that his adversaries feared that his trial in Strasbourg would result in exoneration. They therefore obtained an order from the National Convention that he should be tried in Besançon. At the trial there, in March 1793, he was indeed acquitted, but was not released from prison on the grounds of his classification as an *emigré*. In August he was transferred to Paris; the Jacobins demanded that he be sentenced to death; he was brought to trial again on December 28 and, after a brief hearing, was condemned. He was guillotined on the following day.

At the time of the execution, the Dietrich family was residing at Rothau. When the news came to Oberlin, he mounted his horse and rode across the Perheu and down to Rothau to make a pastoral call,[30] for, both as chief minister of the Ban de la Roche and also—despite the harsh words that had sometimes passed between them—still as a friend, he considered it his duty to minister to the spiritual needs of Jean de Dietrich and his family in that time of anguish over the death of their son, for whom Oberlin himself had had great affection and admiration.

Oberlin's pastoral errand under these circumstances could not in any case have been an easy one; yet it was rendered the more difficult by the fact that he was at that moment full of concern, for on that same day his beloved brother Jérémie-Jacques was being transported to Metz as a prisoner of the Committee of Public Safety.

Jean de Dietrich returned to Strasbourg in March 1794 to petition the authorities to expunge the false listing of his deceased son as an *emigré,* which is to say as a traitor, and to reinstate his family as owners of their property, which had been sequestered. The petition was denied. The Rothau ironworks continued to be managed by Dietrich's old director general, who now, however, was responsible not to him, but to the *agent national* for the district. The forests were patrolled by the district foresters, who were directed to release two cords of firewood to each householder in the Ban de la Roche.

Jean de Dietrich died on New Year's Day 1795, a year after his son's execution. A new petition for release of the property, made in behalf of his widow and children, was granted. Mme de Dietrich lived on for several years in the château at Rothau by a special arrangement with M. Champy, who had become owner of the estate by purchase.

Not only Rothau, but also the other villages of the Ban de la Roche gave asylum to many men, women, and children during the Terror. Even the manse at Waldersbach, though it was already occupied to its normal capacity by the Oberlin family, the maids, the apprentice *conductrices,* and the boarding pupils, also sheltered some of the refugees. The generous way in which Oberlin received those unfortunate guests and the loyal, and sometimes cunning, way in which he protected them is exemplified in the story of one young woman of aristocratic birth, Mlle Adélaide de Villeneuve, both of whose parents had been guillotined at Avignon. In order to make room for her in his house Oberlin had vacated his own bedroom and moved into his study. Ehrenfried Stoeber, who happened to be visiting Oberlin one day when the gendarmerie came to search the parsonage for illicit residents, witnessed the following incident.[31] Oberlin, with his usual courtly *politesse,* accompanied the officer from room to room. As they approached his bedroom, he, knowing that the young lady was within, turned his most disarming smile on the officer and said, *"Citoyen gendarme,* must you enter this room too? I assure you there is nothing suspicious about it except that it is mine." The officer, who had already partially opened the door, on hearing this protest quickly closed it with an apology and withdrew. Mlle Adélaide later said she had been changing her clothes when she heard the men approaching and had hidden behind the door and thus had remained undetected.

Among the several other patrician families of Strasbourg who had come to the Ban as refugees were the Türckheims.[32] The name will capture the interest of readers familiar with the life of Goethe, for Mme Elisabeth de Türckheim was Lili Schönemann of Frankfurt, the inspirer of the magnificent love songs known as the "Lili Lieder." In 1778 Lili married Baron de Türckheim, scion of a family of bankers in Strasbourg. When her husband, a former *maire* of Strasbourg, was taken into custody by the Committee of Public Safety, the elegant and comely baroness, disguised as a peasant woman returning from market, with two children clinging to her skirts and one strapped on her back, eluded the cordon of guards stationed at all the city gates and thus fled on foot to the Ban de la Roche. There she joined the Dietrichs in the château at Rothau.

It was not only aristocrats who found asylum in the Steintal; many a family in all the villages and hamlets shared its cottage and its simple fare with middle-class folk whose lives were endangered in the Terror. Among these, as it happened, was another woman whose name is associated with that of Goethe: Friederike Brion, who in the summer of 1771 had lived out that idyllic love affair with the law student from Strasbourg that is immortalized in the *Sesenheimer Lieder-buch*. In 1787, after the death of her parents, she and her sister Sophie had come to live with their brother Christian, who was then the minister in Rothau. In 1789, Friederike moved to Versailles, where she made her home with a friend of her youth. By 1793, the revolutionary events forced her departure from Versailles and she returned to Rothau. Her brother had meanwhile left that parish, but her sister was still there, eking out a meager existence as a seamstress. Friederike became a friend and companion of the young folk of the Oberlin household and an assistant teacher in the Waldersbach *pensionnat*. In 1801 she moved to Meissenheim in Baden, to take care of a disabled elder sister. She died there in 1813.

It is not possible to say how many persons found refuge from the Terror in the Ban de la Roche. Stoeber says that Oberlin once showed him a large collection of letters that he had received from people who, after returning to their accustomed habitats, remembered with gratitude the time of secure retreat in the parish and their association with its pastor. Since their places of residence were widely scattered throughout France, their sincere testimonials contributed greatly to the spreading of Oberlin's fame as a humanitarian and philanthropist. Especially notable in this connection is Octavie de Berckheim, whose memoirs have been frequently cited in these pages.

As a sample of the encomiums mentioned by Stoeber, I quote here the opening sentences of a letter from Augustin Perrier, who became an influential deputy to the National Convention and a highly successful industrialist. "I shall never forget the thrice blessed, thrice pious man whom I admired in those peaceful mountains. I shall remember until my death, and even beyond, those happy days when that sanctuary of virtue became for me also the sanctuary of friendship."[33]

Early in April 1794, some six weeks after the edict had been issued that all churches were to be closed, the authorities in Strasbourg thought they had reason to suspect that Oberlin had not complied and was still holding services. On May 13, therefore, there came an inquiry, directed to the community council of the Ban de la Roche. It contained three questions: "What is the age of the Lutheran clergyman Oberlin? Has he resigned from his office as minister? To whom and on what date did he hand in his resignation?" To this the council replied that citizen Oberlin was 54 years old; that the council had no knowledge of any resignation; that in December 1793 he had made a declaration to citizen Mainoni who was then president of the Committee of Public Safety at Strasbourg, but at that time, there had been no question asked about his resignation. It declared furthermore that at some time before the hearing at Strasbourg, Oberlin had at a public service of worship divested himself of his clerical gown and his *rabbat,* and that out of the former he had had *corselets* made for poor women in his parish; that after an illness he had again taken up his duties, but since orders had been received forbidding all clerical functions and instruction, he had accommodated himself to them.

Ten weeks later the lightning struck in the Ban de la Roche: Oberlin and his colleague, Pastor Boeckel of Rothau, were both arrested on July 28, 1794. (It happened that this was the very day on which Robespierre was executed.) Details of the arrest were meticulously recorded by Stoeber.[34] On that fateful day, Oberlin, now quite recovered from his illness, had gone to Rothau for the baptism of a child of a distinguished citizen, one M. Bauzel. After the ceremony, the two ministers were sitting at a modest festive meal with the Bauzel family when "the knock at the door," familiar to many a household at that time, came. Thus the two ministers were caught, as it were in flagrante delicto, yet the *commissaire sans-culotte* who was charged with making the arrest (he was from nearby Rosenheim) was visibly embarrassed. Was he awed, perhaps, by the renowned virtues of Oberlin? Or was he perhaps not totally free from some anxiety about his own safety, knowing that in case of necessity the people of the Ban de la Roche would defend their esteemed pastor, even at the risk of their own lives? But knowing also what his office required of him, he ordered the prisoners to prepare themselves for immediate departure. When they asked for time to make certain dispositions for their absence, however, he granted a post-ponement of twenty-four hours.

So they left the next morning, the mayors of their villages escorting them as an unofficial guard of honor. The journey went by way of the valley of Villé to Sélestat, its destination. There Boeckel and Oberlin were consigned to a hotel, although the other curés and pastors, who had been arrested on a general order, were locked up in jail. Oberlin and Boeckel dined at the same table d'hôte with the administrators of the district, all of them rabid Jacobins, who, wearing their red caps, incessantly spoke insulting words to the prisoners and demanded that they abjure the gospel that they had preached. Both ministers responded with courage and vivacity and the debate waxed loud and bitter. There was talk of transporting these two, along with the other prisoners, to Belfort or Besançon; but their steadfastness impressed the administrators so deeply as the evening wore on that they gradually changed their tone and manner and ultimately treated them with respect and consideration.

On the day after Oberlin's arrest, Stoeber went out from Strasbourg to Waldersbach. Arriving in the evening, he went to the parsonage. When there was no answer to his knock, he quietly went in. He found the Oberlin family on their knees with Louise and he joined them in prayers for their father's early release. Daily, during the time of *le cher papa*'s arrest, similar family prayer sessions were held in many of the houses throughout the parish. Those private intercessions were supplemented by more mundane petitions: the five mayors of the Ban de la Roche and the Waldersbach councilmen lost no time in sending a memorandum to the district administrators.[35] They declared that they, like many other good patriots, desired that corrective measures be taken against ecclesiastics who had disdained the decrees and who "by their corrupt morals and invidious preachings" had nurtured the seeds of counterrevolution in their respective communities; but they asserted on the other hand that there were also among the clergy citizens whose republican conduct and complete submission to the laws had always set a good example for their fellow citizens.

"We . . . do not for an instant hesitate," they continued, "to rank among the latter citizen Oberlin, formerly the Protestant minister here, a respected elderly man, father of a numerous family, who has always shown himself to be a zealous defender of the Rights of Man and of the Revolution. Even before that fortunate catastrophe [*cette heureuse catastrophe*] occurred, he had prepared for its success in this region." After a lengthy recital of Oberlin's many benefactions to the community and his sacrificial devotion to the Republic, the document closes with a petition: "In view of these facts and others that are publicly known, we, the undersigned . . . believe that we are not taking a step that is contrary to the public interest . . . by requesting the provisional liberation of citizen Jean-Frédéric Oberlin. We pledge on our personal responsibility that he will remain in the bosom of his family until he is called to be interrogated and judged."

Meanwhile the news of Robespierre's downfall and death had become known throughout the land. Five days after that event, on 14 Thermidor l'an II (August 1, 1794), the community councils of Rothau and Waldersbach received notice from citizen T. Stamm, the *agent national,* who had been well disposed toward Oberlin through the whole affair, that both Oberlin and Boeckel would forthwith return to their homes and that the civil authorities of both Waldersbach and Rothau were enjoined not to molest either of them.

There was great joy among the people, of course, when their minister returned. From Barr and Strasbourg and Paris, however, there continued for several years to come occasional inquiries and challenges concerning Oberlin's political faith. In response to the last of them he wrote in October 1796: "I acknowledge the sovereignty of the totality of the French citizens and I promise to be subject and obedient to the laws of the Republic."[36]

Part 5

The Years of Fulfillment:
1804-1826

13

Happy Endings, New Beginnings

The forests of the Bruche Valley grow lush and tall and have always produced large crops of excellent building material, the value of which has been enhanced by the fact that the harvested logs could be conveniently delivered to the markets of the Rhine plain simply by floating them down the river. The inhabitants of the Ban de la Roche, however, had little benefit from the somewhat sparser forests that grew in the higher reaches of their parish, for they enjoyed only limited rights of exploitation.[1] In fact, they enjoyed none at all until 1570, when the Veldenzes gained control of the fief and granted to the towns and villages certain usufructuary rights to products of the forests. These consisted chiefly of narrowly restricted amounts of timber for buildings, specified quantities of fuel for their hearths, pasturage of livestock in designated areas, fallen deadwood, and nuts and berries. From about 1700 on, however, the people believed that the dimensions of those rights were gradually being diminished. They initiated legal proceedings that dragged on and on through changing times and conditions of proprietorship, and that for a century and more devoured large and ever larger sums of money for lawyers' fees, occasioned by minute investigations into increasingly ramified and inextricable legal complications. So now, in the first decade of the new century, after successive governments, from the monarchy and the States-General through the National Convention and the Reign of Terror, the Directory and the Consulate, had all passed across the scene in

Versailles and Paris and had sent their resolutions of liberation and decrees of reform across the land, there still remained an important piece of unfinished business in the Ban de la Roche. Although the feudal tenure had ended with the death of Jean de Dietrich in 1795, the old uncertainties about the legal rights of the people to the use of pastures and the fruits of the forests remained.

The peasants, for their part, encouraged by the new political climate in the Republic, were more convinced than ever that certain inalienable rights, though they were mentioned in each one of a series of constitutions, were being denied to them. In their simplehearted naiveté, they took literally such popular slogans as "Liberty, equality, fraternity," as well as the orotund phrases about the sanctity of the Rights of Man. They interpreted them, in short, as license to take back for themselves that which they believed had been stolen from them; to trespass on the impounded pasturage; and to poach and pillage in the purloined woodlands.

Such behavior deeply distressed Oberlin, for he expected of his people the same probity in the management of their affairs as he himself practiced; in his view a sense of injury did not constitute a patent for pilfering, and he ceaselessly harangued them about the sinfulness of thievery. But at the same time he remonstrated with the proprietor, M. Champy, in phrases at least as threatening and accusative as those with which he excoriated the sinners in his congregation, for in his heart he shared the people's conviction that their natural and legal rights had indeed been violated.

In the spring of 1806, persons unknown illegally cut down about a hundred beech trees near Bellefosse, burned down two charcoal burners' huts, and shattered the windows in the house of forester Paul Müller. In June, Oberlin preached on Jer. 3:11-12: "Come back to me apostate Israel. . . . I will no longer frown on you. For my love is unfailing. . . . I will not be angry for ever. Only you must acknowledge your wrongdoing, confess your rebellion against the Lord your God. . . ."[2] He called on those who were guilty to confess. He challenged all who could identify others to come forward and do so, citing Lev. 5:1: "If a person is solemnly adjured to give evidence as a witness to something he has seen or heard and does not declare what he knows, he commits a sin and must accept responsibility." He adduced again, as he had in the affair of the *pont de charité,* the Mosaic law that a crime committed in a community must be expiated by the whole community. He decreed that all should sign a declaration that they loathed the crimes and promised to make restitution for them. And, finally, he called on the villages to organize a police force that would be capable of taking preventive and punitive action.

While he was about the business of having the declaration prepared and the signatures gathered, he also wrote to M. Champy, asking him to explain the behavior of his foresters. "Do they really want to stir up the inhabitants to such acts of violence as are the fruits of despair? The people live in the midst of forests, yet have no wood to cook their potatoes and to protect their families from the cruelty of the season. Surely, if God treats each one as he has treated others, those who treat our people so cruelly will be very cold indeed in the other world. Let them read in the books of the New Testament what it means to have mercy."

Some weeks later, Oberlin wrote again to Champy and sent 50.50 francs to him. "Various citizens have made payments to me for damages done by them to your property. Others, who were totally free of any suspicion, have also made contributions. . . . The contributors, both the guilty and the innocent, beg you not to spurn this small sum and at the same time they pray God to bless you and to recompense you for those losses that you have sustained but which they are unable to make up to you." On the copy of the letter that he kept, Oberlin wrote: "Champy brought the entire sum back to me, requesting that I distribute it among the deserving poor of the parish."

At the same time that Oberlin was deeply engaged in dealing with recurring delictions of that kind, he kept trying to devise in his mind some way to put an end to the conditions that seemed to invite and encourage them. The importance that he ascribed to that cause is indicated by the fact that for many years there stood at the head of the list posted on his study door of persons and causes to be remembered in his prayers the inscription, "Oh God, have mercy and put an end to the trial." His study of the long history of the case, however, had convinced him that further resort to litigation could result only in the incurring of still more legal fees, and he therefore now put all his hope in somehow bringing about an amicable settlement without further involvement in pettifoggery. But he knew that to accomplish that end he would need support not only from God but also from human helpers. These would have to include, first, someone who was himself of the people and who could therefore speak most effectively for them; and second, a public personage of high authority and just attitude who could deal persuasively with Champy, but who also had sympathy for the people.

To play the first of these two roles in the drama that he was about to direct from the wings, Oberlin chose one of the brightest and best young men of his parish, Théophile Scheidecker of Belmont, the son of his faithful and beloved Sébastien. To prepare him for his part, Oberlin initiated him into the history of the case and instructed him in the arts of forensics. On every possible occasion he put him forward as a community leader and thus gradually accustomed the people to consider him as such.

The actor of the second role was providentially presented in 1810 with the appointment of Adrien, Comte de Lezay-Marnésia, as prefect of the *département* Bas-Rhin. Lezay—a kinsman of the Empress Josephine—was an exemplary public official, a man of noble character and of even-handed justice who was not content merely to administer from his office desk in Strasbourg, but traveled widely in the area in order to get acquainted with the people. Being also a man of piety and inclined toward mysticism, he was particularly interested in what, as a newcomer in Alsace, he heard about Oberlin. Thus it happened that one of the first trips as prefect took him to the Waldersbach manse.

The two men found themselves *en rapport* from the beginning of their acquaintance. Oberlin honored Lezay as an honest and conscientious public official, while the prefect venerated the parson as a deeply religious man who to an unusual degree showed forth his faith in his good works. When Oberlin was asked, some years later, by the Alsatian journalist Merlin if he had known Count Lezay-Marnésia personally he replied: "Ah yes, and I have often traveled through this region with him. Several times he visited me for several days. He opened his heart to me. Since he wished to have a living faith, but could not always reconcile that desire with the objections that his reason opposed to his will, he submitted his doubts to my judgment. So we often talked about these matters, and whenever I succeeded in putting down the negative arguments that he presented, he was just as happy about his defeats as I was about my victories."[3] Thus Oberlin knew that he had a powerful friend at court when the time should come to adjudicate the ancient dispute.

In the spring of 1812 the eight *maires* came to Oberlin for help in planning their strategy. Oberlin told them "what I would do in your place, and what I wish that you would do":[4] 1. Take Théophile with you and go to M. Champy. 2. Draw up with him the outline of a compromise (for there is no other way to bring the matter to an end). 3. Present these articles to a just magistrate and consult him about them; *do not under any circumstances consult any lawyer;* to do so would mean never to come to a conclusion. 4. If, after you have gone to the magistrate, changes should be indicated, consult again with M. Champy, *always in the company of Théophile.* 5. Continue in this fashion without intermission to the end, making concessions where necessary. "Remember: He who has ordained that we act thus is almighty." 6. When at last an agreement has been reached that is in accord with the magistrate's advice, proceed to the ratification without consulting anyone else concerning what shall be done.

The "just magistrate" in the case was a judge whom Lezay-Marnésia had recommended. All points in dispute were swiftly settled, save only one: the right to cut turf on the Champ du Feu, which Champy refused to concede. On that subject Oberlin, on May 25, 1812, wrote to the mayors: "Here is my advice after reading the answer of M. Champy's lawyer of 16 April 1812 concerning the peat beds. Expect no more of human justice, but implore the help, the grace, and the mercy of the advocate of the oppressed, our Lord Jesus Christ, pleading with Him for the love of God to intervene in behalf of the poor Ban de la Roche, for if the advice of M. Champy's attorneys were followed, the Ban de la Roche, so infertile, so wretched in itself, would be lost, and 700 families of the emperor's subjects would be sacrificed for the benefit of one family, which enjoys not only a pleasant existence, but one of great opulence."

So the matter dragged on for another year, but at last, on June 17, 1813, under the powerful influence of Lezay-Marnésia, who presided over the signing of the agreement, the dispute of more than a century was brought to a conclusion that seemed satisfactory to both sides. The salient features of the settlement were that Champy deeded one-third of the forest lands to the villages; that the villages were to enjoy the rights of pasturage on lands that had been traditionally open to such use; that pasturage would be allowed on the Champ du Feu for a fee of 20 francs per year from each village, provided that such usage did not hinder or inconvenience M. Champy in the extracting of peat.

From the historic meeting in Strasbourg the whole company of the mayors went to Oberlin's home, informed him of the details of the settlement, and gave him as a souvenir the quill with which the instrument had been signed. Oberlin, with a prayer of thanksgiving, attached the souvenir of victory to the wall above his study table. He considered the settlement of that affair as one of the greatest accomplishments of his ministry.

He had managed to come through it without losing the personal respect and good will of M. Champy, who remained a good neighbor and a friend for many years. Unfortunately, however, there remained certain disputes among the several villages that had to be adjudicated internally. All the grants had been made corporatively as concessions of undivided public lands to the combined villages as a single entity. Now each village came forward with its claim to a lion's share of the booty. Attempts to devise a fair system of distribution brought up questions of how to balance such factors as population of each village; the distances between each village and the plots to be granted to it; comparative ease of access; relative productivity of the various plots, and the like. The multitudinous negotiations were further complicated by the fact that political boundaries had been redrawn in such a way that some of the villages now belonged to the *département* Vosges and the district of St. Die, while the rest were in the jurisdiction of Bas-Rhin and Sélestat.

While these disputes were going on, misdemeanors of trespass and wood thievery continued to occur. As late as December 1815 Oberlin felt constrained to circulate a letter addressed to "the wood thieves"—but beginning nevertheless with the salutation "dear friends"—in which he designated those who cut wood illegally as servants of the Antichrist and despicable traitors to their communities. Of those who were apprehended and found guilty he required that they remunerate the rightful owner for the stolen goods. Sometimes that involved a long series of installment payments. Oberlin called such proceedings *"rachats du bois"* and supervised them and kept books on them with the same conscientious and patient dedication that he applied to the retirement of the repudiated assignats, until at last the moral climate changed and the theft of wood was generally looked upon with the same loathing as any other felony or tort by the people of the whole Ban de la Roche.

At the same time that he was actively engaged in the effort to bring the hundred-year trial to an end, Oberlin also was deeply concerned about the necessity of reviving the community spinning and weaving enterprise. The fabrication of cotton textiles that Reber, at Oberlin's instigation, had started as a home industry in the 1770s, as described in chapter five, fell on evil days in the early 1800s. The causes of the decline were several. First, the continental blockade of 1806-1813 hindered the procurement of cotton. Second, in 1806 an English engineer named Heywood, defying a British export embargo on both factory machines and plans for making them, smuggled drawings and specifications for spinning and weaving machines into France. The ruinous competition of machine-made textiles that therewith began to threaten home-based industry on the European continent was carried to the very threshold of the Ban de la Roche when, in 1810, that same Heywood, after an unsuccessful attempt to establish himself in Strasbourg, built a spinning jenny in Schirmeck that had more than 100 spindles powered by the waters of the Bruche.[5] The third mischance, and the one that virtually stilled the sounds of the spinning wheel and the loom in the Steintal villages, was a long and serious illness that incapacitated M. Reber to the extent that he was not even able to move his business into the new building that he had constructed in Fouday.

After Oberlin had prayed and worked for forty years to find a solution to the problem of forest and grazing rights, a man had unexpectedly come to Strasbourg from Paris whose beneficent presence made it possible to settle the long dispute quickly and effectively: Oberlin always believed that God's providence had raised up Lezay-Marnésia and sent him to Alsace to cope with the needs of his parish. Similarly, in 1813 there came directly to Oberlin and the Ban de la Roche a remarkable man, this time from Switzerland, who, from the benefits that the community received from him, seemed the very incarnation of Oberlin's own guardian angel.[6]

Jean-Luc Legrand was born in Basel, May 30, 1755. He attended a private school at Chur and studied theology at

Göttingen and Leipzig, where he preached for a time in the pulpit of his teacher, the theologian Zollikofer. For a year he traveled widely in France and England. After returning to Basel he published two Latin tracts, one on elocution and one on philology. As a student, he, like Oberlin, had executed a "solemn act of dedication," pledging his life to the service of God, of human society, and of his fatherland. But meanwhile, under the influence of the rationalistic philosophers of the time, he had been assailed by doubts concerning the traditional doctrines of Lutheran theology. He consequently considered that his honor and the respect that he continued to cherish for the church demanded that he quit the ministry. For his livelihood he turned to business; but in his continuing devotion to philanthropy and social improvement, he never faltered throughout the eighty-two years of his life.

He established himself as a manufacturer of textiles in Basel. He joined two philanthropic societies there, one for the advancement of the common welfare and one for the promotion of patriotism, and himself founded a society for adult education. He was repeatedly elected to important public offices. He used the influence thus bestowed on him, along with the wealth that his business enterprises brought him, for the improvement of social institutions, with a special interest in education. As a result of extensive correspondence with both Basedow and Campe, he effected (in 1796-1797) a significant reform of the Basel *Gymnasium*.

In the revolutionary years he became very active in behalf of the throngs of citizens of France and other countries who sought refuge in Switzerland and—again like Oberlin—gave asylum to many in his own home. In 1795, when the French government released from prison in Paris Marie-Thérèse, the daughter of Louis XVI, later the Duchess of Angoulême, in exchange for five French noblemen held by the Austrian government, the actual exchange of persons took place in Legrand's home in Basel, as "neutral ground."

When the principles of the French Revolution began to capture the imagination of Swiss leaders, Legrand, together with the senior guild master of Basel, Peter Ochs (incidentally, he was the father-in-law of Frédéric de Dietrich of Strasbourg) founded the Club of the Rhine Bridge for the advancement of democratic government. On February 2, 1798, when, on the model of the French National Convention, the Swiss constitutional convention was formed, Legrand was elected as one of its sixty members. He was forthwith made president of the convention and thus became the head of state in the Helvetian Republic. The immense power that the office conferred upon him filled him with horror. He accepted it only on condition that he could resign at the end of one year to return to his family and his business affairs.

Actual experience soon convinced him, however, that his chief problem was not so much the excessive power that the constitution nominally vested in the office as the hostility of the populace to the new order. He felt constantly balked and frustrated by the unwillingness of the people to accept and to live by a constitution that seemed alien to them and was loathsome because it was favored by the French invaders and occupiers of their fatherland. But he took pride in the fact that he was able to alleviate somewhat the harsh conditions of life in the canton Unterwalden, where military action and a reign of terror had wrought the greatest havoc. His historically most memorable accomplishment there was that he established the institute for war orphans at Stans and appointed Pestalozzi as its superintendent. The experimental projects that Pestalozzi started there and continued later at Burgdorf greatly influenced the development of modern education.

During the time when he was preoccupied with affairs of state Legrand had persuaded his father-in-law to take over the management of his chief establishment, a textile mill in Arlesheim. But when, before the end of Legrand's stipulated year in office, his father-in-law died, Legrand insistently requested his release from the presidency, which was granted on January 29, 1799.

At about the same time a certain officer of the corps of engineers stationed in Poland invented a time-saving new procedure for spinning silk floss into threads. The officer was an admirer of Legrand and wrote to him from Prague, offering to sell his invention to him. Legrand accepted the offer and forthwith converted the factory at Arlesheim from cotton spinning, which had become relatively unprofitable, to silk. Soon thereafter he closed out the mill in Arlesheim and moved his machinery to a former monastery in the village of Saint Morand near Altkirch in Alsace. There he established not only a plant for the manufacture of silk ribbons, but also a colony of Swiss workers that he planned to develop into an ideal industrial community. He treated the workers, along with their wives and children, as members of one large family to which he stood as a father. He managed his business affairs with a light hand and devoted most of his time and energy to the welfare of the community. He was especially interested in the children and young folk. He organized schools for them in which he himself did much of the teaching.

One day, when he was engaged in giving a reading lesson to a group of children, a soldier in the uniform of the medical corps of the French army of the Rhine, his haversack on his back, unexpectedly walked into the schoolroom and introduced himself as Henri-Gottfried Oberlin.

John Frederic Oberlin and Jean-Luc Legrand had never met. It is likely that Henri's visit had been instigated by Lavater, whom Henri had visited in Zurich; possibly also by the Stähling family of Basel, who had taken care of Henri when he had fallen ill while visiting in their home. Henri was enchanted now to find M. Legrand not in the counting house or the factory, but in the schoolroom, looking much like his own father as he had so often seen him, surrounded by children. Legrand for his part, was pleased to receive as his guest the son of Oberlin, whose character and work he knew from conversations with, and published reports of, visitors to the Ban de la Roche. Such reports were now appearing with increasing frequency in France and Germany and Switzerland, and Legrand welcomed the opportunity to talk with "Oberlin's own flesh and blood" about every detail of life and work in the Ban de la Roche.

In Saint Morand Legrand had had one disappointment: the people of that highly productive agricultural area were hostile to the development of industry in their midst and looked upon Legrand and his workers as uninvited intruders and inter-lopers. So when Henri told him about the decline of the textile industry in the Ban de la Roche and the consequent concern of his father to find an experienced manager to take over the moribund enterprise of the incapacitated M. Reber, Legrand decided without hesitation that he would pay a visit to the parson of Waldersbach.

The venerable patriarch, then seventy-two, serene in his unshakable faith and firm in his social purposes, and the distinguished man of affairs, aged fifty-seven, who through the vicissitudes of an active life dedicated to the service of his fellow men had found his way back to the pietistic faith of his youth, both instantly recognized their spiritual affinity and shared social conscience. Immediately there was formed on a foundation of mutual respect and admiration a friendship that was surely unique among all the many friendships of each of those two extraordinary men.

Legrand found the new, still unoccupied building that Reber had constructed on a knoll overlooking Fouday ideally suitable as an office, a warehouse, and a weaving mill. The raw silk could be received there and distributed for spinning in the homes of the five villages. The thread could then be returned to the factory to be woven into finished ribbons, which would then be sent out into the channels of trade. Legrand would have been ready to decide then and there to move the scene of his operations to Fouday, except that he felt a continuing responsibility for his little colony in Saint Morand. So when, less than a year later, the allied troops made their break-through into upper Alsace and requisitioned the former monastery of Saint Morand—the first large building within France on the highway to Paris—for a quartermaster station and hospital, thus making it impossible to continue the manufacturing there, Legrand took the event as the signal to act and forthwith transplanted his establishment to Fouday.

Legrand settled in the Ban de la Roche in 1814 with his wife and two sons, Daniel and Frédéric, and he stayed there until his death in 1836. The Legrand family's coming at just that time seemed particularly providential, for in that year the Steintal had a crop failure that would have been the more disastrous but for the dispatch with which the Legrands set their new enterprise in motion, procured new raw materials, and started the spinning wheels and looms moving and the people working again, for wages that saved many a family from the tragedy of hunger.

From the beginning Legrand took a lively interest in all of Oberlin's many projects and activities. Gradually he turned much of the management of his private business over to his two sons in order to devote his own time and energies more and more to community affairs. He was particularly devoted to the welfare of the children and the young folk and spent much of his time as a volunteer teacher in the schools. Even in the last years of his life, when, as an octogenarian, he had begun to lose his eyesight, he continued his teaching of the children by having them come from the several villages to receive their instruction in his study.

His active participation in the affairs of the community and his generous gifts—made possible by his considerable financial resources—brought about the realization of a long-standing dream of Oberlin's: the founding of a vocational school in which the young men and women of the valley could acquire right on their home ground the knowledge necessary for the improvement of agriculture (which remained the basic industry of the community) as well as the skills that pertained to the manufacture of textiles and the clerical work entailed in the management of the commerce that it brought to the valley. Legrand erected a building for the new school and paid the expenses of instruction.

The Legrands could surely have realized much greater profits from their business operation if they had converted it entirely from hand work to machine production. But the objective of social improvement was more important to them than that of financial gain. They thus were able to maintain a competitive position while continuing to have a large part of the manufacturing process performed by families working in their own homes.

The Legrands accommodated themselves to the life-style of the indigenous residents. They lived in a part of the building from which they conducted their business; the quarters they occupied were nearly as plain and modest as those of their peasant neighbors. The tokens of mutual affection and esteem that passed between the families Legrand and Oberlin were many. The Legrand children joined the other young folk of the parish in addressing Oberlin as *"Papa,"* while the Oberlin children's salutation *"Oncle"* became the name that was generally used throughout the community for Legrand *père.* In addition to the massive help that he gave to Oberlin's educational projects, Legrand gave generously of his time, energies, and money in support of Bible distribution and missionary projects.

After Oberlin's death in 1826, Legrand devoted himself to keeping the memory of the pastor alive in the Ban de la Roche, in Alsace, and abroad. He commissioned a bust by the Strasbourg sculptor Ohmacht, who had distinguished himself as the creator of the imposing sculptured monument to Oberlin's brother Jérémie-Jacques that still stands in St.

Thomas Church. Legrand had many copies of the original marble bust of John Frederic cast in bronze, sold them to fellow admirers of his great humanitarian friend, and used the proceeds for the continuing support of Oberlin's projects. He and his sons created a philanthropic foundation to fund an Oberlin Institute that they established at Schirmeck-la Broque for the training of *conductrices* of infant schools. The resources of the foundation were increased by funds solicited by the Legrands from other admirers of the great educator and by the continuing sale of the Oberlin statues. A second training institute was established in Fouday in memory of Mme Legrand, whose death came a few months after Oberlin's.

When he died at the age of eighty-two, on October 4, 1836, Legrand was buried in the churchyard at Fouday between the graves of his wife and his revered friend. In the annals of Protestant charities in Europe, the names of a triumvirate of humanitarians are closely linked: Stuber, Oberlin, Legrand.

For Oberlin, the years with Legrand were a time of relative tranquility, a season of fulfillment and harvest whose beginning could be dated approximately from the great public celebration of his seventieth birthday on August 31, 1810. On that date many guests came from far and near to extol the manifold attainments of the now famous country parson. It would be a mistake, however, to think of the last sixteen years of his life as an era of contentment unbroken by crises or sorrows. Indeed, the celebration itself had been somewhat shadowed by the death, some ninety days before, of the celebrant's beloved eldest daughter, Fidélité-Caroline. Soon after the festival, sorrow came again to the valley in the form of a fire that left ten families in Belmont homeless; and four months later, Oberlin himself was again struck down by a long and severe illness. In the spring of 1814, the allied powers made their incursion into the interior of France through the valleys and passes of the Vosges, thus making much-beleaguered Alsace once again the theater of Europe's wars and bringing its armies to the very threshold of Oberlin's parish. The famine that was visited upon the whole continent in 1816-1817 brought the greatest starvation of all to that frequently hunger-scourged community, while the worldwide financial panic of 1817 all but destroyed the local economy which had just begun, albeit moderately, to flourish. In the same year the most shattering blow since the death of his wife fell upon Oberlin: Henri-Gottfried died on November 15.

Yet, despite all the crises, reversals, and sorrows, it can still be said that Oberlin's septuagenary years were in fact relatively tranquil. The battles for improvement and reform, which in the early days had been fought alone by the young minister and his wife, had now been largely won. The children who had populated the first infant schools were now middle-aged and active, as housewives, *conductrices,* and deaconesses; as farmers and artisans, teachers and elders. Their children were living in clean and well-kept homes, where prayers and devotions, reading and music, and useful handwork had displaced the morose bickering and the demoralizing idleness of former times. Their grandchildren were attending infant schools under the tutelage of cultivated, competent *conductrices* who were trained by their own predecessors, the pioneers Banzét, Caquelin, and Scheppler. All the children were attending schools built, paid for, and maintained by all the people and taught by the spiritual and intellectual successors of the first *régents d'école,* the Bohys, the Massons, the Scheideckers, the Claudes. The hostility of the early years toward the reforming pastor had faded away, partly because the maturing minister had learned through many a harsh experience that human endeavor is more effectively improved by the amelioration of poverty and care, by messages of hope, and by gentle persuasion than by accusatory preachments and angry fulminations. A general improvement of taste and manners had been wrought by Oberlin's system of education; youthful rowdyism had been refined to sports at school picnics, and destructive Saturday night rampages had been sublimated to athletic contests at folk festivals and village fairs. Communal affairs were now mostly in the hands of a second generation of leaders, men like Théophile Scheidecker, whose sense of civic responsibility, first awakened in Oberlin's schools, had been exalted to a holy fervor of patriotism in the Revolution and tempered in the fire of the wars of liberation.

Oberlin, in his seventies and approaching the fiftieth anniversary of his ministry, was no longer able to work alongside the men of his parish building roads and bridges, planting trees, digging channels, and building stone walls, but he remained mentally and spiritually alert and active. He continued to preach in all three churches and to give religious instruction to all the children, to hold the usual prayer and discussion meetings for adults and the regular training sessions for the *régents d'école*. He attended the meetings of the agricultural society, supplied its members with technical literature, and saw to it that the latest findings of research in agronomy and animal husbandry were accessible to them; and he kept up his own experimental searchings for new and better plant strains and livestock breeds. He personally managed the public lending library and the tool crib, the loan fund, and the assignat retirement project. He was the community's attorney and advocate in prosecuting the matter of forest and pasture rights to its final settlement. He advised and directed the mayors and leaders of the villages in their dealings with higher authorities in Sélestat and Paris during the time when civic affairs seemed endlessly complicated because of several occurrences of military action within the borders of the Ban. He remained the only medical practitioner within his parish except for his faithful assistant Sébastien.

The prosecution of all his projects and tasks required the writing of many letters. It is hard for us, who work with pens and ballpoints, typewriters and photocopy machines, to appreciate the many hours of labor demanded by an extensive correspondence when everything had to be written with the quill—an implement that produced clean and legible writing only with frequent and meticulous trimming—and when a copy of a letter or document could be made only by writing it again in longhand.

Oberlin's correspondence was particularly heavy in the time of the great famine, which in the Ban de la Roche assumed proportions unmatched since the Thirty Years' War. As early as the summer of 1816, some families were forced once more, as they had often been compelled in the old times, to fortify their rations with wild roots, herbs, and grasses. Yet even in that extremity, the people of Waldersbach were still able to collect an emergency fund for the relief of the neighboring Roman Catholic parish of Ranrupt after a midsummer hailstorm had totally destroyed its crops. But when the onset of winter, which came unusually early that year, put an end to the gathering of emergency rations in forests and meadows, the shadow of starvation descended upon every village, every hamlet, and every farmstead in the valley. Oberlin was daily confronted, in the streets, in schools and churches, in his study, and in living rooms and sickrooms around the parish, with drawn faces, emaciated bodies, and desolated spirits. There could be no doubt that here was an emergency that the community simply could not cope with alone.

That insight threw him into a frenzy of activity. He wrote memoranda describing his parish, extolling the virtues of its people, and limning the proportions of the disaster. He sent off letters to be printed in newspapers and church publications in Alsace and Switzerland and Germany. The response was quick, widespread, and massive: Protestant congregations and charitable organizations of Germany and Switzerland made generous contributions; gifts came not only from parishes in Alsace, but also from other *départements:* from Montbéliard and Grenoble, from Anduze in the Cévennes and from Paris; and a generous contribution came from London. Thus the remote little *Gottesvolk* that had made it a habit to cast its own meager bread in charity upon the waters now saw it returning in good measure. Each contribution was promptly and graciously acknowledged by a personal letter from the aged pastor, who still wrote a firm and legible hand, despite attacks of writer's cramp and signs of deteriorating eyesight.[7]

14

From Parochial Obscurity to World Celebrity

But for two small exceptions, Oberlin spent every day of his life in his native Alsace. Leaving aside his occasional preaching in Strasbourg in his student days, he is not known to have appeared anywhere save in his own three churches either as a preacher or lecturer. He never wrote anything for publication. In the face of such parochialism, his fame is nothing less than astonishing, both in the earliness of its emergence and the eventual wideness of its spread. The first country outside of Alsace in which his name became widely known was Germany. The earliest known publication about him there is the anonymous article that appeared in the *Leipziger Intelligenz-blatt* in 1774, the seventh year of his ministry. This piece seems to have been much reprinted and widely distributed in publications of various kinds in Germany and must have motivated some of the early travelers who came to Walders-bach, as it moved Urlsperger in Augsburg to inquire about Oberlin's availability as a missionary in North America.

Another vehicle of his spreading renown was that of private letters, not only Oberlin's own letters, but also those of others. The time of Oberlin's life was the golden age of letter writing. If a thought came to one's head that put one in mind of a friend, one reached for paper and quill as today one reaches for the telephone. Persons with common interests in, say, literature or religion, formed circles of correspondence and wrote incessant letters to each other, exchanging ideas and gossip and the frothy phrases of friendship that characterized the age of sentimentalism. One such group consisted of friends and admirers of Lavater; among its members was the frenetic poet and dramatist Jakob Michael Reinhold Lenz.

To understand the early phase in the spreading of Oberlin's renown, it is necessary to go back to the eleventh year of his ministry and consider an incident that suddenly made him a subject of lively correspondence and gossip within that circle of Lenz's friends, and consequently the object of publicity and of widespread controversy, and eventually the subject of several literary works. After nightfall on January 20, 1778, there came to Oberlin's door a strange figure. He was emaciated, pale, ragged, disheveled, and obviously deeply agitated; he had a suppurating sore on one foot, and, having crossed the Champ du Feu in a howling snowstorm, he was cold. He introduced himself simply as "Lenz, a friend of Kaufmann."[8] When Oberlin asked if he might be the author of "several dramas" that he had read, Lenz replied: "Yes, but be pleased not to judge me by them."

Like all wanderers who came to that house, Lenz was taken into the family circle. Mme Oberlin fed him, bathed and bound his wound, and cared for him as for one of her children. But very soon it became clear that this stranger was as much in need of spiritual solace as of physical restoration. The family had scarcely retired (Lenz being quartered in a guest room in the schoolhouse), when Oberlin was awakened by loud, incoherent shouting in front of the house. Rising hurriedly, he found his guest splashing about in the icy watering trough. Oberlin succeeded in putting an end to that strange behavior and persuading Lenz to go quietly to his room, but from that moment on he knew that, by sending this stranger to him, God was placing a special responsibility upon him for the salvation of the visitor's soul. He therefore arranged his daily work schedule in such a way that Lenz could be with him as much as possible, so that he could comfort and console him in quiet conversations and thus bring tranquility to his troubled mind. Thereafter, during the days, when Lenz was in Oberlin's company reading and writing in his study or accompanying him on his pastoral rounds, and in the evenings, when he shared the pleasures of family life, his behavior seemed unremarkable. But his nights, when he was alone in his room, were marked by wild ravings and repeated noisy simulations of attempted suicide by drowning in the watering trough. Yet after some days of the quietness and peace of the Oberlin household, that condition seemed much improved, and when he requested the privilege of preaching in the Fouday church (he had studied theology at Strasbourg) Oberlin gladly accepted. On that day Christoph Kaufmann, the man who had sent Lenz to Oberlin—after having written Oberlin only that he would soon be visited by a theological candidate who had expressed a desire to preach in his church—came to Waldersbach with his fiancée. In a private conversation Kaufmann interrogated Oberlin on Lenz's behavior since his arrival at Waldersbach, but even then made no comment concerning Lenz's prior history.

When Kaufmann invited Oberlin to attend his wedding in Switzerland, Oberlin considered that the time had come when he could indulge a long-standing desire to go to Zurich, to visit Lavater and other friends there, and to make calls at certain places en route where new agricultural and educational experiments were going forward. After making the necessary arrangements for his absence, he started the journey on horseback. But, alas, he got no farther than the second of the stops that he had planned along the way. This was at Emmendingen in Baden where he was the guest of Goethe's brother-in-law, Johann Georg Schlosser, a public official and a social and educational reformer.[9]

There Schlosser told him truths about Lenz of which Oberlin had had no inkling. For months Lenz had wandered about in Germany, Switzerland, and Alsace, living on the hospitality of his friends. At every station along his erratic way he had, by his eccentric, indeed often crazed, behavior, created frightening scenes of violence. Even the saintly Lavater had lost patience with him; Schlosser himself, a paragon of patience, had pronounced him "a consummate scoundrel"; and Kaufmann, at whose house Lenz was said to have had his first overt attack of obvious insanity, could think of nothing better to do than to send him, in that oddly secretive way, to Oberlin, who had already begun to acquire the spurious reputation of being a healer who, by the use of some extraordinary power, could bring peace to troubled spirits.

After hearing Schlosser's revelations, Oberlin was horrified at the thought of the dangers to which he had unwittingly exposed his wife, who was far advanced in her seventh pregnancy, and he decided to return home forthwith. Upon his arrival, just a week and a day after his departure, he found that frightening incidents had indeed occurred, with wild demonstrations and loud lamentations of remorse by Lenz for imaginary murders that he thought he had committed, and repeated threats of suicide. From that time on his condition deteriorated rapidly. Try as he might, Oberlin could find no way to quiet his demented mind except at times when he was physically in his presence. Oberlin came early to the conclusion that the best thing he could hope to do for Lenz was to persuade him to make his peace with his father, with whom he was in contention, and to return to his Livonian homeland. This, however, Lenz was not willing to do.

One day, when Oberlin had gone on an errand to Rothau, leaving his patient in the care of Sébastien Scheidecker, Lenz engaged in such wild escapades, both in Waldersbach and in Fouday, that the whole community was thrown into turmoil. Oberlin, when he returned, was again able to quiet him for a time. But late in the evening of the same day, when Oberlin had for a moment left the living room, where he and his wife and Lenz were spending the evening together, Lenz managed to lay his hands on the scissors from Mme Oberlin's sewing basket. With a wild shout and a dramatic gesture he made as if to thrust the blades into his heart; only a shriek of horror from Mme Oberlin's lips arrested the stroke. Oberlin, returning to the room, managed gently to take the weapon from him. He now decided that he was incapable of effecting any lasting improvement in Lenz's condition, and, with a heavy heart, made arrangements to transfer him to Strasbourg.

Taking fond leave of the family, Lenz made the sad journey as a prisoner under guard. Soon thereafter one of his brothers came and fetched him back to Livonia. His condition improved somewhat, but he was never capable of steady employment. For a time he lived in St. Petersburg, then in Moscow, where one night in May 1792 he was found dead in a deserted street.

In the perspective of Oberlin's long professional life, the Lenz affair constitutes only a brief episode and is of a kind that would perhaps be scarcely worth the telling, if the man who knocked at the door that wintry night had been just any one among the many travelers who found shelter and friendship there. But Lenz was no ordinary wanderer. To say simply that his name was known to the German reading public would be an understatement. He was in fact one of the literary lions of his time; three of his plays were the theatrical rage of the season; and his popularity everywhere rivaled, and in some places exceeded, even that of Goethe. Thus it happened that stories about his last days in Alsace were widely circulated in newspapers and literary weeklies. These provoked disputes about the treatment that had been accorded him there. There arose a furor that eventually became so great that Oberlin felt constrained to write out his version of the affair; not for publication, but for his own use in answering the many inquiries that came to him, and for that of his friends who wished to speak in his behalf. The manuscript is in German; it runs to nineteen large, closely written pages. It is a moving document, closing with an apologia containing these words: "The only response that I shall make to the contradictory judgments is this: What we have done in this affair we have done before God and as we, on each occasion, believed that it was best to do."

The interest in Oberlin generated by the Lenz affair among the literati endured for many years. Half a century after the event, the German dramatist Georg Büchner saw the manuscript of Oberlin's report in Waldersbach, made a copy of it, and later used it in writing his *Lenz,* which, though it is only a fragment, is accounted one of the great *Novellen* of German literature. To many persons Oberlin was—and even in our time is—known only as the kind and gentle, but frustrated, parson and counsellor of Büchner's memorable account of a mind and spirit going down inexorably to the pit of madness.

There were also other literary productions based on the life and work of Oberlin. In 1828, one Mlle Guizot published a four-volume novel entitled *The Scholar, or Raoul and Victor,* in which a rebellious young dropout is brought back to his boarding school by a priest who reads to him a thirty-page manuscript about Pastor Oberlin. Mlle Guizot's romance is a piously fatuous work of no literary value, which would scarcely be worth mentioning here but for the accident that Honoré de Balzac, while working as a printer, set the type for it, and three years later, remembering the Oberlin episode, used Oberlin as a dual model for the two main characters, the doctor and the priest, in his novel *The Country Doctor.*[10] Furthermore, two years later, when he was inspired by his reading of Mesmer, Lavater, and Swedenborg to write his

rhapsodic romance *Seraphita,* Balzac again turned to Oberlin
as the model for one of his characters—the only Protestant
clergyman in all of his works. Surely neither of these novels
could have contributed to Oberlin's renown, since Balzac
neither used the name of Oberlin in either novel nor anywhere
acknowledged his use of Oberlin as a model. They are
mentioned here merely to document the assertion that Oberlin
was widely known and admired in the literary world.

Quite different is the case of another literary work
influenced by Oberlin, and the only one in which he appears as
protagonist, namely, *Oberlin: Roman aus der Revolutionszeit
im Elsass,* by Friedrich Lienhard.[11] This novel, destined to
make the name Oberlin a household word in German-speaking
Protestant families, first appeared serially in 1909-1910 and
was published as a book in Stuttgart in the fall of 1910. In the
quarter-century from 1910 to 1935, it went through many
printings, finally totalling 169,000 copies. The historical facts
presented in the 450-page book are almost all correct, for the
author, an experienced historian, worked wherever possible
from original documents. Historical characters—Oberlin and
Pfeffel, the Dietrichs, the Türckheims, and others—are
accurately drawn and correctly described. The selection and
arrangement of materials and episodes, however, the emphases
and perspectives, the viewpoints and outlooks are all in the
realm of fiction. The character of Oberlin seems distorted in
that his social milieu seems more that of the aristocratic
Alsatian visitors to the Steintal than of the simple folk of his
parish. It is not a great novel. Its popular success is perhaps
best explained by certain characteristic German attitudes in
the age between the Franco-Prussian war and the First World
War. Its monarchist bias appealed to Germans in the age of
Bismarck and of Wilhelm II; it was a specimen of the *Heimat-
dichtung* (regional literature) that flourished in that heyday of
nationalism; it put forward the Germanic quality of Alsatian
culture at a time when Germans were preening themselves for
having "regained the lost province"; and it catered to the everlasting romanticism of the German mind by translating
Oberlin into an imaginary milieu where he lived more in the
"internal heaven of the mind" than amid the harsh realities of
everyday life in the Steintal.

Aside from the literary community, there was another group
of persons that contributed much to Oberlin's growing fame,

namely, the motley company of eschatologists, millenarians, and visionaries for whom the good life meant the practice of holiness on earth as a preparation for the afterlife. One of these came to visit Oberlin in Waldersbach in 1801.

Johann Heinrich Jung, born in the same year as Oberlin, was reared by his poor parents in the disciplines of fanatical Pietism. He became, successively, a charcoal burner, a tailor's apprentice, a schoolmaster, a *Hofmeister,* a practical surgeon, and finally, at the age of thirty, a student of medicine at Strasbourg. There he happened into a boarding club of which Goethe and Lenz were fellow members. After his student years he published the story of his youth, entitled *Heinrich Stillings Jugend,*[12] and was henceforth known as Jung-Stilling. He wrote a novel on the model of Bunyan's *Pilgrim's Progress,* and several books with titles such as *Scenes from the Realm of Spirits* and *Theory of Spiritualism,* and founded and published a widely read magazine devoted to similar subjects. From 1803 on, he spent his life propagating his own individual kind of sentimental, mystical Pietism, always working against time, for he expected the end of the world to come in 1836. His epistolary style is displayed in his first letter to Oberlin, of April 2, 1801: "To the preacher of righteousness in the Vosgesian desert: Endure as a good warrior of Jesus Christ! Soon the victory will come—then we, the redeemed, shall embrace each other in Solyma and shall be glad to have suffered so much!—but also to have been forgiven so much. From your brother and fellow member in the body of Jesus, Jung-Stilling."

The two men apparently first met each other in 1809, and in August 1812, Jung-Stilling, with his family, visited the Ban de la Roche. He apparently departed from there with very deep and favorable impressions, for on September 8 he averred in a letter to "Papa Oberlin" that he felt "an irresistible calling" to become his biographer and asked for answers to several questions in anticipation of that project. (I join Oberlin's chief biographers, Stoeber and Leenhardt, in expressing regret that Jung-Stilling's book was never written.) The correspondence between the two men continued until Jung-Stilling died, nineteen years before the putative millenium, in 1817. It was probably one of the most meaningful of Oberlin's friendships: in Jung-Stilling's books Oberlin found support for his own deepest views on life and death; in his letters and his companionship he found comfort for his soul. The friendship also contributed much to Oberlin's increasing renown, for through Jung-Stilling's many publications and his countless private letters, Oberlin's name became widely known in the many and varied circles of common folk and aristocrats, of savants and publicists to which Jung-Stilling had access, both in person and through his writings. This friendship also led to a connection with a person through whose intermediation the modest country parson was destined to win personal recognition and admiration from Europe's most powerful sovereign, Alexander I.

Baroness Barbara Julie de Krüdener was one of the most eccentric personalities in that age of exotic characters. Ernest John Knapton, the best of her several biographers, has encapsulated her life in a single sentence:

> [The course of her life] takes us from a simple childhood in Livonia to the butterfly life of France in the last days of the *ancien régime;* from the diplomatic glitter of Venice and Copenhagen to the literary circles of Bernardin de Saint-Pierre and Madame de Staël; from the Paris of the Directory and the Consulate to Berlin and Königsberg; from the Moravian Brethren of Silesia and the Pietists of the Rhineland to the last coalition against Napoleon and to the Czar Alexander's magnificent imaginings; from the economic misery and religious frenzy of Switzerland and southern Germany in the first years of the Restoration to a period of seclusion in Livonia; from a long life of restless activity to an almost mythical end in the distant loneliness of the Crimea.[13]

Oberlin and the Ban de la Roche impinged on that peripatetic life several times. The first of these was in January 1809, when Mme de Krüdener was at Ste. Marie-aux-Mines. Her meeting with Oberlin was initiated by the baroness and took place at Villé, a town about equidistant from Ste. Marie-aux-Mines and Waldersbach. Mme de Krüdener, having recently come from a period of residence at the mother congregation of the Moravian Brethren at Herrnhut by way of a visit with Jung-Stilling in Karlsruhe, was interested in Oberlin not so much for his good works in social reform as for his alliance with mystical prophecies and visions. So the evening was spent in earnest conversation about such matters as the imminence of the millennium and the course and qualities of the life to come. Mme de Krüdener's purpose in coming to Ste. Marie-aux-Mines had been to join a commune that a fanatic religious zealot, Jean-Frédéric Fontaines, had established in the parsonage there; to consort with the commune's resident seeress, Maria Kummer; and to develop a plan that she had conceived to establish an ideal community for the intensive pursuit of the life of holiness. Before she parted company with Oberlin at Villé, she revealed that plan to him and invited him to join forces with her in founding her colony in Württemberg; but he declined, saying that the Lord had placed him in the Ban de la Roche and there he would remain: "one wife, one congregation."

So Oberlin went back to his rocky vineyard where he had already labored for forty years, while the baroness and Fontaines and *die Kummerin* and their motley company, a party of forty persons, went to build their instant utopia at Catharinenplaisir. But it turned out that the visions and prophecies on which their kingdom had been founded were too much of this world: the seeress was exposed as a fraud and the congregation was ordered to leave Württemberg within ten days. Several attempts to reestablish the colony in other places met with similar, though less sudden, failure.

Taking respite from these and similarly wild, sometimes frenzied, occupations, the baroness came several times to the Steintal. She came in the spring of 1812 and stayed on until August 17, living with peasant families and conversing occasionally with Oberlin about his conceptions of the afterworld, while her secretary and travelling companion, a young Swiss theological student named Henri Empaytaz, helped Oberlin with the drawing, engraving, and printing of some of the charts of the heavenly abodes that can still be seen today in the museums at Waldersbach and Strasbourg. She returned for ten days in that year. Her last visit was from August 12 to September 11, 1814.

There is not much evidence now available on which to base a judgment concerning Oberlin's private opinion of Mme de Krüdener. Once, when someone asked him about it, he is said to have used the phrase: "the dear honest baroness." But like his previously quoted utterance about Rousseau—"the dear good man"—it can not be taken as a considered evaluation. There can be little doubt that he approved of her in point of religious zeal; but he must surely have been skeptical, to say the least, about the efficacy, and sometimes the propriety, of her actions. In view of the differences in temperament and personality of these two, and remembering the differing milieus from which each came to their occasional meetings, one can only guess that the modest country parson must often have shaken his head over "the dear honest baroness's" high-flying schemes for the quick creation of a universal kingdom of heaven on earth.

In 1815, not long after her last sojourn in Oberlin's parish, Mme de Krüdener had her first meeting with Czar Alexander I, and therewith began her involvement in those "magnificent imaginings" that won for her the sobriquet Lady of the Holy Alliance. She was at Alexander's side when he and the emperor of Austria and the king of Prussia jointly signed that most visionary of treaties; and Empaytaz preached the festival sermon at the commemorative celebration.

Aside from this indirect association, there were other communications between Oberlin and Alexander, who had heard much about the Ban de la Roche and its pastor from Jung-Stilling, Mme de Krüdener, and other persons within their circle of religious enthusiasts. So in 1813, when his troops first invaded France through Alsace, the czar, being concerned about Oberlin's safety and the welfare of his parish, had sent a messenger to Oberlin's door with a letter of safe conduct and had instructed his General Kolivansky to shun the Ban de la Roche as a possible site for military action.

Again in 1819, another connection was established between potentate and parson. François-Charles de Berckheim, a former pupil and a persistent admirer of Oberlin, had held various positions of public trust in Germany. With the fall of Napoleon he became unemployed, returned to his native Alsace, and, during an extended stay in the Ban de la Roche, met Mme de Krüdener's daughter Juliette, fell in love with her, and soon thereafter married her. Through this connection Berckheim came to the notice of the czar, who subsequently appointed him to a series of increasingly important posts in his far-flung empire. Thus there was established a new route of communication between Petrograd and Waldersbach which set the stage for the following affecting scenes described by Berckheim in a letter to Dr. Christian Barth, head of the Basel Mission Society and also a good friend of Oberlin.[14]

Berckheim wrote that he had seen the czar in Frankfurt and there had received from him a commission that was to take him to a long residence in the Crimea. When he asked leave to go first to the Vosges for a farewell visit with the "patriarch of the region" and to seek advice and strength from him, his old master, for his new assignment, the czar said: "I know Mr. Oberlin and know that he is a true servant of the Lord; tell him that I love him and honor him and commend myself to his prayers."

The sequel is related in the same letter: "On the evening before my departure from Waldersbach, Papa Oberlin came to kiss my hand saying, with deep emotion, 'Bring this to the emperor from me and assure him of my veneration and my wish that the will of the Lord may be fulfilled in him!" Berckheim next met the czar in Riga. When he described his departure from Waldersbach and told him about the "sacred charge" that Oberlin had laid upon him, to express to the emperor his reverential regard, the czar responded: "It is my place to kiss the hand of a priest of the Lord. You know that I never allow anyone to kiss my hand, least of all a priest!'" But ignoring all protestations, Berckheim kissed his hand, saying, " 'Sire, I know that; yet I cannot allow a kiss from the lips of Papa Oberlin to remain upon my hand!' Thereupon the Emperor embraced me three times and said: 'That is for Papa Oberlin.' " Berckheim delivered the message when next he visited Oberlin, accompanying his words with the appropriate actions.

Early in November 1825, Alexander rode from his country château at Taganrog to Karasu-Basar, where the Baroness de Krüdener, after her death on December 24, 1824, had been entombed in a mosque that had been converted to a Christian church. He went down to the crypt and prayed there for an hour. In the night of the same day he fell ill of the "Crimean fever." On November 5 he returned, gravely ill, to Taganrog, and on November 19, 1825, he died, filled with a sense of guilt for his part in the intrigues that had led to the assassination of his father and with remorse over the failure of his grand design to transform not only his own subjects but the whole continent of Europe into a people of God.

Seven months later Oberlin died, also as a humble penitent, but without remorse and universally extolled: his grand design, similar to Alexander's in its conception, though not in its scope, had, in the course of threescore years of unremitting labor, been brought to fulfillment.

If it is sometimes true that a prophet is without honor in his own country, then it must surely be true that a Protestant prophet is not extolled in a Catholic land, even though it be his own. The popular acclaim that Oberlin received in France never even remotely matched that which was accorded to him in Germany, or even in England. Yet it cannot be said that Oberlin was without honor there, for the French government—though only late in his life, to be sure—three times conferred honors upon him. And interestingly enough, the initiator of two of the three awards, and the cosponsor of the other, was none other than the most famous Roman Catholic priest in France at that time.

Henri Grégoire was just ten years younger than Oberlin, with whom he became acquainted when he was a curé at Embermenil in Alsace's sister province, Lorraine.[15] Sharing Oberlin's views on Christian ecumenism, as well as his concern about the unfortunate condition of Jews in Europe, he published a prize-winning essay entitled "The Political, Physical, and Moral Regeneration of the Jews," which played an important role in the development in France of more humane and democratic attitudes toward that oppressed race. In 1789 he was elected to the States-General as deputy for the clergy of Nancy and worked there for the abolition of Negro slavery. He became constitutional bishop of Loir-et-Cher in 1792. He proposed the abolition of the monarchy and demanded the trial of Louis XVI. During the Reign of Terror he was conspicuous for his courageous defense not only of his own church, but of all religious institutions. He steadfastly refused to give up the wearing of clerical dress and he saved many religious books and works of art from destruction. A speech that he made to the convention in December 1794 was instrumental in restoring the freedom of worship. The reorganization of the constitutional church was directed and guided by him. As a senator under the Consulate he opposed the Concordat of 1801 with Rome; he resigned his see in protest against it and became again a simple priest. Although he had opposed both the empire and Napoleon's election, the emperor made him a count. In 1819 he was elected to the chamber of deputies, but as a radical and dissident priest he was refused a seat. He died in poverty in 1831; at his burial there was a great liberal demonstration.

Abbé Grégoire admired Oberlin and through all his preoccupations with national affairs remained loyal to him. He was particularly delighted that Oberlin had used the Bible as the guide to both his social theory and his practical reforms. He honored him also for his spirit of independence vis-à-vis ecclesiastical authority. As one who believed both in international cooperation and in the communion of all believers, he venerated him also for his religious tolerance and his ecumenism, which found its overt expression in his practice of inviting all confessors of Christ to participate in Holy Communion in his churches (at which, to avoid possible pangs of conscience for non-Protestant communicants, he offered both leavened and unleavened bread). The abbé heartily approved of the title Evangelical-Catholic Minister that Oberlin sometimes wrote under his signature, for he himself had assumed the posture of a Roman Catholic *protestant,* using the word in its literal sense, though it is not recorded that he ever used the phrase as a title.

The abbé first came to the Waldersbach parsonage in 1787. In the following years he returned there often, for he found peace and regeneration in the comradely presence of his humble colleague and fellow dissident. According to Stoeber, the priest did not always resist the temptation to proselytize; yet the long and earnest theological discussions that priest and parson held were always marked by mutual respect and affection. The abbé was one of the few correspondents with whom Oberlin used the informal personal pronoun.

The first of the three honors mentioned above was the joint citation (in 1792) of Oberlin and Stuber for their contributions to the "universalization" of the French language that was described in chapter four. The second came in 1818. In March of that year Count François de Neufchatel, member of the French Academy and vice-president of the Royal Agricultural Society, wrote to Oberlin that he, with the support of Counsellor of State Baron de Gerando and of Henri Grégoire, had recommended him as recipient of the annual gold medal award of the society. In his letter of grateful acceptance, Oberlin pleads the infirmities of his age in requesting that the medal to be conferred at the plenary meeting of the society in Paris be presented to Baron de Gerando as his proxy. Many a

French citizen first learned of Oberlin's work in the Ban de la Roche from Count de Neufchatel's explicitly detailed and informative citation and report, which were reprinted in many newspapers and periodicals.

A year and a half later, Oberlin, to his own surprise—and presumably again thanks to the good abbé—received the highest distinction in the power of the nation, the Cross of the Legion of Honor.[16] After his induction, when all correspondence concerning the matter had been completed, Oberlin put together all the documents pertaining to it—the *ordonnance* of King Louis XVIII, the letters from the Ministry of the Interior and from various prefectures, letters of congratulation from countless friends, together with all his responses—wrapped them, tied the packet with ribbons, and wrote on it in a firm hand, and doubtless with a sardonic smile, "A Chevalier!—aged eighty years!"

The extension of Oberlin's fame beyond the boundaries of continental Europe began when he made his first contact with the British and Foreign Bible Society. From his early youth he had taken a lively interest in Christian missions, both at home and abroad. When, in 1774, he had expected to receive the call to Ebenezer, he had seen that prospect as an opportunity to fulfill two desires of his heart: to contribute to the spreading of the Word and the Kingdom, and at the same time to satisfy his yearning for travel to far places. Once he had interpreted the failure of the call to come through as a signal from God that he was to remain at his post in the Ban de la Roche, he renounced his wanderlust, indulging it thereafter only in imaginary journeys, poring over atlases and reading reports and romances of travel and exploration. His interest in missions, however, remained strong and active. He supported the so-called inner mission work of Francke's institutions in Halle; he corresponded with the Preachers' Conference of the Congregation of the Brethren at Herrnhut; he exchanged letters of intimate friendship with Pastor Blumhardt of the Basel Mission Society, one of the greatest among all the many organizations for foreign missions that burgeoned throughout Christendom in the nineteenth century. When Oberlin heard in 1804 that the British and Foreign Bible Society had been founded in London, he wrote to its secretary a letter that marked the beginning of a fruitful collaboration that lasted the rest of his life.[17]

His letter had been motivated by his desire to see that "the beloved, the much beloved Book" was available to every man, woman, and child in both parishes of the Ban de la Roche. The answering letter came quickly. At that time the society had no French Bibles on hand, but the letter contained a gift of thirty pounds sterling. In his letter of acknowledgement, Oberlin described his parish at length and reported on the lives and good works of the persons to whom he had given the first three Bibles purchased with the money received. The reading of that letter, dated November 3, 1804, was a special feature of the first annual meeting of the British society and created such a deep impression that it moved the society to two actions: it elected Oberlin to be its first corresponding member living abroad, and, under the impact of Oberlin's remarks on the contributions of women to the religious life of his parish, it decided to organize a special division for women. Thus the example that Oberlin had set in his remote and primitive villages contributed something to the cause of equal rights for women far away in sophisticated, enlightened London.

In Waldersbach Oberlin formed an affiliate organization of the British society, and with the cooperation of former pupils of his boarding school, including the publisher Treuttel in Paris, he caused similar branch societies to be formed at other places in France. In 1816 Henri-Gottfried Oberlin made an extensive missionary trip through southern France in behalf of the society. Thus it came about that Oberlin, a half-century after his plan to become a missionary in the new world had come to naught, managed still to play some part, albeit vicariously, in the great mission movement of his time, while still remaining faithful to the pledge that he had given in his much-quoted phrase, "one wife, one parish." The persistence of his devotion—and incidentally also of Louise Scheppler's—to the cause of the Bible societies is suggested by the following letter, written by Jean-Luc Legrand on July 17, 1825, within the last year of Oberlin's life. "As all that our venerable patriarch receives and possesses is only employed for the advancement of the Kingdom, he has again remitted to me 100 francs, desiring me to forward them to the Bible Society, in Paris. His Louise has added to it ten francs for the same purpose, and ten for the Missionary Society at Paris. She owns a single acreage, and this is the amount of the rent. May the Lord put a peculiar blessing upon it."[18]

The connection with the society proved to be influential in the spreading of Oberlin's fame in England and eventually overseas. In 1818 the Reverend John Owen, secretary of the society, in the course of a trip through France and Switzerland, came "to testify his veneration for Pastor Oberlin of Waldersbach...this extraordinary man with the simplicity of a Patriarch and the zeal of an Apostle."[19] On his return to London, Owen wrote a long report on his visit. It contained detailed descriptions of the Ban de la Roche; Oberlin and some of his parishioners; the schools; the good works of the *conductrices* and the deaconesses; the churches and the services of worship. It also contained a special section describing the missionary journey of 1,800 miles made by Henri-Gottfried Oberlin in 1818.

In June 1820, two years after Owen, other visitors came from England to Waldersbach: the Reverend and Mrs. Francis Cunningham and the Reverend and Mrs. Karl Friedrich Steinkopf, all personal friends of Sarah Atkins and persons of importance in both the British and Foreign Bible Society and the Society for the Promotion of Christian Knowledge. They stayed nearly a fortnight as guests of Oberlin, of the Legrands, and of other households. Both Mrs. Cunningham and Mrs. Steinkopf kept extensive journals during their stay. These contain detailed descriptions of the people, their personalities, their homes, their schools and churches, what they ate and how their meals were served, how they went about their daily tasks. Like Owen's report, these were printed and were read by many British friends of missions. Mrs. Cunningham's journal also constitutes a significant portion of Miss Atkins's life of Oberlin. The measure of Oberlin's renown in England is intimated by the fact that George Eliot could allude in *Middlemarch* to "the spirit of Oberlin" without any identifying modifier, with confidence that her allusion would be readily recognized and understood.[20]

Through Miss Atkins's book and the many précis and abstracts of it that were widely circulated also in America, Oberlin became so widely known there that Emerson, in addressing the graduating class of the Harvard Divinity School, could, like George Eliot, mention him without considering it necessary to add further identification. His renown in America was amplified with the founding of Oberlin, Ohio, and its college. The story of how it came about that the founders chose Oberlin's name has been told by Robert S. Fletcher in *A History of Oberlin College from its Foundation Through the Civil War.*

Describing the cultural scene on which the foundation was about to appear, Fletcher says: "In the first half of the nineteenth century militant Protestant Christianity saw itself marching to the conquest of America and the World. Rank on rank they advanced with flying banners: the revivalists leading the way, the missionary societies, the Bible societies, the Sabbath reformers, the religious education and Sabbath School societies, and the tract societies. Combined in the same great army and under the same staff were the anti-slavery societies, the peace societies, the Seamen's Friend Society, the temperance societies, the physiological reform and moral reform societies. Closely allied were the educational reformers whose task it was to train a generation for Utopia."[21]

One of the most celebrated among the preachers, leaders, and inspirers of that great wave of moral reform in America was Charles Grandison Finney, minister of the Broadway Tabernacle Church in New York and a mighty hunter before the Lord in his wide-ranging crusades against Satan throughout the northern states.

Among the persons inspired to good works and great enterprises by Finney's preaching was a young man of Granville, New York, named John Jay Shipherd. As a student, he, like Oberlin had dedicated himself to the service of the Lord. He took particular interest in the Sabbath School movement and in the dissemination of inspirational reading material. One of the tracts that Shipherd distributed in many copies was an abridged version of Sarah Atkins's *Memoirs,* published by the National Sunday School Union of Philadelphia.

The specific sector of the front against Satan on which Shipherd felt that he was personally called by God to do battle was the great Mississippi basin, which he often referred to as "the valley of dry bones" and "the vale of moral death." To gird himself for his mission, he apprenticed himself as a minister. After eighteen months of study he was ready to go forth. Following a brief journeyman pastorate in Vermont, he pressed on to the west and came, in February 1831, to Elyria, Ohio, a locality that is actually not quite in "the great valley," but apparently seemed to him close enough to satisfy the specifications of his divine vocation. In Elyria he launched a temperance campaign by which he aroused the hostility not only of the tavernkeepers, just as Oberlin had called down the wrath of his *cabaretiers,* but also the opposition of many conservative church members. By April 1832, he doubted if he could continue long in that place. "The enemy," he wrote to his father, "comes in on me like a flood." And indeed, soon thereafter his congregation asked for his resignation.

Shipherd took this to be a signal for action toward the formulation of a grander scheme for Christianizing the great valley than the mere transformation of Elyria into a terrestrial Elysium. He arranged for a former fellow student, Philo Penfield Stewart, then a lay missionary to the Indians in Mississippi, to join him, and together they talked about what could be done to increase the number of messengers of the Lord in the vale of moral death. The plan, which seems to have been quickly formed, is described in a letter from Shipherd to his brother of August 13, 1832.

> At length, while reading in the *Christian Spectator* a Review of Dr. Henderson's Residence in Iceland, delighted with the intelligence and Christian simplicity of its inhabitants, I proposed to Br. S. that we form a Colony for the promotion of like, or superior, intelligence and Christian simplicity. Pastor Oberlin's Bann de la Roche came up to second the proposal. O! tho't we, how would God be honored in the influence of his religion upon the world if it were divorced from Mammon, and wedded to simplicity and true wisdom! In the examples given by the Icelanders and Pastor Oberlin's Bann, God has been greatly honored, and every one, almost, who has viewed them with a Christian eye has been ashamed of his own conformity to this selfish world.
>
> Now, said we, let us gather some of the right spirits and plant them in the dark Valley, to give such example as Pastor Oberlin's flock, and they will make our churches ashamed of their unholy alliances with earth.

So now they had a name for the new colony, yet to be born; it remained to lay out details of the grand design. These are given in a letter from Shipherd to a friend.[22] They talked, they thought, they prayed, he wrote, and at length decided that they would seek out a favorable place and gather a colony whose regulations would require of each member constant awareness of his stewardship to the Lord; moderation in the acquisition of property; simplicity in dress, diet, houses, and furnishings; industry and economy; promotion of education at home and abroad. Schools would be established "from the infant school up as high as may be, at least as high as the highest High School," with the hope that there would eventually be "an institution which will afford the best education for the ministry." Connected with the institution there would be a farm and workshop where, with four hours of labor per day, students were to defray their entire expense. All the children of the colony were to be "thoroughly taught in English, to whatever service they may be destined"; yet they were to labor so much that "those who are liberally educated for professions, may like Paul and other learned Orientals, acquire the trades which in such fields as many ministers must occupy, will be of great value, and to all of some profit." They projected an institution resembling Oberlin's *pensionnat:* "In addition to the children of the Colony we would educate School Teachers and Ministers from the four winds; for on our plan we can instruct multitudes." They proposed "a manual labor establishment for *females* also, which in our estimation is immensely important."

The site that they finally chose for the new settlement, though its contours were flatter, was no more inviting than Oberlin's Steintal. It was a swampy, nearly trackless area in "the darkness of a deep Ohio forest," nine miles southwest of Elyria. The founding of the settlement; the rapid growth of the colony and of the Oberlin Collegiate Institute—later renamed Oberlin College—under the leadership of the great Finney, who became its president; and its turbulent history in the antislavery movement and the Civil War constitute a separate story. In this context it is sufficient merely to say that through this foundation it came about that within a few decades after John Frederic had died in his obscure Alsatian village, his name became a byword across the continent on which it had been newly planted in Oberlin, Ohio, by Shipherd and Stewart.

In the United States "Oberlin" appears as a geographical name in five places: Oberlin, Ohio, in Lorain County (pop. 8,761); Oberlin, Kansas, in Decatur County (pop. 2,291); Oberlin, Louisiana, in Allen Parish (pop. 1,857); Oberlin, Pennsylvania, a hamlet near Harrisburg; and Mount Oberlin (8,100 ft.) and Oberlin Falls, in Glacier National Park in Flathead County, Montana. Only Oberlin, Ohio, and Oberlin, Pennsylvania, are named after John Frederic; the other names seem to be secondarily derived from Oberlin College.[23]

Another social concern that the founders of the colony in Ohio shared with John Frederic Oberlin persisted well into the twentieth century, namely, the cause of Christian missions. In the 1890s, a group of ten missionaries, all graduates of the Oberlin School of Theology, which was a part of Oberlin College, had gone to Shansi province in China as missionaries. In the course of the uprising against alien influences in China known as the Boxer Rebellion, all of that "Oberlin band," with their families, were massacred. In commemoration of their martyrdom, there was formed an Oberlin Shansi Memorial Association. In 1908 the association erected a living monument to the dead by developing the educational institution that had been projected by them. Eventually a school named Ming Hsien, a college of liberal arts, and an agricultural school and experiment station were established in Taiku. These institutions were generally referred to as "Oberlin in Shansi" or "Oberlin in China." Thus the Oberlin name was again transplanted overseas—this time not from Europe, but from North America—to the continent of Asia. The Oberlin institution in Asia has endured through wars and revolutions and despite forced removals, first from Taiku in Shansi to Chengtu in Zechuan, then back to Taiku, then to Madura in India, and finally to Tunghai University in Taiwan, where it is today.

Meanwhile, another institution, named Obirin, has been founded in Japan, on the general model of the original Oberlin in Shansi, by Mr. and Mrs. Yasugo Shimizu, both graduates of the Oberlin College Graduate School of Theology. Obirin is situated in Tokyo. Its name, meaning "beautiful cherry orchard," describes the grounds that it occupies and at the same time intimates the continuing influence of John Frederic Oberlin and of Oberlin College.

In Europe the name has been perpetuated in several ways. The first establishment honored with it there was the Institut Oberlin, founded by Legrand, for training teachers for infant schools at Schirmeck-la Broque.[24] The (incomplete) list of donors for that cause given by Stoeber shows that contributions came from France, Switzerland, and England, with the last-named group constituting more than one-third of the list. (The most generous donor by a considerable margin was Oberlin's first biographer, who gave her royalties from the *Memoirs*. She appears twice on the list, once as Miss Sarah Atkins of Chipping Norton, and once as Mrs. D. Wilson, née Atkins. The second largest contribution was made by Mrs. Bulwer-Lytton.) In many Protestant congregations in Germany and Switzerland, local organizations called Oberlin Societies have also supported the cause of infant schools. The most significant European institution bearing the name and still existing today, however, is the Oberlin Haus at Neubabelsberg (formerly Neuwawes) near Berlin. It is a deaconess mother house specializing in service to physically disadvantaged children and is especially notable for its enlightened and devoted service to persons deprived of both hearing and sight.

In 1966, the Mouvement de Renaissance spirituelle of Strasbourg, with the agreement of the French Ministry of Youth, Sports, and Leisure Activities, established an international work camp for youth. The site of the camp is near the town of Schoulzbach, in the Vale of Orbey, in the upper Vosges, an area of historic battles and military cemeteries. Its purpose is to promote political, cultural, and spiritual détente among the youth of all nations through shared experience in joint constructive labor. The first camp group, whose motto was "Youth builds in France," prepared the site and laid the foundations of the Maison Jean-Frédéric Oberlin. In the following nine summers, ever larger numbers of young men and women from various countries of Europe have worked together to complete the substantial and handsome home for their organization, the newest of the far-flung humanitarian foundations bearing the still living name of Oberlin.

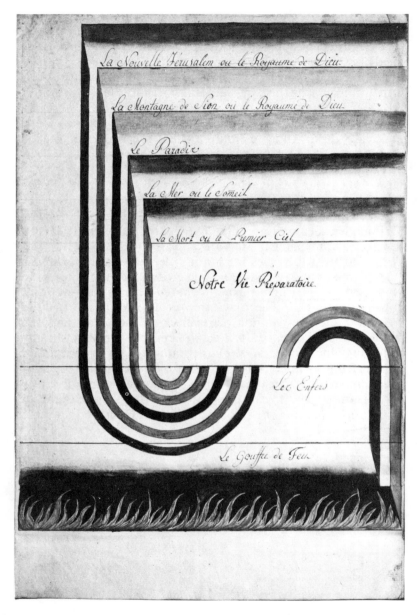

La Nouvelle Jérusalem ou le Royaume de Dieu

La Montagne de Sion ou le Royaume de Dieu

Le Paradis

La Mer ou le Sommeil

La Mort ou le Premier Ciel

Notre Vie Préparatoire

Les Enfers

Le Gouffre de Feu

26   The Seven Worlds. One of many sketches made by Oberlin of abodes of the dead. The stripes, representing souls of persons in various stages of blessedness, are in several colors in the original.

28 Oberlin's Grave at Fouday

27 The Church at Fouday

15

Last Days, Death, and Burial

On November 18, 1825, Oberlin's daughter Frédérique-Bienvenue and her husband, Pastor Louis Rauscher, moved from Barr, where they had lived for about fifteen years, to Waldersbach. Rauscher was to be Oberlin's vicar and after his father-in-law's death, his successor. Thus Oberlin could live out his last days under the care of his youngest daughter, who had been an infant of eight weeks at the time of her mother's death. From her recollections we have a reliable record of the last half-year of her father's life.[25]

The integrity of Oberlin's strictly disciplined personality endured undiminished to the end of his life; his tread remained firm, his posture ramrod straight. Sometimes, when it was hard for him to rise from his chair, he could be heard saying to himself in tones that a sergeant might use in dragooning his recruits: *"Komm, alter Fritz, du Liederlicher* [you lazybones]! Where is your old strength? What has become of you?" Yet, if he happened to be upstairs and required something from downstairs, or vice versa, he would not allow anyone to fetch what he needed, saying that the exercise was good for his old bones. He retired, as always, at ten o'clock, but now rose at six more often than at five. He persisted in his accustomed simple diet, except for one concession. Years ago he had given up the luxury of breakfast coffee with sugar as a protest against the abuse of the black men, women, and children whose labor on the plantations in distant lands made those luxuries available. But now, on waking, he took a few sips of sweetened coffee as a prescribed stimulant, but always under protest and with expressions of revulsion, for every sugar granule and every coffee bean seemed to him to be tainted with the blood of some pitiable mistreated slave. At noon he took soup with vegetables, a small piece of meat, and a glass of wine; in the evening, soup and a compote.

His countenance retained its benignly expressive features, except that his eyes had lost their old luster. He enjoyed his daily walks along the village street because they afforded him contacts with people. When someone approached, he would stop and offer his hand, asking who it was, for the dimness of his vision made him unable to distinguish one face from another. On hearing a familiar name, his countenance became animated again with the old radiance of warmth and affection that friends and visitors had ever and again remarked there. If his acquaintance was a young person, his expression was especially warm; and if it happened to be an old and loyal fellow worker for the Kingdom, he would exclaim, sometimes with tears in his eyes: "God bless you, you too are one who prays for my poor congregation." One boon that seems to grace the last days of some ancients, however, he never experienced: the pleasure of looking back over his long and toilsome life and finding that it was good and satisfying in the fulfillment of its promises. Indeed, when he thought he was alone and unobserved, his attitude often betrayed dejection and discouragement, and Frédérique would hear him murmur, "Oh God, have mercy on my poor parish."

On the morning of June 1 he was no longer able to speak. In the last movement of his limbs he pulled his knitted cap from his head and folded his hands. Five hours he lay—silent, motionless, but still breathing. What, one wonders, was the content of those last hours and moments of life? Had he perhaps already been translated to the first of those seven worlds where dwell the blessed dead, which he had often plotted in manifold graphic drawings during the melancholy yet blissful hours of his solitude? Had he not lost the power of speech, could he now have said whether those eschatological imaginings had been truth or error? We cannot know, for death came to him, as to all men, in impenetrable privacy. He died in silence at eleven o'clock.

His funeral was on June 5, 1826.

Early in the morning travellers begin to come down the hills. The people from the nearby settlements, the people from the towns beyond the mountains, the people from the cities, and the clergy from all Alsace—all are coming to Waldersbach.

Through the morning the corpse lies in state in a glass-covered coffin under the trees in the front yard of the parsonage. At noon the family is joined by the *maires* and elders of the eight villages of the two Ban de la Roche parishes, who are to carry the coffin.

The family, the *maires* and elders, and the assembled clergy form a circle. The president of the Strasbourg consistory lays Oberlin's symbols of office on the coffin; the vice-president deposits the Bible; the *maire* of Waldersbach attaches the medallion of the Legion of Honor. There is singing by a choir.

At two o'clock, amid the ringing of the bells of all the villages, the journey to Fouday begins. The pallbearers are preceded by the eldest of the elders, who carries the wrought-iron cross that is to be planted on the grave. The coffin is carried through the Waldersbach church (which has two portals) with a brief pause before the altar. The people of the parish follow the cortege; the visitors from afar, who will fall in after them, line the road to Fouday. A choir of children sings as it marches, "Non, non, non, nul ne vaincra Gédéon" and other hymns. When, after a half-hour march, the head of the procession arrives at Fouday, the last marchers have not yet begun to leave Waldersbach.

The *place* in front of the church at Fouday is ringed about by the women of a nearby Catholic parish, all in black and kneeling in prayer. The coffin is carried in and set on the platform before the altar. Two curés share the space behind the altar with the officiating Protestant clergy. As many people press into the church as the building will hold; the rest, about three-fourths of all those present, swarm into the plaza, the churchyard, and the street.

There is singing by the congregation. Pastor Jaegle, a close friend of Oberlin and president of the consistory of Barr, occupies the pulpit. He reads the obituary and farewell message to his parish that Oberlin had written for his own funeral, in 1784, when he had confidently expected to die soon after his wife's death. Thereafter Pastor Jaegle preaches on two texts chosen and prescribed by Oberlin: "Bless the Lord, O my soul, and all that is within me, bless His holy name..." and "These are they which came out of great tribulation and have washed their robes, and made them white in the blood of the Lamb."[26] The service closes with a hymn and a blessing.

The coffin is carried through the multitude to the churchyard. The gravesite is on a hillock shaded by a weeping willow that grows on the adjacent grave of Henri-Gottfried. A lengthy graveside address is delivered by Pastor Braunwald, vice-president of the Barr consistory. Ehrenfried Stoeber reads a eulogy in seven stanzas of German rhymed verse. The coffin is lowered: ashes to ashes; dust to dust. But before the first shovelful of earth falls, there is a stirring among the people. A man steps forth, identifies himself as a member of a nearby Catholic parish, and says that he cannot bear to see these ceremonies end without an expression of the sentiments of the Catholic laity. His is the last eulogy.

The grave lies in the middle of the churchyard of Fouday: at its foot there is an open space, carpeted with pine needles, where one stands facing the cross and the stone. On Oberlin's right lies Jean-Luc Legrand; at his left, Henri-Gottfried; at his head, Louise Scheppler. The grave is covered by a massive slab of reddish-brown Vosgesian sandstone. It is inscribed:

ICI REPOSENT
LES
DÉPOUILLES MORTELLES
DE
JEAN-FRÉDÉRIC
OBERLIN
PASTEUR DE LA PAROISSE
DE
WALDBACH
NÉ LE 31 AOÛT 1740
DÉCÉDÉ LE 1er JUIN 1826.

Around the margin of the stone run these words from the last chapter of Daniel: "The wise leaders shall shine like the bright vault of heaven, and those that have guided the people in the true path shall be like the stars for ever and ever."

But the most memorable epitaph is the one on the iron cross that was carried at the head of the funeral procession and then planted on the grave by the people:

PAPA OBERLIN

Appendix

The Curriculum in Oberlin's Schools

Stoeber-Burckhardt's report (2:136), quoted below, is the most complete treatment of the schools. It begins with the subjects taught to the seven-year-olds, who constituted the first class in the *écoles publiques,* and ends with the ninth class, that is, with the children aged sixteen. Stoeber explains in a footnote that a part of the manuscript from which he took this listing was not in Oberlin's hand and that he therefore suspects its authenticity and surmises that the subjects listed in it properly belong among those under "Schools for Adults." The part that is thus put in question is here enclosed in brackets. Oberlin's use of the word *adultes* to include adolescent children of thirteen to sixteen years has misled some writers (e.g., Parisot) to mistake this as the curriculum for adult education in the usual sense.

I. Schools for the Youngest or Beginners

FIRST CLASS. The children are taught: 1. To give up bad habits; 2. to acquire the habits of obedience, sincerity, compliance or good nature [*débonnaireté*], good order, beneficence, good conduct, etc.; 3. to recognize the small letters of the alphabet; 4. to spell without the book; 5. to pronounce well the syllables and difficult words and to strike the right tone in reciting; 6. to give the correct French designation of things that are shown to them; 7. the first concepts of morals and religion.

291

SECOND CLASS. 1. Repetition and further extension of knowledge previously acquired; 2. to spell (more difficult words) from the book and to recognize the capital letters; 3. to know the faculties of the soul; 4. to acquire the concepts of time and the seasons and of the productions of the earth, of animals, and of men, as well as of man's nourishment, clothing, lodging; of the occupations and their wages; of property, donations, exchange, inheritance, money, purchase, borrowing, debts, and interest; of families, villages, market-towns, and cities; of trials and litigations; of magistrates, of states and of public welfare; [of countries and peoples, both near and far; of the course of nature; of the power, the bounty, and the wisdom of God; of the immortality of the soul; of virtues and vices, of the way to salvation by obedience to God and to the stirrings of conscience and by following the example of Jesus Christ; 5. to count to 1,000, both forward and backward, and to use the arithmetic book for the purpose of addition and subtraction of numbers to 100.]

THIRD CLASS. 1. To retain the previously acquired knowledge; 2. to learn to read a book with which the pupils have already become familiar and which has been explained to them, and in such a way that they can read it fluently; 3. to write the small letters legibly, neatly, and uniformly [*avec symétrie*]; 4. to write the numbers to ten on horizontal lines and in columns of various arrangement; 5. to add, subtract, multiply, and to divide abstract quantities on the black slate.

II. The Middle Schools

FOURTH CLASS. 1. To recall the ideas previously acquired and repeat the preceding exercises; 2. to practice reading; 3. to explain the elements of geography, i.e., to identify the concepts: island, strait, sea harbor, promontory, etc.; to talk about fortresses, castles, tolls, and about differences in government, in language, and in religion; 4. to explain a map without text; 5. to learn the second course in arithmetic from fractions to the rule of three for abstract quantities; 6. penmanship in the second degree; 7. to learn the German letters; 8. to sing according to notes.

FIFTH CLASS. 1. To review what has gone before; 2. to practice reading and writing; 3. to read printed material and manuscripts; 4. singing.

SIXTH CLASS. 1. Review of what has gone before; 2. to specify the four rules of calculus for positive quantities; 3. to study geographical maps with text; 4. to read German without spelling; 5. continuation of singing.

III. Schools for Adults

SEVENTH CLASS. 1. To review the exercises of the preceding classes; 2. natural history, especially botany; 3. to learn to write promissory notes, receipts, accounts, etc.; 4. continuation of singing.

EIGHTH CLASS. 1. Review as above; 2. practical arithmetic to the rule of three; 3. more detailed geography; 4. the most notable epochs of world history; 5. to translate orally from German into French; 6. continuation of singing.

NINTH CLASS. 1. Review; 2. principles of agriculture, matters pertaining to registry [*de la greffe*], and of the rules of health; 3. first principles of geometry, of physics, and astronomy; 4. translation in writing from French to German using French characters; 5. to compose letters, receipts, statements of accounts for workmen; 6. religion with its evidences; 7. a general and succinct conception of the sciences and the arts; 8. singing; 9. cutting of quills.

Notes

Part 1

[1]The epigraph on the title page is from a previously unpublished German letter in the collection of Professor Rodolphe Peter of Strasbourg, quoted by Horand Gutfeldt, *Johann Friedrich Oberlin,* pp. 41, 42. The letter was addressed to the Alsatian François Reber. For the baptism in Colmar see Wilhelm Heinsius, *Johann Friedrich Oberlin und das Steintal,* p. 3.

[2]This account of the family in Colmar is based on an article by the late Georg Meyer, "Fort von Colmar," in an unidentified publication. It was sent to me by the author's daughter, Mme Anne-Margrit Meyer. Meyer states that before this time the family name had been Oferle and that, for reasons which he does not mention, this Johannes Oferle changed his name to Oberlin. The latter name is not uncommon in Strasbourg today. The variant Offerlin is documented by Lutz. See n. 4 below.

[3]Johann Wolfgang Goethe, *Hamburger Ausgabe in 14 Bänden,* 5th ed. (Hamburg: Wegner, n.d.), 9:477: "[Professor Jérémie-Jacques] Oberlin directed my attention to the monuments of the Middle Ages and made me acquainted with the ruins and remains, the seals and documents, and even sought to inspire in me an affection for the Minnesingers and the poets of the heroic epics. To this gallant man, and to Mr. Koch, I owe much, and if all had gone according to their wish, I would have owed to them the happiness of my life." Both Oberlin and Koch had urged Goethe to take up the life of scholarship.

[4]Robert Lutz, "Les ancêtres de Jean-Frédéric Oberlin" in *Deuxième Centenaire de l'arrivée au Ban-de-la-Roche de J.-F. Oberlin, mars-avril 1767-1967,* pp. 11-22.

⁵These clerical ancestors were Marx Heyland (c. 1500-1550); Niclaus Florus (1524-1587) of Gotha and Strasbourg, doctor of theology and minister; Johann Albrecht Krauch (1558-1613), minister at Ste.-Aurélie in Strasbourg; Samuel Schallesius (1585-1638); Johannes Bockler, minister at Strasbourg and later professor at Upsala; Johannes Feltz (1628-1691), minister at Ste.-Aurélie and canon of St. Thomas in Strasbourg. The clerical tradition continued in the generation of Oberlin's children: of his four sons, the two who lived to adulthood became ministers, and his four surviving daughters all married ministers.

⁶Stoeber-Burckhardt, *Johann Friedrich Oberlins, Pfarrer im Steinthal, vollständige Lebensgeschichte und gesammelte Schriften,* 2:67.

⁷In "J. F. Oberlin" in *Revue Alsacienne,* 12, no. 11, p. 363, based on family records and recollections of stories and reminiscences related to her as a child by her grandmother. Mme Roerich was a descendent of Oberlin.

⁸Stoeber-Burckhardt, 2:71-74. I have in my possession (a gift from Professor Gustave Koch of Strasbourg) eight leaves from a "comic strip" type of publication (of unspecified date, but obviously mid-twentieth century) entitled "la Superhistoire." They show, in eighty-six frames, "avec scénario de E. Barnard et mise en images de Claude Lapointe," highlights from the life of Oberlin. They include all the scenes of childhood here mentioned, along with others.

⁹Stoeber-Burckhardt, 2:78-79.

¹⁰Edmond Parisot, *Un Educateur moderne au XVIIIe siècle,* p. 26; on Professor Schoepflin, see Franklin L. Ford, *Strasbourg in Transition, 1648-1781,* p. 166.

¹¹Camille Leenhardt, *La Vie de J.-F. Oberlin 1740-1826 de D.-E. Stoeber,* p. 25.

¹²In 1743 Lembke was accused of heresy by the churchwardens of Alsace and was driven out of Strasbourg. He eventually emigrated to America, where he was for many years the head of Nazareth Hall, a boys' school of the Moravian Brethren near Bethlehem, Pennsylvania. His friendship with Oberlin continued throughout his life. See H. Strohl, *Etudes sur Oberlin,* pp. 235-37. Information given below about Lorenz is also from Strohl, pp. 241-44.

¹³Leenhardt, p. 213, fn. 3. The account of the end of the Oberlin-Lorenz friendship farther on is quoted from Stoeber-Burckhardt, 2:81-82.

¹⁴Parisot, pp. 26-27.

¹⁵Sarah Atkins, *Memoirs of John Frederic Oberlin, Pastor of Waldbach in the Ban de la Roche,* p. 24; also Heinsius, pp. 13-14. For

the full text of the "Act of Dedication" see Stoeber-Burckhardt, 2:85-90. The original document was in German.

[16]Stoeber-Burckhardt, 2:106-8.

[17]The record is in the form of a printed proclamation of the University of Strasbourg, preserved as Document 203/10 in the Oberlin collection of the Archives municipaux de Strasbourg. It states that ". . . Joh. Fridericus Oberlin . . . doctoratus philosophici . . . philosophiae laureae non indignos esse judicavit." The dissertation, no longer extant, was on a Leibnizian theme: "De virium vivarum atque mortuarum mensuris." See also Horand Gutfeldt, *Johann Friedrich Oberlin,* p. 15.

[18]Emil Ermatinger, *Deutsche Kultur im Zeitalter der Aufklärung,* p. 219. Some of the details given below about Ziegenhagen are from an unpublished manuscript by Georg Meyer made available to me by Mme Anne-Margrit Meyer. See also Leenhardt, pp. 14-15. The experiences with Ziegenhagen and the reference to Oberlin's diary (now lost) are from Stoeber-Burckhardt, 2:96-102.

[19]Stoeber-Burckhardt, 2:105-6.

[20]I am indebted to Dr. Gustave Koch of the Collegium Wilhelmitanum of St. Thomas in Strasbourg for a mimeograph copy of the *brevis disquisitio* of the thesis, translated into German by Wilfred Stroh and Marlene Kunz. There are eight chapters, the burden of whose argument is that the complexities of theological studies, the exigencies of the ministry, and the responsibilities of those who are charged with the care of human souls are real and great. These are followed by five chapters showing that every such *incommodum* is compensated: by the divine aid that is not withheld from those who have a true vocation; by the advantages which the clergyman is given in his own striving for holiness; and by the recompense which attends the faithful servant, for "they that are wise shall shine as brightness of the firmament; and they that turn many to righteousness as the stars forever and forever" (Dan. 12:3).

[21]Stoeber-Burckhardt, 2:112-14.

[22]Locally it is usually *la Champ du Feu.* Atkins (p. 4) surmises that this name (Field of Fire) derives from the mountain's volcanic origin, but Leenhardt (p. 19, fn. 2), probably more correctly, assumes that the word *feu* is a mistaken classical French translation of the local patois word *fé,* which is a corruption of the German *Vieh,* meaning livestock or cattle. Its summit and slopes, though only sparsely covered with grass, have always been used as pastures by the peasants of the valley. The English translation of *das Steintal,* Valley of Stones, which has been used by some writers, is not acceptable be-

cause it is based on the erroneous notion that the valley derives its name from the stony quality of its soil; Valley of the Rock would be more apposite. Some writers prefer the name Waldbach, but Waldersbach is the generally accepted designation and the one that Oberlin customarily used. Stoeber calls the shorter form *"vulgaire."* See Leenhardt, p. 17, fn. 3. J.B. Masson, *Die Siedlungen des Breuschtals (i. Els.) und der Nachbargebiete,* p. 152, says that the original name was Waltersbach.

[23]Archives, MS 185. The elevations are taken from Masson, p. 29.

[24]Masson, p. 73, 137-42. All the historical data following hereafter are, unless otherwise noted, from Karl Eduard Boch, *Das Steintal in Elsass,* pp. 3-71.

[25]Masson, pp. 137-42.

[26]Stoeber-Burckhardt, 2:31-32. See also Boch, p. 137, 98.

[27]Number of households according to Boch, p. 98:

Village	1655	1700	1771	1777
Waldersbach	8	9	25	68
Bellefosse	12	12	26	65
Belmont	7	9	25	78
Solbach	6	4	10	36
Fouday	5	9	15	46
Total	38	43	101	293

In 1809 Oberlin reported on the number of souls in his parish: Waldersbach, 347; Belmont, 529; Bellefosse, 403; Fouday, 224; Solbach, 203; total: 1,706. *Deuxième Centenaire de l'arrivée au Ban de la Roche de J.-F. Oberlin, mars-avril 1767-1967,* pp. 8-9.

[28]In Alsace the language boundaries are often very sharply drawn. Thus there is a village on the right bank of the Rothaine just outside the Ban de la Roche named Natzweiler whose inhabitants, early in the twentieth century, spoke only German, while in the village of Haute-Goutte, situated on the left bank of the little stream and thus belonging to the Ban de la Roche, the predominant language was French, though the two villages actually form a single settlement. See Masson, pp. 145-46.

[29]Boch, pp. 95-97, lists about 100 patois words and phrases of Germanic origin, of which the following examples are given in patois, German, and French, respectively: buob, Bube, garçon; ehakse,

verhexen, ensorceler; férschi, Pfirsich, pêche; fiéttre, füttern, paitré; haké, haken, crocher; mole, malen, peindre; slaué, schlagen, tuer; stak, Stock, bâton; truric, triste; ça tire, es zieht, il y a un courant d'air.

[30]Georg Meyer, "Kritisches zur Oberlinforschung," *Strassburger Monatshefte,* September-Oktober 1937, 515-18. This article, put at my disposal by Mme Meyer, is a spirited commentary on such exaggerations.

[31]Quoted in Laurin L. Henry, "The Awkward Interval," *American Heritage 19* (October 1968), p. 7.

[32]Boch, pp. 151-52.

[33]Stoeber-Burckhardt, 2:37-38.

[34]Heinsius, p. 22; for the names of the ministers and comments on the language question, see also Boch, p. 192.

[35]The best source of information about Stuber is Baum's biography. Unless otherwise noted, all information given about Stuber in this section comes from it and from MS 185, quoted below, in the bibliothèque municipale of Strasbourg. The manuscript is entitled "Histoire de la Paroisse de Waldersbach par M. Stuber (en 1762)." It is reprinted in Baum, pp. 69-86, in German translation. According to Baum it was written about 1780.

[36]Boch, p. 214.

[37]Stoeber-Burckhardt, 2:48.

[38]Leenhardt, p. 36. Stuber's method and this textbook were later adopted in some schools in Strasbourg.

[39]Heinsius, p. 29.

[40]Archives, MS 185.

Part 2

[1]Camille Leenhardt, *La Vie de J.-F. Oberlin 1740-1826 de D.-E. Stoeber,* p. 25. On prospective brides (below) see Sarah Atkins, *Memoirs of John Frederic Oberlin, Pastor of Waldbach in the Ban de la Roche,* pp. 53-56.

[2]The French term is *grande-nièce à la mode de Bretagne.* Oberlin's maternal grandfather was Mlle Witter's paternal great-grandfather.

[3]W. Steinhilber, *J.F. Oberlin,* p. 16. The following account of the affair is based on the full text of Oberlin's own account reprinted by Leenhardt, app. 2, pp. 421-22.

[4]See Emil Ermatinger, *Deutsche Kultur im Zeitalter der Aufklärung,* p. 271ff.

[5]Archives, MS 203, fasc. 11: "Inventarium über den Wohl Ehrwürdigen J.F. Oberlin . . . und M.S. Oberlinin geborene Witterin 1768."

[6]Wilhelm Heinsius, *Johann Friedrich Oberlin und das Steintal,* p. 34.

[7]Johann Wilhelm Baum, *Johann Georg Stuber, der Vorgänger Oberlins im Steinthal und Vorkampfer einer neuen Zeit in Strassburg,* p. 99.

[8]Archives, MS 185, p. 50. For the letter to Dietrich, ibid., pp. 141-42.

[9]Baum, p. 91. The quotation below is from Martha Buch, *Die pädagogischen und sozialpädagogischen Ideen Johann Friedrich Oberlins,* p. 44.

[10]Pestalozzi did not start his educational experiment at Neuhof until 1774. There is no doubt, therefore, about Oberlin's priority, quite aside from the differences in the nature and the success of these two programs. Oberlin's notation that he furnished the lodging of Sara Banzét is contradictory to the stipulation in the agreement quoted. Of the two versions, the one stated in the legal document is, of course, the correct one. The document is printed in facsimile as Illustration 11. The figures agreed to as wages are illegible.

[11]Information about the *poêles à tricoter* is from Leenhardt, pp. 58-71, and Buch, pp. 30-94. See also the description of the *poêles* by Louise Scheppler, with facsimile, in Erich Psczolla, *Louise Scheppler, Mitarbeiterin Oberlins,* pp. 97-101; on Oberlin's report cited below, see ibid., pp. 115-16.

[12]Leenhardt, pp. 477-78. Another cause for embarrassment—not mentioned by Oberlin—might have been the fact that early in his ministry he had wanted to make German the language of the Ban de la Roche. It was Stuber who dissuaded him from that purpose.

[13]Froebel opened his first kindergarten at Bad Blankenburg in 1840. His comprehensive work, *Die Menschenerziehung (Education of Man),* first appeared in 1826, the year of Oberlin's death. On "magic tricks" (below) see Psczolla, pp. 165-66.

[14]Robert R. Rusk, *A History of Infant Education,* pp. 162, 171.

[15]J.-J. Rousseau, *Emile,* trans. Barbara Foxley (London and New York: Everyman's Library), pp. 13-14. See also Ernst Schering, *Sternstunde der Sozialpädagogik,* pp. 14-15. It would not be correct to claim that Oberlin's *conductrices* were the first females ever to be employed anywhere as teachers, for the Ursuline Sisters, a Catholic order founded in Brescia in 1555, had been employed as early as the seventeenth century as teachers of girls, and *die englischen Fräulein* (a Roman Catholic congregation founded in Munich in 1630 among genteel female refugees from England) had from that date on

conducted schools for girls in German cities. (See Alfons Rosenberg, *Der Christ und die Erde,* p. 191.) There is apparently no record, however, of the employment of female lay teachers, either Catholic or Protestant, in public schools before Oberlin's *conductrices.* Thus Sara Banzét was the first laywoman ever employed as a teacher. Her years as a *conductrice,* however, were only four; she died on April 24, 1774, aged twenty-eight. Several others among the early *conductrices* are known to us from silhouettes cut by Oberlin and from character analyses of them made by him. See Psczolla, pp. 44-67, 78-79.

[16]Leenhardt, p. 37.

[17]A copy of Meyer's manuscript was kindly sent to me by his daughter, Mme Anne-Margrit Meyer.

[18]Baum, pp. 105-6; also Heinsius, pp. 34-35.

[19]Leenhardt, p. 38.

[20]Stoeber-Burckhardt, *Johann Friedrich Oberlin, Pfarrer im Steinthal, vollständige Lebensgeschichte und gesammelte Schriften,* 2: 123-24.

[21]Leenhardt, pp. 40, 41; also p. 37.

[22]Georg Meyer, "Kritisches zur Oberlinforschung," p. 516.

[23]Archives, MS 185, p. 72.

[24]Leenhardt, pp. 41-42, fn. 4.

[25]Ibid., p. 42, fn. 1.

[26]Archives, MS 185, p. 73.

[27]Leenhardt, pp. 42-43. The *présentateur* was the person who, in lieu of instrumental accompaniment, led the congregational singing.

[28]Ibid., p. 44.

[29]Ibid., pp. 38-39.

[30]Buch, p. 76.

[31]Leenhardt, p. 39.

[32]Archives, MS 54.

[33]Leenhardt, pp. 44-45.

[34]Rusk, p. 131.

[35]Both the code of behavior and the Neuvillers story are in Leenhardt, pp. 45-47.

[36]Stoeber reproduces from the Waldersbach archives several pages of a no longer extant manuscript entitled "Schools." Although he identifies it as a list of the subjects taught in each of the nine classes in the Steintal schools, it seems upon close scrutiny to be more a general statement of teaching and learning objectives than a systematic specification of courses or subjects. Furthermore, its authenticity seems questionable, since part of it is said to have been in a hand other than Oberlin's. For Stoeber's list of courses see the Appendix,

p. 291; also Stoeber-Burckhardt, 2:136-39; Leenhardt, pp. 47-48, fn. 2; Buch, pp. 117-18; Gutfeldt, pp. 157-61. The daily schedule is from Stoeber-Burckhardt, 2:142.

[37]Baum, p. 107.

[38]Karl Eduard Boch, *Das Steintal im Elsass*, p. 221.

[39]Stoeber-Burckhardt, 2:140.

[40]Leenhardt, pp. 51, 52.

[41]See Rousseau, *Emile*, pp. 341-42, where this point is illustrated by a dialogue between a nurse and a child.

[42]Ibid., pp. 278-328.

[43]Heinsius, p. 41.

[44]Stoeber-Burckhardt, 2:338-40.

[45]Erich Psczolla, "Pädagogische Impulse in den Predigten Oberlins," in *Evangelische Kinderpflege* (Witten/Ruhr: Luther Verlag, 1966), pp. 1-7.

[46]Mme Ernest Roerich, "J. F. Oberlin," *Revue Alsacienne* 12, no. 11, p. 363. The author gives a list of thirty-five children of Strasbourg families who were *pensionnaires;* all of them have distinctly German names. The Stoeber quotations below are from Stoeber-Burckhardt, 2:356-57.

[47]From *Middlemarch,* chapter three. On disputes about the climate see Meyer, "Kritisches," p. 515, and Wilhelm Scheuermann, *Ein Mann mit Gott,* pp. 312-13. The documentations of poverty below are from Boch, p. 153.

[48]Oberlin's letter is not extant; for Stuber's reply of February 1768 see Baum, pp. 93-94, and Heinsius, pp. 46-47.

[49]Leenhardt, pp. 142-43.

[50]Ibid., pp. 352-53.

[51]Quoted by Leenhardt, p. 92, from Fallot's article on Oberlin in Buison, F., *Nouveau dictionnaire de pédagogie,* 2 (Paris, 1887), p. 145.

[52]The two letters of Stuber quoted here are from Heinsius, pp. 46-47.

[53]Basic documents pertaining to this subject are: a letter written by Jean-Luc Legrand to a Parisian bookseller named Treuttel, and a report made to the Royal Agricultural Society by Count François de Neufchatel; its most explicit treatment in the Oberlin literature is that of Leenhardt, pp. 91-101; see also Stoeber-Burckhardt, 2:235-54.

[54]Stoeber-Burckhardt, 2:243-44. Information given below about the cultivation and utilization of potatoes in the Ban de la Roche and Alsace comes chiefly from Boch (pp. 155ff.), and from an unpublished essay by Georg Meyer, put at my disposal by Mme

Meyer. Meyer refers to Girard's *Alsace à table* as his chief source of information.

[55]The fact that patois words are used here suggests that Mme Rauscher was paraphrasing her father rather than quoting him literally; Oberlin would have avoided using such words in communicating with the people. (*Kmatiar* is the patois word for potato.)

[56]Heinsius, p. 48.

[57]Stoeber-Burckhardt, 2:247-48.

[58]Stoeber specifically states that in 1817, which was a year of crop failure in all of Alsace, such deaths occurred in the Alsatian Rhine plain, but, thanks to Oberlin, not in the Ban de la Roche; Stoeber-Burckhardt, 2:137-38. In the Musée Oberlin in Waldersbach as well as in the Musée Alsacien in Strasbourg, there are large collections of plant specimens, gathered, mounted on paper, and identified by Oberlin, and sketches in ink made by him, many of them drawn with considerable artistic skill.

[59]The manuscript came to the museum in 1949, a gift from M. Emil Walter of Zabern. The dissertation is mentioned by Boch, with the list of twenty-two edible plants. The two specimens unique to the Ban de la Roche are listed in Friedrich Kirschleger's *Flore d'Alsace et des contrées limitrophes,* 3 vols. (Strasbourg, 1852-1862), 2:111. On wine making see Sarah Atkins, *Memoirs of John Frederic Oberlin, Pastor of Waldbach in the Ban de la Roche,* pp. 76-77.

[60]Leenhardt, pp. 99-101.

[61]In the Ban de la Roche the hymnal was customarily used as a family record book.

[62]*Encyclopedia of the Social Sciences* (New York: Macmillan Co., 1930), article by Nelson Antrim Crawford on "Agricultural Societies." In America, the Philadelphia Society for Promoting Agriculture was formed in 1785. George Washington, Benjamin Franklin, and Timothy Pickering were members.

[63]Information about mining given here is from Boch, pp. 156-68; see also Archives, MS 185, p. 128.

[64]General information about trades and industry is given by Leenhardt, pp. 102-6.

[65]Leenhardt, p. 104.

[66]Ibid., pp. 112-46. Specimens of such parables and anecdotes are included in Leenhardt's chapter on lawsuits, debts, and charity. This is one of the longest and most explicitly documented sections of Leenhardt's biography. It is the general source of the information given here on these subjects.

[67]Ibid., p. 115. In the Musée Oberlin in Waldersbach there is a ledger on 313 crowded pages, written mostly in Oberlin's hand, which contains the individual accounts of borrowers from the fund.

[68]The rules are given in full by Leenhardt, pp. 115-16.

[69]Neither Stoeber nor Leenhardt specify the year. The value of a livre was three francs.

[70]Leenhardt, p. 359.

[71]Ibid., p. 120.

[72]Ibid., p. 125. Leenhardt remarks that he had once had in his hand the rough draft of this letter, which had been previously quoted by Stoeber. The letter is apparently no longer extant. It is not included in Stoeber-Burckhardt. Was the addressee perhaps Jean-Luc Legrand?

[73]The documents quoted or paraphrased in this paragraph and the next two are from Leenhardt, pp. 129-36.

[74]This incident is related in a manuscript in the collection of Mme Meyer.

[75]The importance of this passage as a basis for Oberlin's views on charity was pointed out to me by Mme Meyer, who has made a thorough study of Oberlin's sermons and translations of many of them from French to German.

[76]Stoeber-Burckhardt, 3:191-92, quotes Oberlin's account of the incident in full.

[77]Leenhardt, pp. 106-7.

[78]The amount of money is not specified here because the figure is illegible in the document.

[79]For a complete list of similar accomplishments see Horand Gutfeldt, *Johann Friedrich Oberlin*, pp. 43a-43b.

[80]Franklin L. Ford, *Strasbourg in Transition, 1648-1789*, pp. 10-11.

[81]The document was first published as "Die Besitznahme der Grafschaft Steintal durch den Stettmeister Johann von Dietrich. Aus den unveröffentlichten Schriften Johann Friedrich Oberlins, herausgegeben von Marie-Joseph Bopp," in *Extrait de l'Annuaire de la Société historique, littéraire et scientifique du Club Vosgien*, n.s.1, 1933. Quotations given here are from Heinsius, pp. 54-61. The original document is in German.

[82]Leenhardt, p. 297. The nature of the "indiscretions" is not specified.

[83]Alfons Rosenberg, *Der Christ und die Erde*, pp. 197-98.

[84]Buch, p. 96. The second quotation from Martha Buch below is also to be found here.

[85]Leenhardt, p. 95.

[86]For the following three quotations see Leenhardt, pp. 154-56.

[87]Quoted by Jean Paul Benoit, *Brücke der Barmherzigkeit*, p. 163.

[88]The Niclas affair, with its sequel, is related by Leenhardt, pp. 285-89. Leenhardt also discusses at length certain bits of conflicting evidence on Oberlin's beliefs concerning *les peines éternelles*. His final conclusion: Oberlin did indeed believe that all souls can be, and are, eventually redeemed. The quotation that follows on "fifteen minutes in hell" is from a poem by Will Carlton, "Gone With a Handsomer Man."

[89]This detail and quotations in the following paragraphs concerning the services are from Stoeber-Burckhardt, 2:155-96.

[90]Leenhardt, p. 148.

[91]Ibid., p. 148, fn. 2. Leenhardt believes that one of the hymns from this collection, later ascribed in the *Recueil synodal des églises réformées de France* to Oberlin's authorship, was actually written by Stuber. The Oberlin manuscript quoted below is cited by Leenhardt but has since been lost. It was seen, however, by Mme Meyer some years ago, when it was in the possession of the late Pastor Beltrando of Waldersbach. Some details about church services were kindly conveyed to me by Mme Meyer. In the British Museum Library there is a book entitled *Chansons Spirituels*. The book is ascribed to Oberlin's authorship by the Department of Printed Books of the Museum Library. This ascription is probably wrong. It may be a copy of the hymnbook compiled by Stuber. Authors of the individual hymns, many of which are translations of familiar German Lutheran hymns, are not identified. There is no evidence that Oberlin ever wrote a hymn.

[92]Leenhardt, p. 149, fn. 2. For the comments on preaching below, unless otherwise noted, see Leenhardt, pp. 150-53.

[93]The "theological student" was the poet Lenz, whose visit in Waldersbach is described in chapter fourteen. The passage quoted is in a manuscript in the Oberlin collection of the bibliothèque municipale of Strasbourg. The manuscript is in Oberlin's hand and constitutes his report on the Lenz affair (see also p. 269 below). Oberlin's critics are nowhere identified. One suspects that these scoffs may have been circulated by Oberlin's archenemies, the *cabaretiers*.

[94]Archives, MS 4. Jean-Daniel Wohlfahrt, 2:2, gives the numbers of sermon manuscripts in the several repositories as follows: Archives municipales de Strasbourg, 349; Musée Alsacien de Strasbourg, 258; Musée Oberlin, Waldersbach, 19; Bibliothèque de la société du protestantism français, 7; Bibliothèque Nationale et Universitaire de Strasbourg, 1; Privé, 32; total, 711. Of these, 22 are printed by Leenhardt, pp. 503-50, and all of the funeral sermons, totalling 138, are to be found in the second and third volumes of Wohlfahrt's

dissertation. Facsimiles of sermon manuscripts are given by Leenhardt, opposite p. 150 and by Wohlfahrt, 2:4 and 6.

[95]The first example is from Leenhardt, p. 161; those below quoting Mlle Berckheim are from Mme Anne-Margrit Meyer's German translation (in manuscript) of Mme Ernest Roerich's article.

[96]Wohlfahrt, 2:11 and 12, fn. 21-37. Also Leenhardt, p. 158, fn. 2.

[97]Such miraculous happenings are recorded at various places in the journals. Those quoted here are conveniently brought together by Benoit, p. 160.

[98]Benoit, pp. 145-47.

[99]Wilhelm Scheuermann, *Ein Mann mit Gott,* pp. 310-11.

[100]From Mme Meyer's translation of Mme Roerich's memoir. See also W. Steinhilber, *J. F. Oberlin,* p. 50.

[101]While he surely could not believe that his bellowing could drive death away from his patient, he may have thought that it would at least scare hell out of the superstitious bystanders.

[102]Steinhilber, p. 46.

[103]Alfred Stucki, *Johann Friedrich Oberlin, der Vater des Steintals* (Basel: Verlag Friedrich Reinhardt, n.d.), p. 56.

[104]The "Annales" of Waldersbach, in a section entitled "Nouveaux arrangements," give, on p. 141, a list of "young people with excellent abilities." The date is 1773.

[105]Leenhardt, pp. 258-63. Oberlin read German, French, Greek, Hebrew, and Latin. Works originally written in other languages he read in French or German translations.

[106]Leenhardt, pp. 208-12 and 434-36, gives a full account of the *Société chrétienne* from its beginning to its dissolution, including either the full text of, or ample quotations from, each of the documents referred to here.

[107]Stoeber-Burckhardt, 2:320-29; also Leenhardt, pp. 225-33. There were more than 30,000 Protestants living in the province of Salzburg. Firmian's decree (mentioned in the next paragraph) forced them to choose between conversion to Catholicism and emigration. About 22,000 chose to emigrate. All but the Ebenezer group went to European countries, chiefly Prussia, Finland, the Netherlands, and Württemberg. The Ebenezer colonists are known to history as "the Salzburgers." Their story is told in P. A. Strobel, *The Salzburgers and their Descendants,* reprint (Athens, University of Georgia Press, 1953); Jones, Charles Colcock, "The Dead Towns of Georgia," Morning News, Savannah, 1878; Urlsperger, S., *Detailed Reports on the Salzburger Emigrants,* G. F. Jones, ed., Athens: University of

Georgia Press, 1968-1972; Urlsperger, J., *Amerikanisches Acker-werk Gottes.*

[108]This error of Oberlin's has been perpetuated by his biographers. Of those who mention Ebenezer at all, two (Leenhardt and Rosenberg) identify it only as being in North America, while seven (Stoeber-Burckhardt, 2:312-36; Atkins, p. 175; Heinrich Lutteroth *Aus Oberlins Leben, nach dem Französischen des Hrn. Heinr. Lutteroth,* p. 94; Steinhilber, p. 59; Heinsius, p. 68; Marshall Dawson, *Oberlin, a Protestant Saint* (New York: Willett, 1934), p. 86; and Augustus Field Beard, *The Story of John Frederic Oberlin,* p. 81, locate it in Pennsylvania. The error persisted uncorrected and without editorial comment even in American editions of Miss Atkins's book and in the only American biography, namely, Beard's, as well as in the German translation of Atkins, which was published in Pennsylvania with an introduction by S. S. Schmucker, a professor at Gettysburg Lutheran Seminary in Pennsylvania (this book constitutes vol. 1 of Stoeber-Burckhardt).

[109]See Leenhardt, p. 225, fn. 1. The name of Oberlin does not appear anywhere in the *Detailed Reports* of Urlsperger. In the journal that H. M. Muehlenberg kept during his four-month stay in Ebenezer in 1774-1775, in which the history of the parish in the preceding ten years is recorded in detail, there is no statement that either Oberlin or any other minister had been either considered or called during that period other than the incumbent second minister, Mr. Triebner. Furthermore, as far as I have been able to ascertain, there is no record in any archives concerning Ebenezer, either in America or in England, in Augsburg or in Halle, that shows any trace of correspondence with or about Oberlin. For help in making my inquiry about the call to Ebenezer I am indebted to Professor George Fenwick Jones of the University of Maryland, translator and editor of the three volumes of Urlsperger's *Detailed Reports;* Gerlinde Frank of the University Library of Erlangen-Nuremberg; J. Storz, director of the library and archivist of the Franckesche Stiftungen in Halle; and Arthur E. Barber of London, archivist and librarian of the Society for Promoting Christian Knowledge.

[110]There was actually a direct connection between Urlsperger and Oberlin that is not mentioned in any Oberlin biography. In the Musée Oberlin at Waldersbach ("Annales," p. 78) there is a copy of a letter from Oberlin to Urlsperger, thanking him for "gifts for the extension of the Kingdom in the Steintal" and describing the schools, the churches, and the general condition of the parish. There is nothing in it about Ebenezer. The date is November 11, 1773.

[111]As soon as the British had taken Savannah and established their headquarters there, Triebner went there, proclaimed his loyalty, took the oath of allegiance to the crown, and a few days later escorted a detachment of British troops in an easily triumphant assault on his own town and against his own people. From then on the story of Ebenezer is one of dissipation, decline, and ultimate extinction as a community. It is remembered now as the first, and one of the noblest, of "the dead towns of Georgia."

Part 3

[1]"Ich bin kein ausgeklügelt Buch,/Ich bin ein Mensch mit seinem Widerspruch,"; I am no contrived book/ I am a man with his contradictions. (C. F. Meyer).

[2]Detailed descriptions of the presbytery, of Oberlin's appearance, his courage, his manners and idiosyncracies are to be found in Stoeber-Burckhardt, *Johann Friedrich Oberlins, Pfarrer im Steinthal, Vollständige Lebensgeschichte und gesammelte Schriften,* 3:234-41; Camille Leenhardt, *La Vie de J.-F. Oberlin 1740-1826 de D.-E. Stoeber,* pp. 246-47; and Sarah Atkins, *Memoirs of John Frederic Oberlin, Pastor of Waldbach in the Ban de la Roche,* pp. 127-35.

[3]Edmond Parisot, *Un Educateur Moderne au XVIIIe siècle,* p. 23.

[4]Archives, MS 41. The probable date of the MS is 1817.

[5]Ibid., MS 185, p. 153; for the incident related below, ibid., p. 146.

[6]Leenhardt, p. 191.

[7]Ibid., p. 243.

[8]Portions of the diary were discovered by Mme Anne-Margrit Meyer among the papers of the late Georg Meyer. The incidents related here are quoted by Meyer in a fictionalized version of Mlle Diemer's original manuscript. The Meyer story has been put at my disposal by Mme Meyer. The Sommerhof that is mentioned was a leasehold estate, the largest in all the region of the Ban de la Roche.

[9]From a description by Mme Roerich in "J. F. Oberlin," *Revue Alsacienne* 12, no. 11, p. 363.

[10]Leenhardt, p. 159.

[11]Atkins, pp. 220-23.

[12]Rev. 21:11-21; also Stoeber-Burckhardt, 2:295.

[13]Stoeber-Burckhardt, 2:195-96. The manuscript quoted by Stoeber is in the Waldersbach museum.

[14]*Deuxième Centenaire de l'arrivée au Ban de-la-Roche de J.-F. Oberlin, mars-avril 1767-1967,* p. 28.

[15]The title of the book is *Propositions géologiques pour servir d'introduction à un ouvrage sur les éléments de la chorographie, avec exposé de leur plan et leur application à la description du Ban de la Roche* (Strasbourg, 1806). See Edmond Parisot, *Un Educateur Moderne au XVIIIe siècle*, p. 118, fn. 1. The book is a revised version of the author's doctoral thesis.

[16]Georg Meyer, "Kritisches zur Oberlinforschung," pp. 516-17.

[17]This quotation and the two following are all to be found in Leenhardt, pp. 246-47. See also Georg Heinrich von Schubert, *Die Symbolik des Traumes*, p. 281, and Stoeber-Burckhardt, 2:301-02.

[18]Leenhardt, pp. 249-51; Stoeber-Burckhardt, 2:351-53. Stoeber's version is also reprinted by Leenhardt, app. 16, pp. 449-50. Stoeber erroneously gives the death date as January 27.

[19]This letter, in German translation, is in Erich Psczolla, *Louise Scheppler, Mitarbeiterin Oberlins*, pp. 72-75. The second letter cited is translated from a facsimile of the French original manuscript, Psczolla, p. 76. It is also reprinted in full in Leenhardt, p. 362, fn. 1. The later letter, quoted below, is also printed in that place. It is dated "New Years 1793."

[20]Cuviér's statement is quoted in Stoeber-Burckhardt, 3:182. See also Leenhardt, p. 361, fn. 2; Psczolla, pp. 82-83.

[21]The complete document is printed in Leenhardt, pp. 361-64. It was signed by Charles-Conservé Oberlin, Jean-Luc Legrand, and Pastor Rauscher, and certified and attested by a dozen public officials, including the burgomaster of Bellefosse and the regional deputies to the National Assembly.

[22]A teacher training institute was established at Schirmeck-la Broque in 1827, the year after Oberlin's death. It was named the Oberlin Institute for the Training of Conductrices. In its early years it was administered by Louise Scheppler and Mme Rauscher. It continued to function until the establishment of a similar institute in Strasbourg made it superfluous. See Psczolla, pp. 112-13.

[23]Joseph Sweeney alias Gordon Johnstone, "There is no Death," stanza 3.

[24]Alfons Rosenberg, *Der Christ und die Erde*, p. 149.

[25]Jean Paul Benoit, *Brücke der Barmherzigkeit*, p. 197-98.

[26]Archives, MS 4 and 97.

[27]See Wilhelm Heinsius, *Johann Friedrich Oberlin und das Steintal*, p. 80, for the comments on both Bengel and Oettinger. Leenhardt quotes them in French translation from the German on p. 261, together with Oberlin's comment, which Heinsius omits. For the

quotation from Heinsius below see Heinsius, p. 115, fn. 149; for Oberlin's letter to Lavater see Leenhardt, pp. 263-65.

[28]The full text of the critique is in Leenhardt, pp. 259-61.

[29]The titles are: *A Summary of the Writings of Swedenborg* (being chiefly an abstract of *The True Christian Religion,* published in 1778 and purchased in the same year, much used and copiously underlined in green); *The Doctrine of the New Jerusalem* (acquired 1785, also much underlined); *Intercourse of Soul and Body* (published and acquired in 1785, also underlined); *Divine Love and Wisdom,* 1786 (an abridged edition of the oddly entitled book *Marital Love*), purchased 1787. There are also two excerpts of *Divine Love* in Oberlin's hand, in the bibliothèque municipale de Strasbourg: one entitled "Divine Metaphysics," the other "A Visit to Paradise." Data about these books are from Horand Gutfeldt's article, "Oberlin and Swedenborg," pt. 1, p. 57. Readers who are interested in reading more about Oberlin and Swedenborg are referred also to Anne-Margrit Meyer's *Licht und Schatten über dem Leben des Johann Friedrich Oberlin,* pp. 27-30.

[30]Archives, MS 13, 35, 42, 56, 61, 70, 77, 81, 97, 102, 113, 116, 118, 135, 155, 202.

[31]One such fabrication, entitled *Zion and Jerusalem,* was first published separately and subsequently republished in part 4 of the Stoeber-Burckhardt biography. The title page and a "Nachwort" falsely identify it as one of Oberlin's posthumous papers. It is a dull book of 487 pages. It has absolutely no connection with Oberlin.

[32]Leenhardt, pp. 290-92.

[33]Leenhardt, pp. 430-31. It is not clear which of the several balloon ascensions that occurred in the 1780s, after the Montgolfiers had sent up their first linen bag in 1783, is referred to here. The complete title is: *Rapport spirituel de ces machines pour aller en l'air, c'est-à-dire des ballons aérostatiques.*

[34]After Benoit, pp. 195-96.

[35]The remaining sermons in the series were preached on January 26, February 16, February 23, March 2, and March 18, 1783. All are to be found in Leenhardt, pp. 453-64.

[36]Quotations from Oberlin's private journal on this subject are translated from Rosenberg, *Der Christ und die Erde,* pp. 255-69. Some of the entries are quoted also, in French translation, by Leenhardt, pp. 256-58.

[37]Rosenberg, *Der Christ und die Erde,* pp. 257-58.

[38]Ibid., pp. 266-67.

[39]Leenhardt, pp. 253-54.

[40]Ibid., p. 294.

[41]Ibid., p. 294, fn. 2. Charles-Conservé was eventually unfrocked by the Strasbourg Consistory.

[42]For readers who may have a further interest in Oberlin's "visions" there follows here a précis of the treatment that other writers have given the subject.

Sarah Atkins, 1829, probably had no specific information about the visitations; she closes her account of Mme Oberlin's death with the words: "... Oberlin had not ceased to live in her society. ... Every day he devoted whole hours to communicating with her in those abstracted frames of mind which make us almost imagine ourselves in the presence of those whom we love." With one exception, books in English about Oberlin, all of which are based on Miss Atkins's *Memoirs,* are devoid of any information about his visions. The exception is Dawson (1934), who devotes to the subject about two pages of somewhat maudlin prose. (E.g., p. 103: "Meanwhile, his bride was leaning over the parapets of the sky," etc., etc.)

Stoeber, in 1831, tells about Oberlin's "dreams," in which his wife visited him, and of the "series of notebooks" in which he kept a record of them, but quotes nothing from them, saying that they were "written only for his intimate circle of friends and are therefore not suitable for publication."

In 1837 Gotthilf Heinrich Schubert published the second edition of his popular book, *The Symbolism of Dreams,* and—"in response to a widespread public demand, but not without considerable hesitation"—added a section entitled *Berichte eines Geistersehers* (Reports of a Visionary), which consists of a brief sketch of Oberlin's life and thirty-two pages entitled "Oberlin's Conversations with the Soul of his Deceased Wife," in which he quoted full length a "handwritten copy" of Oberlin's journal. Thus the posthumous visits of Mme Oberlin first became widely known beyond the borders of Alsace. The cause of Schubert's "hesitation" was apparently the question of the propriety of publishing such private papers, rather than any doubt about the authenticity and actuality of the events related.

Leenhardt, in 1911, says that he would have preferred to agree with Stoeber that these notebooks "are purely intimate and do not admit of publication," but he feels constrained to give the subject a fuller development because "several passages, even from manuscripts which we have had in our hands, have recently been published." He treats Oberlin's notes sympathetically, as a recital of actual dream experiences, but censures him for "not having sensed the danger that lies in developing these preoccupations" and for encouraging the simple folk of the parish to bring him their stories of similar experiences, which, in the undiscriminating minds of the peasantry, became "unhealthy and unfortunate curiosities."

Rosenberg, in *Der Christ und die Erde,* gives Oberlin's visions the most extensive treatment since Schubert's (on which it is largely based) and displays toward them the same positive attitude of credulity and uncritical acceptance that, in the 150 pages of his book preceding the 150 pages devoted to Oberlin, he accords to a wide variety of egregious speculations, theophanies, and fantasms that took possession of many impressionable minds in those times.

In 1971, Mme Anne-Margrit Meyer, in *Licht und Schatten,* a privately published pamphlet of forty-seven pages, sprang to Oberlin's defense against what she considered to be unfair and defamatory representations and adumbrations by Rosenberg against Oberlin as a visionary and an "occultist." Her spirited defense is based on certain premises: (1) that some human beings have the attribute or faculty of medianship, i.e., the ability to communicate with the souls or spirits of the dead; (2) that this attribute is more a burden than a boon (its possessor is said to be *medial belastet—* cursed with medianship); (3) that Oberlin was thus burdened; and (4) that the curse was inherited by him from his maternal grandfather, according to the revelation of Mt. Sinai (Exod. 20:2): ". . . for I, the Lord your God . . . punish the children for the sins of the fathers to the third and fourth generations. . . ."

Part 4

[1] The new residence that Dietrich built is even now the finest structure in Waldersbach; it still serves as the pastor's residence and also houses the Oberlin museum.

[2] The letters from Dietrich are printed in Camille Leenhardt, *La Vie de J.-F. Oberlin 1740-1826 de D.-E. Stoeber,* app. 23, pp. 469-75. Dietrich's first letter is dated October 27, 1788, Oberlin's reply, October 31; to Dietrich's second letter of November 6 no reply has survived.

[3] No petition has been found in any document. Whether Oberlin was aware of its existence at this time is not known.

[4] Apparently Dietrich had been a student of Oberlin's father at the *Gymnasium.*

[5] Oberlin's response to the council is printed by Leenhardt in French (pp. 298-99) and in German by Stoeber-Burckhardt, *Johann*

Friedrich Oberlins, Pfarrer im Steinthal, vollständige Lebens-geschichte und gesammelte Schriften, 2:361-64. It is dated April 23, 1786.

[6]Leenhardt, pp. 299-300. The sermon is printed without date.

[7]Oberlin's argument is based on Matt. 20:27 and 23:11, and on Mark 10:44.

[8]Sarah Atkins, *Memoirs of John Frederic Oberlin, Pastor of Waldbach in the Ban de la Roche,* pp. 143-46.

[9]Wilhelm Heinsius, *Johann Friederich Oberlin und das Steintal,* p. 82.

[10]Stoeber-Burckhardt, 3:371-77. See also Leenhardt, pp. 304-6, and Heinsius, pp. 82-83.

[11]The sermon is extensively quoted by Leenhardt, pp. 308-10. The date was August 5, 1792.

[12]The Oberlin documents concerning the assignats are printed in full in Leenhardt, pp. 329-34 and app. 26, pp. 480-82. See also Stoeber-Burckhardt, 3:442-58, and Heinsius, pp. 83-84.

[13]Thomas Carlyle, *The French Revolution* (London: Chapman and Hill, 1837), 2:13-14.

[14]Leenhardt, p. 308.

[15]Stoeber-Burckhardt, 2:394-97.

[16]All documents cited here on the revolutionary events in Alsace and the Ban de la Roche are, unless otherwise noted, in Leenhardt, pp. 311-15. For the memorandum of December 18 see also Stoeber-Burckhardt, 2:403-4. A *rabbat* or *rabato* is a wide, stiff collar worn over the shoulders, or open in front and standing at the back. It was standard clerical garb among the Lutheran clergy of Alsace. Thus Oberlin gave up simultaneously the vestments and titles of office; the only title allowed to men and women in revolutionary France were *citoyen* and *citoyenne.*

[17]Unless otherwise noted, documents quoted here about the *Club populaire* are from Leenhardt, pp. 316-19.

[18]Leenhardt, pp. 317-18. Participation in the actual meetings of the club was restricted to men. The *Klingelbeutel,* a collection pouch suspended from the end of a pole and with a small bell attached, is standard equipment in Lutheran country churches.

[19]Ibid., pp. 321-23.

[20]Ibid., pp. 325-26; Heinsius, p. 90.

[21]Leenhardt, pp. 55-56.

[22]The complete list is in Leenhardt, pp. 425-30.

[23]Ibid., p. 58.

[24]Paul Philippi, *Die Vorstufen des modernen Diakonissenamtes (1789-1884) als Elemente für dessen Verständnis und Kritik,* p. 12, fn. 1. The title of Spangenberg's book, cited there, is *Von der Arbeit der evangelischen Brüder unter den Heiden* (1782). For the biblical reference about deacons, see Phil. 1:1 and I Tim. 8:12, 13.

[25]The Oberlin documents on this subject are to be found in Leenhardt, pp. 206-7, and Philippi, pp. 12-14, in the original French; they are also given in an exact German translation by Philippi in the Appendix, pp. 243-47. Philippi's copies of Oberlin's manuscripts are more complete and more accurate than Leenhardt's. The comments on the character of a deaconess are from Philippi, pp. 14-15 and 244-45.

[26]Karl Eduard Boch, *Das Steintal im Elsass,* pp. 139-41.

[27]Philippi, pp. 16-20 and 245-47.

[28]Atkins, pp. 162-64. For a definitive presentation of Oberlin's significance in the history of the deaconess movement, see Philippi, pp. 10-42 and 245-47.

[29]Stoeber-Burckhardt, 2:422-24.

[30]Jean Paul Benoit, *Brücke der Barmherzigkeit,* p. 228.

[31]Stoeber-Burckhardt, 2:426-27.

[32]Rosenberg, *Der Christ und die Erde,* pp. 269 and 290-93.

[33]Heinsius, pp. 89-90. See also Leenhardt, pp. 328-29, and app. 15, pp. 445-48.

[34]The following is excerpted from the accounts of Leenhardt, pp. 213-14, and of Stoeber-Burckhardt, 2:408-14.

[35]Leenhardt, pp. 314-15.

[36]Stoeber-Burckhardt, 2:405-6.

Part 5

[1]Information given on the history of the rights to the use of forests and pastures is from Karl Eduard Boch, *Das Steintal im Elsass,* pp. 120-23, and from an article by Georg Meyer, which came to me from Mme Anne-Margrit Meyer in the form of a clipping of unidentified origin, but apparently from a newspaper. It is an essay of about 2,000 words entitled "Um Wald und Weide im Steintal." The documents pertinent to the settlement of the case are quoted in full and in the original French by Boch and by Camille Leenhardt, *La Vie de J.-F. Oberlin 1740-1826 de D.-E. Stoeber,* app. 30, pp. 493-94.

[2]Leenhardt, pp. 350-51.

[3]Stoeber-Burckhardt, *Johann Friedrich Oberlins, Pfarrer im Stein-thal, vollständige Lebensgeschichte und gesammelte Schriften,* 3:219.

[4]Leenhardt, pp. 348-50. The eight *maires* included the five from the Waldersbach and the three from the Rothau parish.

[5]In 1828, Heywood added a mechanical weaving mule and converted his plant to steam power. On the history of the textile industry in the Steintal, see J.B. Masson, *Die Siedlungen des Breuschtals (i. Els.) und der Nachbargebiete,* pp. 147-49.

[6]Information given here on Jean-Luc Legrand is from G. Wyss, "Legrand, Jean-Luc," in *Allgemeine deutsche Biographie,* 13:128-32, from Leenhardt, pp. 367-70; and from Stoeber-Burckhardt, 3:221-29.

[7]Leenhardt, pp. 354-55.

[8]Christoph Kaufmann of Winterthur, physician and satirist, self-styled "Hound of God" and "Apostle of Power," was one of the charlatanic characters who resided on the broad lunatic fringe of the Sturm und Drang movement. All information about Lenz in the Ban de la Roche is from Oberlin's manuscript report (in the bibliothèque municipale of Strasbourg) on the incident referred to below. For information about Lenz's life before and after the sojourn at Waldersbach see: Johannes Froitzheim, *Lenz and Goethe* (Stuttgart, 1891); M. N. Rosanov, *J.M.R. Lenz, Sein Leben und seine Werke,* translated by C. v. Gutschow (Leipzig, 1909); and August Stoeber, *Der Dichter Lenz und Friederike von Sesenheim* (Basel, 1842), which also contains the complete text in German of Oberlin's manuscript report. See also Max Winkler, "Lenz und Goethe," *Modern Language Notes,* 9 no. 22, 65-78; and Goethe's *Dichtung und Wahrheit,* Books 11 and 14. The fullest account of Lenz in Waldersbach given in any Oberlin biography is in Rosenberg, *Der Christ und die Erde,* pp. 283-90. Lenz was the theological student referred to in chapter six, page 134.

[9]On the two trips to Baden, see Wilhelm Heinsius, *Johann Friedrich Oberlin und das Steintal,* pp. 69-76. Earlier writers mention only one trip, in 1780. Heinsius's report is based on an unpublished Oberlin manuscript found among the family papers of the late Robert Jung in Strasbourg. It consists of Oberlin's journal of the journey made in 1778 and contains extensive comments on the educational and social work done by Sander in Köndringen and by Schlosser in Emmendingen. MS 203 in the Strasbourg bibliothèque municipale contains a list of journeys made by Oberlin. Though the earliest date mentioned is 1770 and the latest is 1819, there are entries for only

twenty-four of the intervening years. All destinations mentioned are within Alsace save three: two trips to Baden are listed, and then there is the following enigmatic fragment quoted from a letter written on September 3, 1804, to "candidate Blumhardt": ". . . I still marvel that I have been in Basel, it seems like a sweet dream to me, and yet it is true." This bit of evidence has never been remarked by any writer on Oberlin, and nowhere have I found any other mention of it, nor corroborative information about the visit such as its duration, the persons he met, the sights he saw, etc. If the words had been written during the time when he was having his "visions," which he often referred to as "dreams," one might explain the anomaly by a surmise that he had visited Blumhardt in the spirit only, not in the flesh. Is it possible that this might be a hint that visions did occasionally recur after the putative date of their cessation?

[10]The subject of Oberlin's influence on Balzac is exhaustively covered by Mme Claire Richardot, "Oberlin, Balzac et Swedenborg," in *Evangile et Liberté,* July 8, 1971, pp. II-VIII.

[11]Stuttgart: Greiner und Pfeiffer, n.d., 447 pp.

[12]Dieter Cunz, ed., *Heinrich Stillings Jugendgeschichte* (Stuttgart: Reclam, n.d.). See also Leenhardt, pp. 268-69, and app. 18, p. 469, where the letter to Oberlin quoted below is reproduced in the original German.

[13]Ernest John Knapton, *The Lady of the Holy Alliance,* pp. 3-4. Biographical data adduced here are chiefly from this excellent book. The first meeting between Oberlin and Mme Krüdener has escaped the notice of all Oberlin biographers. It is detailed and documented by Knapton, pp. 118-19, after A. Bossert, *Etudes historiques et figures alsaciennes* (Paris, 1919), pp. 239-54.

[14]Stoeber-Burckhardt, 2:512-16.

[15]On the Oberlin-Grégoire friendship see Stoeber-Burckhardt, 3:194-99.

[16]Ibid., 3:119-29.

[17]Two letters from Oberlin are recorded in English translation in the *Reports of the British and Foreign Bible Society:* one in the *First Report* (1805), pp. 40-41, under the heading, "A Letter from a Respectable Clergyman in Alsace," dated Nov. 3, 1804, and one in the *Second Report* (1806), dated June 17, 1805. Quotations from Owen's remarks on his visit are from John Owen's *History of the British and Foreign Bible Society,* (London: Tilling and Hughes, 1818-1819), pp. 419-45. All these documents are reprinted or excerpted in Sarah Atkins, *Memoirs of John Frederic Oberlin, Pastor of Waldbach in the Ban de la Roche,* pp. 167-78 and 224-30.

Owen's travel report was also printed as a separate brochure: *Extracts of Letters on the Object and Connections of the British and Foreign Bible Society from the Rev. John Owen, A.M., During his Late Tour in France and Switzerland.*

[18] Atkins, pp. 304-5.

[19] Owen, pt. 5, pp. 423-25. Some writers on Oberlin have mistakenly identified this John Owen as Robert Owen of New Lanark in Scotland and have thus been misled to overestimate Oberlin's influence on the famous British industrialist-educator-reformer. The error was compounded by Robert Owen himself, who in a report on a European journey spoke of having visited "Father Oberlin's schools at Fribourg." The correct name of the Fribourg educator is Father Girard. There is no evidence that Robert Owen ever visited the Ban de la Roche. See Robert R. Rusk, *A History of Infant Education*, p. 120.

[20] The passage from Eliot alluded to here is quoted as the epigraph of chapter five above. For the reference to Emerson I am indebted to my friend and colleague Andrew Bongiorno, who in an article entitled "The Coming Age and the Departing Age" (*Oberlin Alumni Magazine,* July-August 1973, p. 16) quotes the following passage from Emerson's address: "Let me admonish you, first of all, to go alone, to refuse the good models, even those that are sacred in the imagination of men. . . . Friends enough you shall find who will hold up to your emulation Wesleys and Oberlins, Saints and Prophets. Thank God for these men, but say, 'I also am a man.' "

[21] Robert S. Fletcher, *A History of Oberlin College from its Foundation Through the Civil War* (Oberlin: Oberlin College, 1943), 1:207. Fletcher's book has recently come out in a new printing in one volume. See also Fletcher's chapter on John Jay Shipherd, pp. 58-69. All information given here about Finney and Shipherd and the founding of Oberlin College is from this history.

[22] The unabridged letter is in Fletcher, 1:87-89. About the alacrity with which the scheme was developed, Fletcher says, "The plan was certainly not an entirely original one," and points to Rochester, New York, and Royalton, Vermont, as places where, under Finney's inspiration, similar projects had been considered. Ebenezer Henderson was a clockmaker of Edinburgh who became a Congregational missionary and colporteur in Iceland. The review mentioned was an abridgment of his *Iceland: or the Journal of a Residence in That Island During the Years 1814 and 1815,* Edinburgh, 1818. In abridged form it was reprinted in Boston in 1837. The review read by Shipherd and Stewart is in the *Quarterly Christian Spectator* 4 (June

1815), 187-207. The source of Shipherd's information about John Frederic Oberlin was by Sarah Atkins's *Memoirs,* first published anonymously in London in 1829 and reprinted in abridged form by the American Sunday School Union in 1831. A copy of that booklet is in the Oberlin College Library.

[23]See *Webster's New Geographical Dictionary,* s.v., 1972; also George R. Stewart, *American Place Names* (New York: Oxford Book Co., Inc., 1970). Information about Oberlin in China, below, is from a pamphlet entitled "Fiftieth Anniversary: Oberlin Shansi Memorial Association 1908-1958," by Wynn C. Fairchild. On Obirin in Tokyo see Jasugo Shimizu, "The Story of Obirin" (Tokyo: Obirin-in-Tokyo, 1951), 49 pp.

[24]Stoeber-Burckhardt, 3:338-45.

[25]This description of Oberlin's last days, his last illness, his death and burial is based on the ninth book of Stoeber's biography, a collocation of Stoeber's own recollections, the description of the funeral by Oberlin's Strasbourg friend Rieder, and of notes written, at Stoeber's request, by Mme Rauscher. Stoeber-Burckhardt, 3:296-332.

[26]Ps. 103:1-4, and Rev. 7:14. The gravestone inscription reads, "Here repose the mortal remains of Jean-Frédéric Oberlin, Pastor of the Parish of Waldbach, Born the thirty-first of August 1740, Died the first of June 1826."

Notes on the
Oberlin Literature

No comprehensive collection of archival materials on Oberlin now exists. I have studied the collections of surviving Oberliana at the Musée Oberlin in the Waldersbach parsonage and at the Musée Alsacien and the bibliothèque municipale at Strasbourg. Manuscripts in Waldersbach and in the bibliothèque municipale are cited in the notes and the bibliography under "Annales" and "Archives," respectively. Aside from these, there is a considerable collection of Oberlin's letters in the archives of St. Thomas Church in Strasbourg. These have for some years been in the process of preparation for publication by Pastors R. Peter and G. Koch. Some private collections of Oberlin papers are described by Buch (pp. 120-26). Neither these nor the St. Thomas collection have been accessible to me.

Daniel-Ehrenfried Stoeber's *Vie de J.-F. Oberlin, pasteur à Waldbach, au Ban-de-la-Roche, chevalier de la Légion d'honneur,* published in Paris in 1831, is a basic sourcebook. Although I have had an opportunity to inspect a copy of it in Strasbourg, it was not otherwise available for my use. (Augustus Field Beard, in the preface to his *Story of John Frederic Oberlin,* says that the copy he owned in 1908 was "perhaps the only one in this country.") I have, however, had the use of a copy from the Oberlin College Library of a German translation made by W. Burckhardt and included as parts two and three in the two-volume book that I refer to as Stoeber-Burckhardt. The translation is good, as far as I have been able to ascertain, and reasonably faithful to the French original. The content of Stoeber's book, being based on intimate personal acquaintance of the author with Oberlin and on unlimited access to documents that have long since been lost, is authentic and reliable. In its arrangement, however, the book is a hodgepodge that is difficult to read and to use.

In 1911, Camille Leenhardt, a clergyman of Nancy, published *La Vie de J.-F. Oberlin 1740-1826 de D.-E. Stoeber.* This is the nearest thing we have to a definitive biography of Oberlin. It is indispensable to students of Oberlin because many basic documents are now available only in the form in which Leenhardt reproduced them. Three books—Atkins, Stoeber-Burckhardt, and Leenhardt—have furnished a large portion of the basic material for this study.

Dr. Horand Gutfeldt has put together a reasonably complete bibliography on Oberlin and published it as a supplement to his University of Vienna dissertation of 1968. In the fifteen decades since the 1820s, 101 books have been written about Oberlin. Of these, 14 appeared in the 1830s; 13 in the 1900s; 9 each in the 1930s and 1950s; 8 each in the 1820s and 1940s. The remaining 40 are scattered through the other nine decades in numbers ranging between six and two per decade. Most of them are inspirational, hortatory, and propagandistic in purpose and in style; and all are derived from the three chief works mentioned above.

Dr. Gutfeldt has included in his study an analysis of the geographical distribution of publications on Oberlin. In making that analysis he has taken into account not only the number of titles, but also the number of editions or republications of each title. Thus, if a book was printed only once, it is counted as one unit; if it was published in, say, five editions, it is counted as five units. His study (pp. 61-62) shows the following distribution of units: Germany, 285; France, 183; England, 40; United States, 34; Switzerland, 12; Holland, 3; Brazil, 3; Iceland, Japan, Lithuania, Madagascar, Mexico, and Norway, 1 each.

Of the original studies published in the United States, only two constitute substantial volumes: Beard's *The Story of John Frederic Oberlin* (1908) is an acceptable adaptation of Atkins and Stoeber, while Dawson's fictionalized biography (1936) is of little value, either as biography or as literature.

Annotated Bibliography

"Annales du Ban de la Roche surtout de la Paroisse de Waldersbach. Commencées l'an 1770." This is a lengthy manuscript in Oberlin's hand, with references to narrative notes written by Stuber, deposited in the Musée Oberlin in Waldersbach.

Archives. All manuscripts cited from the Archives municipaux of the bibliothèque municipale in Strasbourg are documented in the footnotes under the entry "Archives."

Atkins, Sarah. *Memoirs of John Frederic Oberlin, Pastor of Waldbach in the Ban de la Roche.* 3rd ed. London: Holdsworth and Paul, 1831. The source book from which all previous Oberlin biographies in English are derived.

Baum, Johann Wilhelm. *Johann Georg Stuber, der Vorgänger Oberlins im Steinthal und Vorkämpfer einer neuen Zeit in Strassburg.* Strasbourg: Silbermann, 1846. The only published biography.

Benoit, Jean Paul. *Brücke der Barmherzigkeit: Das Leben Johann Friedrich Oberlins.* Constance: Christliche Verlagsanstalt, 1956. Translated from the French original by Marguerite Wolf and F. W. Gerhard Schneider. One of the best of the inspirational books. The author was a descendant of Oberlin.

Beard, Augustus Field. *The Story of John Frederic Oberlin.* Boston: Pilgrim, n.d. Introduction by Henry Churchill King.

de Berckheim, Octavie. *Souvenirs d'Alsace: Correspondance des demoiselles de Berckheim et de leurs amis (1797-1846) précédée d'un extrait du Journal de Mlle. Octavie de Berckheim (1789-*

1795). 2 vols. Paris: Monnerat, 1889. Since this book was not available to me, all quotations from it are either as found in Leenhardt, or in Mme E. Roerich's *Le Ban-de-la-Roche: Notes historique et souvenirs.*

Boch, Karl Eduard. *Das Steintal im Elsass: eine geschichtliche Studie über die ehemalige Herrschaft Stein und deren Herren, sowie über die Entwicklung des gesamten Wissenschafts- und Geisteslebens im Steintal.* Strasbourg: Trübner, 1914.

Buch, Martha. *Die pädagogischen und sozialpädagogischen Ideen Johann Friedrich Oberlins.* Berlin: Beltz, 1932.

Dawson, Marshall. *Oberlin, a Protestant Saint.* New York: Willet, 1934.

Deuxième Centenaire de l'arrivée au Ban de-la-Roche de J.-F. Oberlin, mars-avril 1767-1967, edited by Roger Henninger, Gustave Koch, Robert Lutz, Rodolphe Peter, and Georges Wild, with the collaboration of Mme Claire Richardot. Strasbourg: Editions Oberlin, 1967. See also Lutz, R., in this bibliography.

Ermatinger, Emil. *Deutsche Kultur im Zeitalter der Aufklärung.* Potsdam: Athenaion, n.d.,

Fletcher, Robert Samuel. *A History of Oberlin College from Its Foundation Through the Civil War.* 2 vols. Oberlin: Oberlin College, 1943.

Ford, Franklin L. *Strasbourg in Transition, 1648-1789.* Cambridge: Harvard University Press, 1958.

Gugenheim, Georges. "Balzac et Oberlin." In *Etudes alsatiques I.* Publications de la Faculté de l'Université de Strasbourg. Paris: Mélanges, 1947, pp. 121-25.

Guizot, Pauline. *L'Ecolier, ou Raoul et Victor.* Paris: Ladvocat, n.d. The Oberlin episode is in chapter 17, vol. 2, pp. 1-45.

Gutfeldt, Horand. *Johann Friedrich Oberlin. Eine wissenschaftliche Untersuchung seiner Gedankenwelt, seiner Pädagogik und seines Einflusses auf die Welt, mit einer kurzen Biographie.* Vienna: Author, n.d.

_____. "Oberlin and Swedenborg." *New Church Magazine* 638 (Oct. 1966): 55-58; ibid., 639 (Nov. 1966): 11-15.

Heinsius, Wilhelm. *Johann Friedrich Oberlin und das Steintal.* Lahr: Schauenburg, n.d.

Hermelink, Heinrich. *Das Christentum in der Geschichte der Menschheit.* Vol. 1. *Die Restauration 1789-1835.* Stuttgart: Metzler, n.d.

Knapton, Ernest John. *The Lady of the Holy Alliance: The Life of Julie de Krüdener.* New York: Columbia University Press, 1939.

Leenhardt, Camille. *La Vie de J.-F. Oberlin 1740-1826 de D.-E. Stoeber: Refondue sur un plan nouveau, complétée et augmentée de numbreux documents inédits, avec neuf planches hors texte.* Paris: Berger-Levrault, 1911. Important source book for all Oberlin studies.

Lienhard, Friedrich. *Oberlin: Roman aus der Revolutionszeit im Elsass.* Stuttgart: Greiner und Pfeiffer, 1910.

Lutteroth, Heinrich. *Aus Oberlins Leben, nach dem Französischen des Hrn. Heinr. Lutteroth.* Translated and revised by C. W. Krafft. Strasbourg: Treuttel, 1826. Lutteroth was a friend of Oberlin. This brief obituary and eulogy appeared within the year of Oberlin's death. The original French version was not available to me.

Lutz, R. "Les ancêtres de Jean-Frédéric Oberlin." In *Deuxième Centenaire de l'arrivée au Ban de-la-Roche de J.-F. Oberlin.* Strasbourg: Editions Oberlin, 1967.

Masson, J. B. *Die Siedlungen des Breuschtals (i. Els.) und der Nachbargebiete.* Zabern: Fuchs, 1911.

Meyer, Anne-Margrit. *Licht und Schatten über dem Leben des Johann Friedrich Oberlin.* Strasbourg: Editions Oberlin, 1971.

Meyer, Georg. "Kritisches zur Oberlinforschung." *Strassburger Monatshefte,* Sept.-Oct. 1937, pp. 515-18.

_____."Um Wald und Weide im Steintal." This article was available to me only as a clipping from a periodical publication of unknown title and date.

Parisot, Edmond. *Un Educateur moderne au XVIIIe siecle: Jean-Frédéric Oberlin (1740-1826).* 2nd ed. Paris: Colin, 1907.

Philippi, Paul. *Die Vorstufen des modernen Diakonissenamtes (1789-1884) als Elemente für dessen Verständnis und Kritik. Eine motivgeschichtliche Untersuchung zum Wesen der Mutterhaus-diakonie.* Neukirchen: Erziehungsverein, n.d.

Psczolla, Erich. *Louise Scheppler, Mitarbeiterin Oberlins.* Witten: Luther Verlag, 1963.

Richardot, Claire. "Oberlin, Balzac et Swedenborg." *Evangile et Liberté,* July 8, 1971, pp. I-VIII.

Roerich, Mme Ernest. *Le Ban-de-la-Roche: Notes historiques et souvenirs.* Paris: Fischbacher, 1890.

Rosenberg, Alfons. *Der Christ und die Erde: Oberlin und der Aufbruch zur Gemeinschaft der Liebe.* Freiburg im Breisgau and Olten; Otto Walter, n.d.

———. *J. Fr. Oberlin: Die Bleibstatten der Toten.* Bietigheim: Turm Verlag, 1974.

Rusk, Robert R. *A History of Infant Education.* London: University of London Press, 1933.

Schering, Ernst. *Sternstunde der Sozialpädagogik: Johann Friedrich Oberlin, Gründer der ersten Kindergärten und Wegbereiter der Inneren Mission.* Bielefeld: Bechauf, 1959.

Scheuermann, Wilhelm. *Ein Mann mit Gott: Das Lebenswerk Joh. Friedr. Oberlins.* Berlin: Deutsche Buchgemeinschaft, n.d. A fictionalized biography.

Schubert, Georg Heinrich von. *Die Symbolik des Traumes.* Leipzig: Brockhaus, 1814. The second edition was published in 1821. The third and fourth editions, 1837 and 1862, contain a supplement entitled "Berichte eines Geistersehers über den Zustand der Seelen nach dem Tode" (pp. 276-309), which purports to be based on a manuscript by Oberlin.

———. *Züge aus dem Leben des Johann Friedrich Oberlin gewesenen Pfarrers im Steintal.* 7th ed. Nuremberg: Raw, 1842.

Steinhilber, W. *J. F. Oberlin: Sein Leben und Wirken im Lichte der Bibel.* Strasbourg: Editions Oberlin, n.d. Steinhilber, alias Steinhilber-Oberlin, is a descendant of John Frederic Oberlin.

Stoeber, Daniel-Ehrenfried. *Vie de J.-F. Oberlin, pasteur a Waldbach, au Ban-de-la-Roche, chevalier de la Légion d'honneur.* Paris: Treuttel, 1831. An important source book, rare, and largely superseded by Leenhardt, which is based on it. Stoeber, a Strasbourg attorney, was a graduate of Oberlin's *pensionnat* and a lifelong friend of the Oberlin family.

Stoeber-Burckhardt. *Johann Friedrich Oberlins, Pfarrer im Steinthal, vollständige Lebensgeschichte und gesammelte Schriften: Herausgegeben von Dr. Hilpert, Stoeber und Andern.* edited and translated by W. Burckhardt. 2 vols. Stuttgart: Rieger und Sattler, 1843. Part 1 consists of Sarah Atkins's *Memoirs of John Frederic Oberlin;* parts 2 and 3 comprise Stoeber's life of Oberlin;

part 4 consists of a spurious book entitled *Zion und Jerusalem,* whose authorship is falsely ascribed to Oberlin.

Strohl, H. *Etudes sur Oberlin.* Paris: Alcan, 1926.

Wohlfahrt, Jean-Daniel. *Le sort des trepasses dans la theologie de Jean-Frédéric Oberlin (1740-1826).* 3 volumes. Mimeographed. Ph.D. dissertation, University of Strasbourg, n.d. Volume 1 contains the dissertation proper; volumes 2 and 3 consist of transcriptions of Oberlin's sermons.

Index

John Frederic Oberlin is referred to throughout as JFO.